The Business and Practice of Coaching

Also by Lynn Grodzki

Building Your Ideal Private Practice:
A Guide for Therapists and Other Healing Professionals

12 Months to Your Ideal Private Practice:
A Workbook

The New Private Practice:
Therapist-Coaches Share Stories, Strategies, and Advice (Editor)

A Norton Professional Book

The Business and Practice of Coaching

Finding Your Niche, Making Money, and Attracting Ideal Clients

Lynn Grodzki and Wendy Allen

W. W. Norton & Company
New York • London

For information about permission to reproduce
selections from this book, write to
Permissions, W. W. Norton & Company, Inc.,
500 Fifth Avenue, New York, NY 10110

Production Manager: Leeann Graham
Manufacturing by Quebecor World Fairfield Graphics

Library of Congress Cataloging-in-Publication Data

Grodzki, Lynn.
    The business and practice of coaching : finding your niche, making money,
    and attracting ideal clients / Lynn Grodzki and Wendy Allen.
        p.   ; cm.
    "A Norton professional book."
    Includes bibliographical references and index.
    ISBN 0-393-70462-9
    1. Consultants—Marketing. 2. Executive coaching—Practice. 3. Personal
    coaching—Practice. I. Allen, Wendy, 1953- II. Title.

HD69.C6G74 2005
001'.68'8—dc22   2005047294

W. W. Norton & Company, Inc., 500 Fifth Avenue, New York, N. Y. 10110
www.wwnorton.com

W. W. Norton & Company Ltd., Castle House, 75/76 Wells St., London W1T 3QT

5 7 9 0 8 6

Contents

Part III. Entrepreneurship

Part IV. Profiles in Coaching

Appendix of Helpful Information

Acknowledgments

This book is a family affair: The authors are sisters as well as professional colleagues. As family, we want to extend our appreciation to our extended family within the coaching community—those coaches who so generously mentored, encouraged, and informed our work and this book. We also thank Deborah Malmud, director of publishing at Norton Professional Books and editor extraordinaire, and Michael McGandy and Kevin Olsen at W.W. Norton for their combined efforts to make sure the book reads well, looks good, and reaches the people who need it. Additional thanks go to:

(From Lynn)
The coaches I mentor who constantly remind me what it means to be a new coach on the front lines; the CoachU community; my husband for his patient, sage advice; and Wendy, for her lighthearted coaching perspective and steely sense of purpose.

(From Wendy)
My clients who inspire me every day; my wonderful husband and family who weren't really 100% interested in this text, but were 200% interested in me and supported me in all the important ways; my sister, Lynn, who so generously asked me to participate; my fun next-door neighbors who were always glad to see me during my necessary and unnecessary breaks; and my dog, Rubby-the-Tummy, who loved this whole endeavor because he got to lie down at my feet without me moving, for hours at a time—his snores gently kept me focused.

The Business and Practice of Coaching

A Coaching Approach for the Coach in Business

Building a thriving coaching business is a challenge. With an estimated number of 30,000 coaches worldwide, and with the majority hanging out their coaching shingles since 1999, the coaching market is definitely growing. But data show that these same coaches are finding that despite their best efforts, the business side of coaching is not as financially viable as they had initially hoped. In the latest industry-wide survey conducted by the International Coach Federation (ICF), the largest professional association of coaches, 70% of all coaches surveyed report that even though they are working hard to build their businesses, they are making less than a living wage. Coaches need help in order to succeed in the business of coaching, and they need it now.

Whether you are a veteran coach, a brand-new coach, or someone still undecided about coaching, this book is written with your business success in mind. If you have questions about what it takes to start a coaching business or how to expand your ongoing coaching business, we have answers that have been tested in the marketplace. If you are at a loss as to how to attract clients, retain clients, or earn what you need, we have strategies that will shorten your learning curve. If you love being a coach but don't yet love being in business and feel stuck or burned out, we can help you find an easier way to thrive in this challenging business.

To make money as a coach in business today, you need to be both a skilled coach and a capable entrepreneur. As a business owner, you need to select the right coaching specialty, target your ideal market, build a reputation, use the most leveraged marketing strategies, know how to set and raise your fees, develop multiple streams of income, and ultimately build a six-figure business not just to own but to sell. You need to develop a business mind-set, so that you can stay resilient and optimistic, even in the face of inevitable setbacks. All the while you must know how to stay risk-adverse and safe, promoting the core principles and ethics that are essential to the practice of coaching. This book will show you how to do all this, and more.

We have been involved in the coaching profession since 1996 in our own coaching businesses. One of us is a *mentor coach*—a teacher-trainer for a large coach training organization, and editor of a previous book on coaching. Our research for this book included a review of the coaching literature and of several prominent coach training curricula. We also interviewed and tracked well over 100 new coaches as they worked to build their businesses and met with dozens of senior, successful coaches to hear about their best business strategies. We regularly attend coaching conferences, present workshops internationally on the business of coaching, and sit on panels and advisory boards as coaching experts.

Despite the challenges of the current coaching trends, we feel optimistic about the possibilities and opportunities available today for new coaches. But we also maintain a strong pragmatic stance. We want to correct the myth and hype that have unfortunately caused many new coaches to feel misled or disappointed as they start into business, and help you stay grounded in reality so that your coaching business is viable.

Because so many coaches are in trouble financially, books and courses on how to market a coaching practice are currently flooding the coaching world. Unfortunately, most of these offer a solely strategic approach, focusing on the "how to" of business, which presumes that you, the coach, are only in need of information. But we coaches know that information is never enough to help someone make real change. As the coach, you also need coaching about your business that is as much *who* based (speaks to who you are) as it is *what* based (suggests what you can do). Based on our experience as business coaches and workshop leaders who have shown thousands of your colleagues how to become more entrepreneurial, we have seen that even the most reluctant entrepreneurs can accomplish significant business goals when offered a coaching approach.

Our approach is to work with each reader as though you were our individual coaching client. Through the words and exercises in this book, we will walk along side you to guide you through a multifaceted process of entrepreneurship, one that specifically addresses the business of coaching. Chapter by chapter, we make direct suggestions, ask provocative questions, encourage you to take big steps, and then help you to determine your next set of goals. We give you a road map in the form of a business model that takes into account where you are starting, informs and educates you by offering clearly interpreted data, evaluates the many directions possible, and then helps you to decide your own entrepreneurial path.

We know the terrain (as coaches in business ourselves) and will help you evaluate your right steps and educate you about the possible mistakes to avoid. In the process, you can grow yourself as you grow your business. Then we send you on your way with a full tool kit of information so that you can take ownership of your progress: we offer you a coaching approach to the business of coaching.

Business consultant Michael Gerber (1995) wrote that those in small business must spend time working *on* the business, not just *in* the business. You may be drawn more to the task of service provider—coach—than to the role of business owner. But having a profitable business will allow you to do your best work as a coach. The reverse will also be true: a weak and floundering practice will drain your energy and adversely affect your creative and inspired coaching work. By the end of this book, we believe you will be many steps further in the direction of being a better coach by becoming a much smarter entrepreneur.

To make any external change, in this case building or improving your coaching business, you will need to open your mind to new possibilities. Throughout this book, we will show you how to develop an entrepreneurial mind-set—the distinctive thinking that small business owners need to succeed. With the right mind-set, every business decision and strategy gets easier to achieve. With the right mind-set, questions turn into solutions and normal business anxiety lessens. We believe in a holistic approach to business and offer exercises and suggestions to help you develop emotionally, creatively, cognitively, spiritually, and strategically. As business coaches, we often work with non-business-oriented professionals (therapists and other healers, coaches, and consultants) and we see the profound healing and maturation that small business ownership can effect. We want the same for you.

Overcoming Obstacles

Because we have helped so many of your colleagues walk their own business paths, we know that building a coaching business can be a daunting experience at first. Your start-up years of building a coaching business will include establishing yourself in your community and defining your unique specialized services, and will probably involve more marketing than you like. Starting and sustaining any new business is tough, which is why failure rates on new businesses are so high, but a coaching business is especially vulnerable to collapse. Here are four reasons why:

- First, you are selling something new. Coaching is an unfamiliar service for much of the public. You may have to do double duty: Create a market and then sell your services. You will need to be part educator, part salesperson, part leader in the field—and be ready to demonstrate coaching to people you meet, at a moment's notice. This takes assurance.
- Second, since you are selling improvement and achievement services, you will be held to a higher standard of self-care and self-actualization than if you were selling something more material or mundane. Coaches need to be a model of their services in order to have integrity. If you are a life coach, you need to make sure you are having a very good life yourself. If you are a leadership coach, you need to be an unmistakable leader. If you are a creativity coach, you need to be fully engaged in your own creative ventures. This takes commitment.
- Third, you have to become highly articulate. You must impart the value and consequent expense of your coaching services primarily through your words, written materials, and presence. You have to hone your language and your speaking. This takes preparation and poise.
- Fourth, you need to be skilled in your craft. Clients, many of whom pay for their coaching out of pocket, want to see results fast. As a coach, you need to be very good at what you do. Your services and programs must add clear, tangible value. This takes know-how.

Assurance, commitment, preparation, poise, and overall coaching know-how—a tall order for anyone engaged in a small business, but especially challenging for those coaches who may be new to coaching, new to business, or new to the business of coaching.

Strategic Model

In order to overcome these challenges, it helps to have a strategic business model that addresses both the business and the practice of coaching. Our business model is a road map to help you anticipate the coaching territory, make choices, create a plan, take action, and stay motivated. This book is structured to follow our business model and consists of four distinct sections:

Positioning

You need to build your coaching business so that it has relevance to the larger community around it. In Part 1 of the book, we help you incorporate a set of basic coaching and business concepts so that you feel grounded and aligned with the reality of today's marketplace.

Coaching has a short history, starting in the 1980s, and yet in that time the coaching industry has gone through rapid and sometimes unsettling changes. There is considerable hype about coaching that you need to sort through. The profession is not yet standardized and few of the coach training organizations across the world are accredited or agree on what constitutes a solid coaching curriculum. For your coaching business to succeed, you need to understand the current climate of coaching, how to recognize the coaching trends, and how to avoid the coaching fads.

We will position you to move forward in this direction by explaining the changing trends and market forces that affect coaching today. We also clarify the differences among three professions (coaching, therapy, and consulting) that often get confused, so that you can explain what coaching is and is not to the public. We explore the decisive factors that separate average coaches from their more masterful colleagues and note the competencies, skills, and coaching principles that can move you to the top of your field.

Differentiation

As marketing expert Jack Trout (2002) explained, being different is the key to survival in a crowded marketplace. *Start Up Magazine* calls coaching the number-one home-based profession and the number two growth industry, right behind information technology. All coaches are faced with a growing field of eager competitors. As a coach, your survival will depend on your ability to stand out.

Using a series of insightful questions, we guide you step by step to focus on defining your coaching specialty so that you build a practice that plays to your existing strengths. We show you how to target a niche—the client base that needs your exact services and, as a result, will pay your fee. We offer you strategies to become articulate and a stronger presenter of your coaching services. Then we highlight the marketing strategies that work best to bring in a flow of coaching clients. Our approach to differentiation works to highlight the essence of who you are and what you do so that your business stands out from others.

Entrepreneurship

If you want to build a coaching business that will last, you must become entrepreneurial. We will show you how to develop an entrepreneurial mind-set and the emotional business intelligence to help you overcome the at times emotional roller coaster that owning and operating a coaching business creates. We explore the issue of money and coaching, looking at why even great coaches go broke and what you need to do to become highly profitable so that you earn a good income while doing the work you love. Finally, we help you assess the risks inherent in coaching by highlighting ethical considerations, the complex issues of confidentiality, how to avoid dual relationships, how to implement the best business practices, and how to determine liability insurance options. We offer a template to help you design a solid coaching contract so that you stay safe and legal as a coach in business.

Profiles in Coaching

A business model is only a vague theory unless you can see it in action. In Part 4, we offer you an inside look into case studies of coaches who are in business, making money, and enjoying their work. We present the most profitable coaching specialties and show you how each type of coaching works in the real world so that you can assess if it's the right direction for you. We also offer you a tool kit of additional resources—books, Web sites, sources for coaching assessments, training, and more, to help you take ownership in building your business to the level you desire.

So on to Positioning: To feel grounded in the coaching business, you need to stand on a solid foundation by understanding the relevance of your coaching business to the overall coaching profession. Since coaching's inception, the profession has changed radically. In Chapter 1, we look at the history of coaching and then bring you up to date on the important trends and realities of coaching today.

PART I

POSITIONING

CHAPTER I

Coaching: Trend or Fad?

The profession of coaching has been on a fast track since the 1980s, going through several sea changes. We want you to make sure that your business is well positioned to fit within the coaching industry as it operates today. We predict that the coaching industry will continue to evolve quickly, leaving behind those coaches who can't distinguish the coaching trends from the fads.

Much of the initial hype about coaching, both from the media and within coach training organizations, has deflated. The at times wild expectations about coaching put forward by the coaching industry itself—in terms of earnings, results, and impact on society—have started to come down to earth. This speaks to the maturing of the profession from a business perspective and bodes well for its long-term stability. In this chapter we review the history of coaching and then anticipate the trends and realities that influence the coaching business today.

The History of Coaching

In the 1980s, corporate downsizing across the United States resulted in the reduction of internal managerial training within corporations. With reduced budgets, corporations could not continue to invest in the education of executives, especially when much of middle management was getting laid off. Not only did management education lessen, but a long-standing culture of in-house mentoring relationships that helped executives climb the corporate ladder also disappeared.

If executive coaching and mentoring were to continue in corporate America in the downsized economic climate of the 1980s, it would have to be outsourced. Consultants saw a need that was not being met internally in the corporate culture and added "executive coaching" to their list of services to fill this void. Corporations hired external coaches to groom midlevel executives for promotion or to improve the productivity of problem executives. Management consultants and human resource firms, who formerly offered training or organizational development, became the front line of coaching services.

A few of these consultants recognized early on that not only was there a market of potential customers for their coaching services, but that a second, untapped market was emerging at the same time. An army of well-educated but unemployed or unhappily employed professionals read about the new coaching profession and signed on for coach training in the hopes of creating meaningful work in an autonomous setting. Coach trainees wanted to use their people skills and work for themselves in a solo entrepreneurial business instead of staying within a corporate or bureaucratic setting.

With a flurry of intense activity, a half-dozen schools of coaching emerged in the late 1980s and early 1990s, competing for coach trainees. The schools were all privately held, for-profit companies. The urgency to get the schools up and running made quality control very uneven; some employed newly minted coaches, themselves barely established in a coaching business, as teachers of other coach hopefuls, or offered newly made up, untested curricula. At several coaching schools, this just-in-time teaching atmosphere meant that the curriculum was being cocreated with the coach trainees themselves, on the spot. The trainees came into the schools wondering: What is coaching? How does one coach? Where do coaches find clients? Often, the teachers had few definite answers. The coaching profession rushed to invent itself.

One of the most robust early training schools, CoachU, was created in 1992 by a dynamic former financial planner named Thomas Leonard. Leonard, a mercurial thinker and gifted teacher, attracted a core group of executives, actors, psychotherapists, and human resource consultants, all intrigued with the idea of helping to create a cutting-edge training program for the new profession of coaching.

Leonard and his core group of trainers developed the first comprehensive curriculum for coaching, integrating and refining methods from related lines of work, including organizational development (OD), which relies on a coaching style for team building and leadership; human resources (HR), whose assessments and methods use a coaching approach to help employees increase effectiveness; counseling, a coaching style incorporated since Carl Rogers's 1950s client-centered approach; and personal growth seminars, such as EST, the Forum, Landmark, and Lifespring. Leonard, known for his amazing productivity, was able to use these related concepts of OD, HR, counseling, and personal growth as a springboard for new thinking about coaching. He created dozens of coaching checklists, many detailed coaching programs, and an intensive course curriculum that required at least 2 years to complete. Each CoachU student received an 11-pound coaching manual through the mail upon registration, and more curriculum was continually developed and dispersed.

Leonard insisted that coaches first address their own self-improvement through an 8-week personal foundation course, where all coach trainees went through 25 lessons to dramatically enrich their own lives. Lessons included how to simplify one's life, create daily positive habits, raise personal standards, set good boundaries, eliminate tolerations, get one's finances in good shape, and learn to be *at choice*—to live life with a proactive, value-based attitude. Only after completing this foundational level of coaching would students be considered ready to go further in the curriculum. The next level of courses taught new coaches how to coach a variety of clients—creative artists to sales people to CEOs—based on an exhaustive checklist of client needs, personality quirks, and common coaching goals according to situation. Coach trainees learn coaching skill sets, such as challenging, advising, relating, and strategizing, and specialized skills to use in business settings. Finally came courses to teach business skills for the coach so that new coaches could market and manage their own coaching businesses.

As a virtual coaching school (the training courses were offered primarily by phone and Internet), CoachU used the technology of "bridgelines"—low-cost, easily accessed telephone conference calls to allow students from all over the world to access the teleclasses. Students only needed a phone and a computer to be part of the CoachU ever-growing community. CoachU relied on the immediacy of e-mail to disseminate communication quickly about program changes, new course offerings, and changes in overall direction. Leonard's inventiveness and enthusiasm about coaching were contagious, and his comfort level with new technology positioned coaching as a fast-growing, sophisticated service industry. He set standards for coach training, in both content and format, and wrote several books to outline his coaching concepts. Today, many coaching schools offer virtual training via teleclass based on the CoachU early model.

CoachU envisioned a career for its graduates that would be both satisfying and financially rewarding. One of Leonard's popular teleclasses, "The

Million Dollar Coach," introduced an enterprising business plan suggesting how students could leverage their coaching services to generate an annual income of $1 million. But Leonard admitted in a *Fortune* article (Hyatt, 2003) that the average CoachU graduate would more likely earn far less, perhaps only $60,000 in annual business revenue after 3 years of starting a coaching practice. Unfortunately, as we will see, even that modest prediction was too optimistic.

By the late 1990s, at least a dozen privately held, for-profit coach training organizations competed aggressively with CoachU to train new coaches. Some targeted special coaching niches: The Newfield Network, founded by Julio Olalla, trained executive coaches using methods of philosophy, sociology, and organizational development. Coaches Training Institute (CTI) offered coaching workshops focusing on the elements of rapport and relationship between coach and client. TherapistU (now Institute for Life Coach Training) and MentorCoach both targeted mental health professionals who wanted to become coaches. A few public institutions also began to offer coach certificate programs in executive coaching and leadership, among them Georgetown University and George Washington University, both in Washington, DC. By 2003, International University of Professional Studies, a long-distance learning university, granted Ph.D. status to those who completed its program in professional coaching and human development, and the UK College of Life Coaching offered a master's in coaching in conjunction with the University of Wolverhamptom in West Midlands, UK.

Coaching and the Media

In the mid-1990s, an orchestrated PR campaign within the coaching industry helped to fuel the explosive coaching market: CoachU and its newly formed professional association, the ICF, hired a media consultant to place positive stories about the new profession of coaching in magazines and newspapers. In just 2 years, from 1998 to 2000, the two organizations successfully placed 1,000 mentions about coaching in national magazines and newspapers. Public awareness of coaching grew. As the concept of coaching found its way into the general media, the desire for coaching spread from the boardroom to the living room.

Business owners read about the benefits of hiring a business or leadership coach in *Money Magazine, Fortune,* and *FastCompany. New Age Magazine, Time,* and *Newsweek* ran articles about coaching. In 2000, *Oprah* viewers watched a full year of "life makeovers" with life coach Cheryl

Richardson. Books on coaching authored by Richardson, Tony Robbins, Laura Berman Fortgang, and others hit the best-seller lists.

Coaching Today

Coaches today are finding that the once smooth ride of coaching is developing some bumps and potholes. Take the public impression of coaching. Although the coaching profession benefited from past media stories and mentions, today the media focus is bringing some unwanted results. Life coaching has begun to be criticized based on its inclusion on a few TV shows, notably *Starting Over*, a reality show that follows a group of women who want to change their lives and use the services of two nationally known life coaches. In an attempt to make the process of life coaching more "visual," the TV coaches end up suggesting silly exercises for the women, which has left some in the viewing public scoffing at the idea of life coaching. As one review of the show noted, "I am having a hard time trying to figure out just what each woman's goal is. I'm sorry, but when Jennifer [a contestant on the show] crawled up in that life coach's lap . . . I burst out laughing and just shook my head."

Some in the coaching industry fear that the unusual portrayal of coaching in this show and others (the life coach character on the cable TV drama *Nip/Tuck* is a postoperative transsexual who, in the season finale, admits to having had affairs with her client's son and her own son!) will cheapen the perception of coaching, until it becomes the stuff of jokes.

Seen from a lens of standardization, the coaching profession today resembles the Wild West of early American history. Anyone and everyone can call themselves a coach and it's a buyer-beware marketplace for coaching clients who want to hire a skilled coach and those new coaches looking for coach training. Coach certification is lagging far behind the numbers of newly minted coaches. According to ICF, of the purported 30,000 people calling themselves "coaches" in business worldwide, fewer than 2% have achieved ICF certification as either a Professional Certified Coach (PCC) or Master Certified Coach (MCC). The ICF acknowledges that tens of thousands of people operate as coaches with no coach training and no certification. Others received minimal training, perhaps as little as a 3-hour course. Of the small percentage of coaches who graduate an accredited program, fewer still go through the arduous process of ICF certification.

A bit of history about the ICF: The Professional and Personal Coaches Association (PPCA) was already in existence in 1994 when Thomas

Leonard decided to start a second professional coaching association, the ICF, to standardize coaching, certify new coaches, and accredit coach training programs. Leonard encouraged CoachU trainees and graduates to join the ICF, and within a few years the heavily subscribed ICF merged with the PPCA, keeping the ICF name. The ICF now claims 137 chapters worldwide in 30 countries, and a membership of 7,000 coaches. With head-quarters in Washington, DC, the ICF provides accreditation for coach training organizations, and certification for coaches. It promotes local and international events and conferences. The ICF lists two dozen accredited coach training organizations on its Web site, with another two or three dozen on a waiting list for accreditation. At this time, only one is an academic institution; the others are privately held, for-profit companies, most often solely owned. It's difficult to know how many more unaccred-ited coach training programs are in various states of operation. Determining the validity of any coach training program is challenging for potential students. Since the training programs are most often private, not public, institutions, data regarding student satisfaction, detailed information about curriculum, and results of postgraduate placements and earnings are considered confidential and rarely available.

Sobering Statistics

In 2003 the ICF published the findings of its first membership survey, compiled in 2002. Surveys are one of the only ways an industry can keep track of its members, and the ICF survey revealed some fascinating and sobering statistics about its roughly 6,000 coaches. After reading the survey and participating in ICF-sponsored discussions of its findings, we group the results into six key areas:

- Competition within the coaching market
- Credibility for coaches
- Certification concerns
- Importance of training
- Earning power
- Best business practices

Competition Within the Coaching Market

The findings: The majority of all coaches are newly in business and searching for clients. Seventy percent have been earning money as coaches for fewer than 5 years. The local concentration of coaches is split equally between the East and West Coasts, with California having the most coaches. Seventy percent say they work nationally as well as locally.

What this means for you: Most of your coaching colleagues are brand-new to the profession. Everyone is hungry, trying to start up a new coaching business or sustain one that is relatively untested. Although the greatest number of coaches are primarily concentrated on the two coasts, coaches in most major cities may feel the competition. If you are a pessimist, this finding confirms your sense that the marketplace consists of a lot of hungry sharks (coaches) at feeding time. If you are an optimist, this finding can feel supportive: with so many new coaches having the same business agendas, the opportunities for alliance and collaboration abound. Beyond sharpening your coaching skills, being a skilled business person will be essential.

What we suggest: Become a pragmatic optimist. Collaborate, but keep yourself differentiated in a competitive marketplace. Learn to do two things well: (a) use the specialization exercises in this book to make sure you find the right niche so that you differentiate and promote your uniqueness, and, (b) network with a select group of coaches for support to maximize your marketing abilities.

Credibility for Coaches

The findings: Many coaches have existing or prior experience as business consultants or managers, and a smaller number have some experience as teachers, counselors, psychologists, or mental health professionals. Seventy percent have prior experience as consultants, executives, or managers, and 20% of coaches report a background in mental health. Coaches are, as a rule, well educated: 44% report a graduate degree.

What this means for you: Your prior experience adds credibility and importance to selling yourself as a coach. Business and mental health professionals are well represented in the coaching industry, but financial advisers, teachers, lawyers, and physicians are not. Incorporate and highlight your prior experience, training, and academic achievements. Your track record counts.

What we suggest: In business coaching settings, knowing how business operates is essential. Your prior business background and accomplishments will be your calling cards if you are an executive coach, and you need to spell them out. An advanced mental health degree can be a plus in coaching, especially if you have additional experience, such as business experience, to combine with it. A graduate degree in human behavior is helpful for a coach, and a prior background in law or teaching can be a big plus for certain niches. For those reentering the job market after a long hiatus, or those without a solid résumé, prior work experience, relevant training, or coaching certification, it may take time and effort to find clients and build a track record as a coach.

Certification Concerns

The findings: While becoming certified as a coach is not necessary for building a successful coaching business, the tide may be turning. Most new coaches have yet to achieve certification, although 50% say that they are on a credentialing path. At this time, 18% of the ICF membership has certification, with more than half of those achieving certification in the past 3 years.

What this means for you: Certification may not mean much now, but if this profession follows others, it may become important to your credibility over time. Start your certification efforts early in your coaching career. Join a professional association that has a certification process. Keep records of your coach training and client contact hours. As soon as you have completed all the steps required, apply for certification. There are several coaching associations to consider joining and they have their own separate certification requirements. See the Appendix for a list of associations.

What we suggest: Joining a professional coaching association gives you a standing in the industry and helps you stay current with industry changes. Make sure that you train with an accredited program, since that will be important when you begin the certification process.

Certification through the ICF requires that each coach become familiar with and demonstrate his or her ability to use eleven "core competencies." At the time of certification, a written and oral test will be administered and each coach will be evaluated, in large part, on his or her mastery of the competencies. A complete description of the competencies is available free from the ICF (http://www.coachfederation.org/credentialing/en/core.htm). The competencies, in brief, are:

1. *Meeting ethical guidelines and professional standards:* understanding coaching ethics and standards and ability to apply them appropriately in all coaching situations.
2. *Establishing the coaching agreement:* Ability to understand what is required in the specific coaching interaction and to come to agree-

ment with the prospective and new client about the coaching process and relationship.

3. *Establishing trust and intimacy with the client:* Ability to create a safe, supportive environment that produces ongoing mutual respect and trust.

4. *Coaching presence:* Ability to be fully conscious and create spontaneous relationship with the client, employing a style that is open, flexible, and confident.

5. *Active listening:* Ability to focus completely on what the client is saying and is not saying, to understand the meaning of what is said in the context of the client's desires, and to support client self-expression.

6. *Powerful questioning:* Ability to ask questions that reveal the information needed for maximum benefit to the coaching relationship and the client.

7. *Direct communication:* Ability to communicate effectively during coaching sessions, and to use language that has the greatest positive impact on the client.

8. *Creating awareness:* ability to integrate and accurately evaluate multiple sources of information, and to make interpretations that help the client to gain awareness and thereby achieve agreed-upon results.

9. *Designing actions:* Ability to create with the client opportunities for ongoing learning, during coaching and in work/life situations, and for taking new actions that will most effectively lead to agreed-upon coaching results.

10. *Planning and goal setting:* Ability to develop and maintain an effective coaching plan with the client.

11. *Managing progress and accountability:* Ability to hold attention on what is important for the client, and to leave responsibility with the client to take action.

Certification through the ICF is rigorous and demands many years of documented training and coaching hours. Start now.

Importance of Training

The findings: Most coaches in the survey have received formal training and have hired a mentor coach. Seventy percent are graduates of a coach training program and the same number report having been coached by a mentor coach before trying to coach others. Two accredited programs attract almost 50% of these coach trainees: CoachU and CTI.

What this means for you: The majority of coaches in the ICF recognize that they need training of some kind prior to coaching others. If you resist training, you will be in the minority and may lose credibility. Some corporations require executive coaches to be trained and certified before adding them to their referral lists. Get trained as a coach so that you have a clear coaching model and an abundance of skills to use with your clients. Along with the already established providers of coach training, some interest in offering coaching programs is now occurring at the community college level and at a few universities (see the Appendix for training programs). We expect to see more dissemination of coaching into the traditional academic venues in the future as coaching becomes a more established profession.

What we suggest: The market for coach training is filled with accredited and unaccredited schools, most of which are private, solely owned businesses of short duration. Take your time, ask for referrals, and pick a school that has been accredited by the ICF. Remember that, with a few exceptions, all of these schools are businesses, not public institutions. The profit motive is in operation and the "teachers" who coach you may be brand-new coaches themselves. Check carefully and ask questions so you won't be disappointed. If you are a coach and have never been coached yourself, get a referral to find a mentor coach—one who has been successfully working as a coach for several years—to coach you and offer you a firsthand experience of the kind of coaching you want to offer to others.

Earning Power

The findings: Despite promises of a lucrative business, coaches report that the coaching business functions similar to any small start-up, with slow growth and slow earnings in the first few years. Almost 100% of those responding say they primarily offer one-on-one coaching. Seventy percent are self-employed and sole practitioners. Seventy percent earn less than $50,000 per year of gross annual income. Thirty-seven percent earned less than $10,000 in gross income in 2002. Only 1 in 10 earns the magic number of $100,000 annually.

What this means to you: Finally, we see the financial facts of coaching and they are not pretty. There are too many underpaid coaches in the ICF. There are several reasons why. Most of the coaches in the survey don't charge a full fee, instead offering a sliding scale, pro bono sessions, or bartered sessions. Over 50% said it took them up to 2 years of marketing to get their first paid coaching client. Fifty percent said that they are working with only one to six clients per month. From this we can surmise that a coaching business is similar to most other types of small service-oriented businesses. According to small-business statistics, most small businesses take 3 years to show profitability. Three years may also be a fair assessment of how long it will take to develop a full-fee coaching practice. The research shows that filling a coaching business is a slow process. Regardless of what you may be promised by a training organization, you may need a day job or substantial financial reserves in order to supplement your coaching in the first several years.

What we suggest: Have a business plan to build a coaching business over time, one that can last. Recognize that it takes time to develop a market niche and make good money. Develop your business skills to stay knowledgeable and current about good business practices. Be patient. Learn to network, find the right specialty, know how to target a profitable market, and become an organized and efficient entrepreneur. Be sure you have adequate financial reserves. Don't quit your day job too soon.

Best Business Practices

The findings: The most successful coaches are good marketers. Forty percent say that their primary client target markets are businesspeople, professionals, entrepreneurs, and executives. Twenty percent target the nonworking market (college students, stay-at-home moms, retirees). Business-related activities for the coach in practice, such as administration, marketing, and professional development, require an average of 6 to 20 hours a week, in addition to whatever time coaches spend delivering actual coaching services, which may be as little as 2 hours a week to start. Few coaches spend more than $100 per month on marketing. The majority, 68%, carry no liability insurance.

What this means to you: As a coach, you need to become expert in finding a way to market and network. You also need to learn to organize and manage your time in order to advance your business. You need to adopt professional, cost-effective methods to run a business, not a hobby.

What we suggest: Plan to spend as much time as possible marketing, networking, and organizing your business when you start. As you get more successful and have a full client load, continue to reserve at least 10% of your overall working time for business-related activities. Get ready to wear a number of hats: CEO, coach, marketer, administrator, program designer, manager, maybe even bookkeeper. Develop an entrepreneurial mind-set to make this pleasurable. Identify and use good management skills, and rely on a business model and a business plan. Sound complicated? Don't worry. As the book progresses, we will walk you step-by-step through the process of building your ideal coaching business.

Trends Versus Fads

The major difference between a trend and a fad is that one lasts and the other doesn't. Some wonder if coaching is a trend or a fad. Our answer: it depends on the type of coaching.

An article on coaching in the respected psychotherapy magazine, *Psychotherapy Networker* (2002) cautioned that coaching can go in several possible paths: it might proceed on the path to professionalism, or it might take another route and become a field of lightly credentialed practitioners, similar to certified public accountants versus store-front tax preparers. If the price of coaching stays high, it may be an upper-middle-class phenomenon. But if the coaching profession can prove its effectiveness, it can become a resource for the worried well—higher-functioning adults who would rate themselves as "content" but want more or feel blocked in some area of their lives, who up until now might have chosen psychotherapy as the vehicle for resolving their problems.

Terri Levine (2003), founder of the Coaching Comprehensive, an as-yet-unaccredited training organization, is one of the few in the industry who countered this optimism and wrote openly of her concerns about the viability of the coaching profession. She said that the coaching industry is on shaky ground, having attracted thousands of unsuitable people, who received training via impersonal telephone classes and were taught by coaches who, themselves, never reached financial success. According to Levine, the schools they attended didn't teach them to be in business and didn't provide solid sales and marketing training. She thought that prospective clients care less about what organization you belong to, and more about the quality of your coach training, current and prior experience, and resources that a professional coach brings with them. Above all, they care about receiving positive outcomes for their money.

Her solution? She believed that as the poorly trained coaches and those afraid to sell or market their services leave the industry, this further clears the way for the new people being trained by quality programs, people who have excellent coaching skills and can learn to grow a coaching business.

Executive coaching has been around long enough to be considered a trend, not a fad. Executive coaching has been a strong market since the 1980s, and the business world is increasingly comfortable with the idea of executive coaches in the workplace. The *Economist* (Anonymous, 2003) reported that the coaching market is a $1 billion market worldwide. Harvard Business School expects that number to double in the next 2 years.

Today, within the corporate world, coaching is moving full circle, back to in-house status. For example, Lockheed Martin, a technology company that employs 130,000 people worldwide, has begun an ambitious program to train in-house coaches. At Lockheed, HR managers are being trained to take a coaching approach in their general HR work, to bring coaching skills down the chain of command. Executives are assigned coaches and also train to be coaches themselves. Whereas the initial coach training was delivered by outside consultants, the new HR coaches will be able to lead their own coaching programs and train managers and other leaders in adopting a coaching style. This idea of bringing a coaching culture into a large corporation is becoming increasingly popular within organizations that want to effect better management results and aid employee retention, since a coaching culture values partnership and constructive action.

Teri McCaslin (2002), the executive vice president for human resources at the ContiGroup Companies, a huge agribusiness corporation, estimated that half of the middle and senior managers at their New York headquarters have undergone company-sponsored executive coaching. She said, "Every one of our businesses, across the board, uses executive coaching in one capacity or another, from the top down, starting with senior management."

A quick search of the American Psychological Association Web site shows 30 articles published about executive coaching in only one journal, *Consulting Psychology*, between 1995 and 2005. Several of these are studies demonstrating the effectiveness of coaching in a corporate setting using case studies or the polling of customers. Many coaches promoting executive coaching like to cite a study done by Manchester Inc., an executive coaching firm from Jacksonville, Florida, that polled its own client base and found that 100 executives from Fortune 1000 companies cited a return of six times the initial coaching investment. According to Manchester, this return included gains in productivity, quality, organizational strength, customer service, and reduced customer complaints. Additional studies of other companies suggested that in the workplace, coaching resulted in improved group relationships and retention of executives.

Life coaching is less well studied. One research study, conducted by Anthony Grant, director of the Coaching Psychology Unit at Sydney University, Sydney, Australia, examined the application of life coaching to overall life performance. Grant analyzed a commercially marketed life coaching program, Coach Yourself, and its effects on 20 adults. The study resulted in empirical data showing that a life coaching program can facilitate goal attainment, improve mental health, and enhance quality of life (Crawford, 2000).

Another article suggested that life coaching might be the "next step" for those in 12-step recovery programs (Williams, 2002). Williams, author of several books on coaching, suggested that life coaching can help those in recovery achieve their goals and successes, by showing them how to move into a future-oriented mind-set of constructive thinking and behaving.

USA Today reported, (Petersen, 2002) in an online article, that life coaches are a new option for men. "It is OK for a man to see a coach," said Martha Beck, a popular life coach who guests on *Oprah* and writes a column for O — *The Oprah Magazine*. "It is not OK for a man to see a therapist."

In June 2003, *The Washington Post* called life coaching "the wave of the future" and noted that although life coaching seems like a fad now, it might be in a similar situation to psychotherapy in 1910, at the beginning of *its* profession (Simon, 2003).

Other coaching specialties that we explore in Part 4 of this book, "Profiles in Coaching," also show the promise of being more trend than fad: wellness coaching incorporated into health plans, sessions with a health coach as preventative medicine by a few health insurance companies, and career coaching, which finds a sponsoring market within organizations retraining or laying off employees.

Your Future in Coaching

With the industry of coaching in a state of rapid change, what should a new or experienced coach, or a professional considering transitioning into coaching, do to stay viable? Here is a list of suggestions:

Stay informed about the coaching profession. Subscribe to one of the many coaching e-mail newsletters. Join a coaching association and attend local meetings of national conventions. Stay current on trends in your local area and society at large. Build a library of coaching texts, so that you are conversant in your industry.

Become a masterful coach and play to your strengths. Hone your skills, opt for training where needed, and get coaching from a mentor coach to improve your coaching ability. Rely on your prior experience as you build a business, and integrate all previous strengths and skills to compliment your coach training.

Target a market. The trend in coaching is toward specialization. Find yours and then target a market. Aim to be the best and brightest coach within your niche. Plan to "own" your target market and build a reputation.

Be an entrepreneur. All current data indicate that you will need to be well versed in coaching and business to succeed. Small business ownership has a failure rate of 44% within the first 3 years. Don't be a statistic. Make getting business information and business support part of your priority.

Minimize risk factors to stay safe when working as a coach. Even though coaching isn't a licensed profession, you are still liable for lawsuits or client complaints. Structure your business well and work safely with a minimum of risk. Follow the ethics of the profession and get insurance to protect your assets.

Chapter by chapter, we will point you in the direction of information, self-assessment, and action, so that you learn to accomplish all of the above goals. But first, let's move forward with more positioning for your coaching practice, by making sure that you are clear about the nature, range, and limits of coaching. In the next chapter, we spell out the differences and similarities between two professions that the public often confuses by the public with coaching: therapy and consulting. Since all coaches must become educators about coaching, this is a chance to deepen your understanding of what coaching is and is not, and learn to articulate coaching in a way that attracts ideal coaching clients.

CHAPTER 2

The Differences Among Coaching, Therapy, and Consulting

Coaching as an industry may be recent, but coaching as a style of relating to others is ancient. Examples of coaching, in the form of mentoring, assisting, advising, supporting, or training, can be found documented throughout literature and practiced within many professions including sports, business, academics, and psychotherapy. Because coaching is a new and separate profession, coaches have needed to define the range and boundaries of coaching in order to distinguish it from similar vocations such as therapy and consulting. But since a *coaching style* is often used in these other vocations, it can become confusing for the public to understand what coaching actually involves.

As you promote your services as a coach, a common question you may hear is "How is coaching different from therapy or consulting?" To help you fully understand what coaching is and is not, we look at not only the definition of coaching, but also at its emerging knowledge base. By knowledge base, we mean that coaching has a growing body of theory, insights, methodologies, primary elements, and research that defines it as a separate profession. It's because of this knowledge base that coaching generates results with clients that are different from those generated by either therapy or consulting. First, let's sort out the three professions of coaching, therapy, and consulting.

Coaching Versus Therapy

Since its inception as a new profession in the 1980s, coaches have been trying to explain the difference between coaching and therapy to the

24

public. They often do this with a short, snappy sound bite such as "Coaching focuses on the present and the future. Psychotherapy focuses on the past." Or "Coaching is about achieving goals and therapy is about developing insight." But these definitions are simplistic and, as a result, inaccurate. Psychotherapy can't be compressed into a single sentence so neatly. Neither can coaching.

Here's why: Psychotherapy as a profession has been in existence for over 100 years. At last count, it contains over 100 "schools"—not institutions but distinct methods. These schools vary in approach. One school of therapy, cognitive behavioral therapy, is currently gaining popularity within the media and the therapeutic community because it is so well researched. Cognitive behavioral therapy helps clients focus on specific behavioral changes that they can effect within their present and future situations; therapists using this method do not focus on past issues with clients. This school of therapy uses the technique of goal setting, accountability to the therapist for all goals, and developing clear, tangible solutions to any and all client problems.

Another well-defined school of therapy, brief solution focused therapy, also popular with managed care companies because it results in short treatments with specific results, helps clients contract with a therapist to set concrete goals in a few sessions. There are dozens of other schools of therapies using similar methods. The sound-bite definition (given above) that coaching is about achieving goals, while therapy is about developing insight would be false when comparing coaching and any one of the many solution-based methods of therapy.

Comparisons between coaching and therapy get even more complicated. Consider the thousands of books that have been published detailing the hundreds of therapy methods and the fact that psychotherapy graduate programs regularly teach not one method, but several, as a basis for being a therapist. With 500,000 psychotherapists practicing in the United States, most of whom trained in more than one school or method of therapy, it's even more misleading to try to reduce psychotherapy to a packaged, reductionistic phrase.

Can coaching be reduced to a short sound-bite? Given the range in curriculum within coach training programs, it's likely that there are as many methods of coaching as there are training organizations. So rather than use a single sentence to define the difference between therapy and coaching, we offer you five criteria to help you develop a more informed understanding about the two professions. We focus on the following areas:

- who (population)
- what (purpose)
- where (setting)
- why (intent)
- how (skills)

Who (Population)

Therapy: Therapists treat a vast client population, with one common denominator: the majority of those seeking therapy are at a low point in their lives, facing distress and emotional pain. They range in functioning from seriously impaired to functional, but regardless of how well particular clients fair in general, they seek therapy for the part of their lives that are dysfunctional, wounded, or hurting. The issues that bring people to a therapist are often entrenched and complex, and, as a result, therapy often follows a medical model: An expert diagnoses and then treats a client or patient, and hopefully the outcome is either a cure or a marked improvement in symptoms.

The therapist–client relationship is usually a hierarchical one for good reason; sometimes the therapist, in the role of expert, needs to make a hard call to protect the life or well-being of the client, or to set a course of immediate medical action. The hierarchy also encourages the emergence of transference, one of the powerful methods that some therapists use to help clients work through unconscious material. Based on the inherent hierarchy of therapist to client, therapists who also work as coaches must choose one role with a given client. See Chapter 10 for a further explanation of the need to minimize dual relationships as a coach.

Coaching: Coaches work with a narrower client population that economists call the worried well. According to Marisa Domino (2002), assistant professor of health economics at University of North Carolina, 85% of the worried well don't seek psychotherapy or counseling even when they have personal problems, because they don't identify themselves as psychologically "ill." The worried well, underserved by therapy, are considered the target market for coaches because when they seek help with relationships, parenting, career change, boredom, or unhappiness—the same issues that cause others to seek counseling or therapy—they may be open to considering coaching instead.

The coaching relationship is one of partnership and collaboration. Although the coach may be an expert in certain skills or areas, as a coach she positions herself as an equal with her clients. She asks perceptive questions rather than gives advice. Her clients define their own goals, choices, and decisions, with her input. Then the coach uses accountability, motivational strategies, and constructive support to help her clients meet and at times, exceed their desired goals.

What you need to consider: Coaching clients have challenges, but they are usually quite well functioning and looking for a fast fix to a specific situation, not a personality overhaul. They can be more demanding than therapy clients, bringing high expectations about the outcome of their sessions. Therapy clients "see" or "consult with" a therapist for treatment (medical model), but coaching clients "hire" a coach (consumer model). As a result, these consumers want to see concrete results. Most coaching clients ask to be challenged and will be uncomfortable with a slow tempo, long silences, or vague language that might be very normal in a therapy session. To satisfy a coaching client, coaches need to be articulate, interactive, and direct, and get their points across clearly. We look further into the specifics of the relationship between coach and client in the section of this chapter called "Primary Elements."

What (Purpose)

Therapy: Martin Seligman, past president of the American Association of Psychology, wrote an article on the usefulness of psychotherapy. He defined the purpose of psychotherapy as "the improvement in the general functioning of clients/patients, as well as amelioration of a disorder and relief of specific, presenting symptoms" (1995, p. 970). When therapy works, he wrote, clients report robust improvement with treatment in the specific problem that got them into therapy, as well as in personal growth, insight, confidence, well-being, productivity at work, interpersonal relations, and enjoyment of life. Based on Seligman's assessment, the purpose of therapy (removing symptoms and improving functioning) may generalize into aspects of life and work enhancement that mirror common life coaching goals (confidence, well-being, productivity at work, interpersonal relations, and enjoyment of life).

However, the process of therapy—how the therapist and client get to these goals—may differ dramatically from coaching. The process of therapy is rarely linear; during treatment, some aspects of a person's functioning improve while other aspects stay the same or change more slowly. When the therapy goal is broad—say, to help a person gain insight, heal emotional wounds, eliminate self-destructive behaviors, or bring about characterological development—therapists must take a long view of progress. A therapist might consider the therapy successful if, after treatment, a client has made substantial internal shifts in thinking, feeling, and behaving, even if the client is still functioning in the world in a low to moderate range.

Coaching: Thomas Leonard, one of the early founders of the coaching movement, defined the purpose of coaching as threefold: to help people (a) set and reach better goals, (b) do more than they would have done on their own, and (c) improve focus so as to produce results more quickly (Leonard & Byron, 1998). He characterized coaching as a collaborative relationship that allows clients to become self-generative and productive, and leverage their talents. In process, coaches see themselves as partners, ready to work in tandem with a client to solve an interesting challenge. The issues that coach and client address are rarely life-and-death, so the coach uses a less diagnostic, analytical approach.

To sum up, although the purpose may be similar for therapy and coaching in some cases, the process differs: In therapy, emphasis may be placed on helping a client resolve past issues and grieve loss in order to be more functional in the present. In coaching, emphasis is placed solely on a person's present state of mind and future potential. Whereas some therapists don't want clients to take action, but instead to reflect on a situation and develop insight first, *action* is the byword of coaching. Most coaches rely on markers for concrete outcomes, since coaching is less about process and more about doing. A coach might see success only if a client has made substantial external change and is functioning at a high level.

What you need to consider: When three therapist-coaches surveyed 30 colleagues working as coaches to find out how they saw the differences and similarities of coaching (Hart, Blattner, & Leipsic, 2001), they concluded that the focus of coaching is prospective, and oriented to untapped potential and critical success factors in a person who seeks to maximize fulfillment in life and work. They found that the focus of therapy is retrospective, dealing with both conscious and unconscious identifiable issues, as well as interpersonal relationships.

In practice, the distinctions between therapy and coaching are less black and white, and more of a continuum. At one end of the continuum is the traditional version of psychotherapy, say, psychoanalysis, and at the other end the traditional version of coaching, say, sports coaching. Looking at the ends of the continuum, one can easily discern many differences between the two approaches. In psychoanalysis, there is little expectation for a patient to take action or meet goals; uncovering unconscious material and developing insight is tantamount. The analyst acts as a neutral presence, is nondirective, and wants to help the patient weaken defenses as a way to develop self-awareness and feel repressed emotions.

Contrast this to sports coaching, at the other extreme of the continuum. The feelings and inner desires of the athlete are not examined; winning is the sole focus. The coach is tenaciously influential, directive, opinionated, and expressive, trying to strengthen—not weaken—defenses.

As one starts to move toward the middle of the continuum, away from the classic approaches of psychotherapy and coaching toward the middle ground, the differences begin to blur. Helping a client to feel happy, self-actualized, and more productive? Building a person's confidence, self-awareness, or ability to have better relationships? These goals could fit into the stated purpose of either therapy or coaching. At the very center of the continuum we might see an area of shared common territory simply described as "personal growth."

Although the differences between therapy and coaching tend to overlap in the center of the continuum, many coaches and therapists use methods that place them more toward the ends. The distinctions between therapy and coaching become sharper when we add to the discussion the other categories of where, how, and why.

Where (Setting)

Therapy: Most therapists agree that to provide optimal therapy they need a controlled, consistent, private setting so that they can have confidential face-to-face sessions with a client at regular, anticipated intervals. Licensed therapists adhere to the ethical and legal guidelines of their professions to protect the client and promote safety and trust.

Coaching: Coaching is notable for its flexibility in regard to setting. Coaching sessions can and do take place in the coach's office, the client's office or workplace, a hotel, a restaurant, in the field, on the phone, or over the Internet. It's not necessary for coaches and their clients to have ever met face-to-face for the sessions to be effective. Sessions may be regular, infrequent, or packaged to fit the terms of a specific contract.

What you need to consider: The coach may need to keep the professional boundaries of the coaching relationship firm or somewhat loose, based on the nature of the coaching. Coaches often seek to keep relationships flexible, somewhat self-revelatory, and mutual to make it possible to work within varied settings and flexible conditions. See Chapter 10 for a further discussion about how to set professional coaching boundaries, uphold coaching ethics, and write a coaching agreement.

How (Skill Set)

Therapy: Therapists spend years, during their education and afterward, developing methodology for their clinical work. They rely, at least in part, on cognitive-behavioral methods—asking questions, listening carefully, establishing rapport, verbal mirroring, reframing, observing, challenging, giving some advice, making suggestions, making interventions (offering provocative statements designed to promote insight), proposing assignments—to help clients think and behave differently. But therapists add to this a vast number of additional techniques, many of which are designed to elicit deep feelings, insight, awareness, and kinesthetic or sensory shifts. Most therapists work eclectically, mixing and matching a variety of approaches to fit the needs of their client base.

Coaching: Some coaches use a specific coaching model learned from their coach training. Coach training organizations provide students with coaching tools (assessments, checklists, exercises, and full programs). Other coaches design or collect their own tools and approaches. Similar to therapists, some coaches work eclectically whereas others use a structured approach based on pre- and post measurements and assessments.

What you need to consider: Whereas therapists draw on a century of methodology and development, coaches have limited "pure" coaching approaches to use because the field is still in its infancy. As a result, coaches have borrowed from other disciplines, such as HR, OD, spiritual practices, counseling, psychotherapy, and personal growth. In the end, what we think distinguishes a method as a coaching tool versus a therapy tool is not the skill used as much as how it is applied, in what setting, with what population, for what intention, and with what results.

Why (Intent)

Therapy: Therapists are taught to determine the intention or objective of a therapy session before the sessions begins. They often make use of a treatment plan for a client, with defined objectives, and carefully decide which therapeutic methods and interventions they will employ to foster the session goals. Common therapeutic intentions for individual psychotherapy are to help a client heal, get in touch with feelings, resolve past issues, make unconscious thoughts and behaviors more conscious, relieve symptoms, review behavior, and solve problems.

Coaching: A coach's objective for a coaching session will help determine the effectiveness of the session, and can further discern the distinction between coaching and therapy. Common coaching intentions for a session are to help a client stay grounded in current reality, further daily progress, take constructive action, set and reach big goals, create a vision and mission, become highly effective or productive in a work setting, manage time better, do more, focus, and produce results fast.

What you need to consider: In every session, a coach is presented with a myriad of choices about what to do. The coach decides, often in the moment, what to say and when, how best to respond to a given situation, what questions to ask or when to be silent, how to challenge a client's statement or strategize a course of action, what suggestions to make that can help a client become motivated, or when to suggest a client stop and think. The choices are vast. Coaches need to start a session with a game plan in mind so that the coaching is not random or purely improvisational.

Eclectic coaches may borrow techniques from their other professional training, but need to use them selectively, given the population, setting, and goal of the coaching. The intention of the coach is to move a client forward into action to achieve stated results and gains. For example, some coaches use the method of guided imagery, a closed-eye exercise where the client imagines a future situation and outcome. Therapists use this technique as well. A therapist may use guided imagery with a therapy client to promote insight and gain closure for a painful past memory. But a coach would use the same skill, not for dealing with emotional material or for insight, but to foster a dress rehearsal for a proposed plan of action.

Based on all these criteria, the population, purpose, setting, skill set, and intention all weigh heavily on the distinctions between therapy and coaching. Now complete the following exercise to incorporate this information into an explanation of the objectives you use to define your coaching practice.

Exercise: Coaching Objectives

Fill in the following statements.

I coach this population:

_____

_____

_____

I coach in this setting:

_____

_____

_____

I coach with this purpose in mind:

_____

_____

_____

I coach using these skills:

_____

_____

_____

I coach with this intention for my clients:

_____

_____

_____

I summarize the difference between my coaching and my understanding of therapy as:

_____

_____

_____

Coaching Versus Consulting

Many coaches combine consulting with coaching, creating what some in the coaching profession refer to as "con-coaching." There is nothing wrong with this combined approach, but you need to be aware of what you are offering and why. The consultant assumes three roles:

- provider of expert information
- diagnostician and prescriber of remedies
- adviser who strategically helps a client.

Consultants, as experts and analysts, generally have specialized skills and knowledge. Clients hire consultants for their expertise, their ability to diagnose and resolve organizational problems, and their knowledge and data to propose solutions. Consulting services may include one-on-one time with clients, but more often involve a needs assessment, a program for training, proposals for retooling, and a written report of recommendations. Consultants usually work and bill on a project basis rather than at an hourly rate, and they may focus on the larger system of a work environment rather than working one-on-one with individuals. A consultant's client may be an individual or an entire organization (Schein, 2000). For some consultants, coaching is considered a subset of their consulting services, a "consulting intervention," according to Schein.

Coaches focus on helping specific individuals make targeted change. They do not focus on organizational systems. As a result, coaches must be experts in people and the process of individual change. Coaches understand what helps people become motivated to take action. Coaches want to help grow people, often from the inside out, not just fix a business situation (although that may be part of the coaching results). Coaches know how to ask good questions, be agenda-free sounding boards, help people expand their ability to take action, stay motivated, and successfully accomplish a desired goal.

As we suggest above, one major distinction between consulting and coaching depends on who the client is. Who initiated the request for services—an individual, or an organization? If employees are having problems and their boss recommends the employees get some targeted help, and this help is going to be confidential and individualized for the employees, this fits the definition of coaching. If a boss wants a seminar or training program for several employees at once and a report on the progress of the program, then the situation fits the description more of consulting than coaching, because the client is now the organization.

Another distinction is hierarchy. To be effective, the coach can't be a subordinate of the client, or a boss of the client: the coach must be lateral to the client so that the relationship can be between equals. If coach and client have a similar status or standing, then the coaching can have an impact and the coach's words and suggestions have merit. In contrast, consultants may be brought in for a project and can advise a CEO, but need not be at the same rank or status as the CEO to complete their consulting mandate and to be valuable.

Other distinctions concern the timeline in regard to coaching or consulting: Consultants may finish their work long before a project reaches completion. Coaches are hired to implement changes in individuals, and often work with those people long enough to see evidence-based results. Coaches most often get hired to strategize with clients, but then stay to help clients overcome obstacles, fine-tune the process of change, and observe the progress until the clients achieve their vision and identified goals.

In this way, coaching can be seen as a complement to consulting. Both coach and consultant are service-oriented positions. Both offer advice, expertise, and strategic process. Both may have special understanding of the clients' needs. Both may work with individuals or groups. Both may undertake some training duties. The differences occur based on the nature of the relationship (coaches are accountable primarily to the clients, consultants may be accountable to other people within the hiring organization); the hierarchy required (coaches must be at the same level as the clients to ensure authority; consultants need not have a mutual degree of rank to be effective); the type of work that is offered (coaches work more with helping individuals help themselves; consultants may work more as outsourced, hands-on employees on a project); and the time frame (coaches work over time to see goals implemented; consultants may work on a per-project basis without seeing implementation).

Coaching Knowledge Base

The knowledge base of a profession includes the theories, insights, methodologies, primary elements, and research studies that define and inform that profession. Even though coaching is a young profession, there are three aspects that indicate an emerging knowledge base. These help further distinguish coaching from therapy or consulting. They are:

- methodology: the content of the coaching conversation
- research: social science investigations into the field of happiness
- primary element: the coaching relationship and the unique positioning of the coach and client

Methodology: Content of the Coaching Conversation

We conducted a review of coaching literature, including published articles, books, and coach training curricula where available, and found that one aspect of coaching methodology, the content of the coaching conversation, held true across the literature. Coaching conversational topics include: vision, purpose, and mission; spiritual path; mastery and excellence of work; setting and achieving far-reaching goals; leadership; effortlessness; success; effectiveness; financial independence; attraction; legacy; passion; joy; integrity; abundance; ease; action; money; pleasure; community; flow; creativity; love; clarity; achievement; and dreams.

While some of these topics may be discussed in other client-professional relationships—such as money and financial independence when talking with an accountant or financial planner; creativity and dreams when talking with a spiritual adviser; purpose, integrity, clarity, and goals when talking with a therapist; leadership, achievement, and excellence concerning work when talking with a trainer/consultant—we found that coaches regularly talk about *all* of these topics to their clients, sometimes touching on almost all of them over the course of a month of coaching.

As such, the breadth and depth of the content of a coaching dialogue seems to us to be unique to the profession of coaching, based on the integration of lofty, affirmative, philosophical concepts and pragmatic, strategic tracking of action steps. Not every coach-trainee is competent to initiate discussion on the full range of these topics, but most senior coaches handle them with ease. We find that the most complete coach training curricula teach these topics to student coaches. The best coach training programs teach strategic thinking, methods of empowering others, effective goal setting, life planning, how to find one's spiritual path, financial independence, business and managerial skills, how to help clients achieve states of flow and peak performance, supporting leadership, and furthering passion and happiness.

Coaching conversations are distinct based on *what* topics are discussed and *how* the coach talks about the topics. Senior coaches we interviewed discussed their verbal styles during a coaching conversations, and each made use of the following methods:

- *Challenging clients to stretch their capacity by asking for far more than they have done before.* One life coach says that she asks each client to list the ten goals that they would like to achieve in ninety days, then reverses the list so that the last goal listed is placed at the top of the list. Then she asks the client to "double" that top goal, either by making it happen in half the time or, if the goal has a value to it, such as "I want to make $90,000 this year," doubling the figure offered to $180,000. This willingness to ask for a lot from a client goes beyond the normal stance for therapy or consulting, which is more likely to be satisfied asking for smaller behavioral steps from clients.
- *Adopting a nonjudgmental attitude when responding to clients, to "make the client right."* A business coach who works with clients who want to grow their mid-level businesses asked a client with several franchises to list the obstacles that prevented further business growth. The client said he could not expand and purchase another franchise because his reading of the Bible was that no one person should have too much financial power. Rather than debate the client, the coach agreed with the client's assessment and asked the client for five possible strategies to overcome the obstacle. With this degree of support from the coach, the client began to strategize how to expand by "sharing" power—ultimately bringing in a series of partners and family members to co-own additional franchises. The client felt that this was an excellent solution to his desire to expand, because it stayed within his belief system of right and wrong. This stance of unconditional approval allows the coaching conversation to be one among equals, not always the case in therapy or consulting, which is more hierarchical.
- *Speaking openly and honestly with clients, withholding no thoughts or intuitive feelings.* Several coaches spoke about their use of intuition when coaching clients, that they tracked their own internal dialogue and feelings during the course of a coaching session, and at the end of the session offered concrete suggestions for the client as well as their vague impressions or inklings about what was not said during the coaching session. One coach told her client at the end of a career coaching session that she felt unsettled about the client's decision to take a job offer after a recent interview, but she (the coach) wasn't sure why. Something felt "off" to her, and she just wanted the client to know that she was getting a sense that although this job offer sounded pretty good

on the surface, she recommended that the client take some time and really be sure it was what she wanted. The client listened and said little at the time, but then contacted the coach shortly after the session to say that she had withheld an important piece of information: the interviewer had made several inappropriate statements during the interview and the client was feeling very uncomfortable herself about the offer, but had little to base it on and was loathe to mention it. Based on her coach's comment she reevaluated her initial impressions and was able to clarify her discomfort with the interviewer. Ultimately she refused the offer and found a better job. The coach's decision to be open and transparent in conversation is different from the stance of neutrality that may be exercised by a therapist or consultant.

- *"Gapping" a client—defining a wide disparity between a client's current situation and the desired goals, as a motivator for change.* We discuss this important skill in the next chapter. Coaches explained that the gap between current reality and the stated goal must be big—large enough to give the client a sense of excitement and to allow for advancing quickly toward the goal—but not too big, or it would cause a client to feel overwhelmed. One wellness coach's client made a New Year's resolution: she wanted to lose a lot of weight for the coming year. The client weighed 205 pounds and wanted to weigh 145. But the goal was so large that after the first month, the client shared that she could not get started; it just felt hopeless. The coach helped her client cut her goal in half and set a target of 175 pounds by the Fourth of July. The client loved this new goal and was able to start the program: it felt substantial but not impossible for her to achieve. Allowing sufficient tension to build within a client defining a gap between what is desired and one's current state of being is common to coaching, but not common to therapy or consulting, which may seek to reduce tension rather than create it.

- *Using definite language and "edge"—a type of tough questioning and clear communication to provoke a client into action, not just discussion.* Many coaches said that one of their primary methods in conversation was their ability to get tough with a client, to be direct and "real." Executive and leadership coaches mentioned using an edge in conversation as a necessary tool in coaching senior executives, who responded well to being challenged and confronted as needed. One executive coach who had a prior career as a therapist summed this up by saying that as a therapist he would use coaxing, softness, and understanding to help a client to feel understood, and when ready, shift behavior. "But as an executive coach, I am confrontational," he says. "I need to move faster in coaching so I don't hide my reactions, as I did as a therapist. If I see an opportunity to say something important, I take it. I laser my communication to my clients, to make it short and on-target. My clients really like this and often tell me that this is part of my value. I stand up to them and tell them what I think." The brevity and focus of the coaching conversational style is considered the norm in coaching. Brevity may be used in therapy sessions at times, but it is not the norm since a process of unfolding is important—allowing enough space and time within a session for a client's full narrative to emerge. In consulting, brevity may also be a problem because the information being gathered by the consultant may be highly technical and require time to be explained completely. The consultant's solutions to problems often need a full hearing to be understood and considered, including reports and written suggestions.

Research: Social Science Investigation into Happiness

The research into the efficacy of coaching is still slight. At the 2004 ICF Conference, a full-day research event featured presentations originating from several different countries, including studies on executive coaching, wellness coaching, the impact of coaching following a leadership development program, and a pilot coaching program for Native American students.

But one avenue of more defined research is making its mark within some coaching circles. Social science research that has been conducted for the past decade by a variety of academic institutions under grants from the National Institute of Mental Health has focused on findings about well-being, happiness, and longevity. This research, which is known as positive psychology, studies positive subjective experiences (happiness, pleasure, gratification, fulfillment, well-being, success, longevity) and constructive individual traits (character, talents, interests, values) that enable affirmative experiences. Positive psychology contributes to the knowledge base of coaching when it is used to further coaching aims. The leading force behind much of the current research into positive psychology is Martin Seligman and his team of senior researchers (Seligman, 2002). The Authentic Happiness Coaching Program has graduated 1,000 professionals from a twenty-four-week training program during the past 4 years, and uses the positive psychology research and exercises based on the research as the basis of its program. The Authentic Happiness Coaching Program does not "train coaches." Rather, it prepares professionals across a wide array of disciplines to use the theory, tests, exercises, and interventions of Positive Psychology in their ongoing work within their areas of professional expertise.

Although Seligman has spearheaded much of the research into happiness, additional studies contributing to this perspective can be found in a number of recently published books. Foremost is Vaillant's (2002) longitudinal study of the life span of Harvard graduates from the classes of 1939 through 1943, along with a large group of men from the inner city of Boston. Valiant found that the "mature defenses" of men, defined as "altruism, ability to delay gratification, future-mindedness, and humor" were the direct correlates of the men's physical health, joy in living, and longevity. Peterson and Seligman (2004), Easterbrook (2004), and Schwartz (2004), all promote additional fascinating perspectives into personal well-being.

One goal of the positive psychology is to promote a client's "voluntary control" of happiness, based on a happiness formula of "set range, plus circumstances, plus voluntary control" to equal happiness. *Set range* refers to an unvarying degree of self-reported happiness that does not vary much despite varying life conditions. Seligman (2004) cited numerous published studies to support this formula, explaining that many aspects of life that one would think would affect happiness actually have little long-lasting effects, including:

- climate—no effect
- education—no effect
- money—above poverty level, very small effect
- age—very small effect
- health—very small effect
- negative events and emotion—very small effect
- marriage—slightly greater affect
- practice of religion—moderate effect
- social life—correlates strongest to happiness

What does seem to have the largest effect on happiness, according to Seligman, are three areas of voluntary control:

- degree of satisfaction about the past (gratitude and forgiveness)
- optimism about the future (optimism and hope)
- happiness about the present (pleasure and gratification, including states of flow, meaning, and purpose)

The professionals trained in the Authentic Happiness program are taught skills and exercises for clients that promote measurable change within the three areas of voluntary control, since they correlate to the greatest increase in a person's level of well-being. The research points the way for coaches to enhance the "good life" of clients, including purpose, growth, productivity, self-determination, genius, legacy building, creativity, future-mindedness, parenting, courage, empathy, wisdom, and philanthropy.

Primary Element: Positioning of the Coaching Relationship

A knowledge base also consists of primary elements, the core fundamentals that comprise ontology. In coaching, the coach-client relationship is a primary element, and it is distinct from the therapist-client relationship and the consultant-client relationship. The coach-client relationship focuses on partnership and collaboration rather than hierarchy and expertise. The coach-client relationship actively diffuses the kind of transference that often surfaces in a therapy-client relationship and acts to directly empower a client, which is not the focus of the consultant-client relationship. Unlike therapists, who may well need to keep some hierarchy within a working relationship, coaches need to promote:

- Genuineness (as opposed to detachment)
- Guidance (as opposed to a nondirective approach)
- Mutuality (as opposed to authority)
- Empathy (as opposed to neutrality)
- Support (as opposed to analysis)
- Present and future focus (as opposed to past concentration)
- Ego strengthening (as opposed to ego regression)
- Transparency (as opposed to not revealing)
- Cognition (as opposed to emotion)

Consultants who are transitioning to being coaches need to shift from a position of

- Expert to equal
- Information-based to process-based
- Fixing problems to supporting change in people
- Examination to implementation
- Aloof analyst to close-in and caring helper

Leadership coach Hannah S. Wilder, a psychotherapist turned coach, explained her former role as a therapist as being engaged in the "archaeology of the heart" as she looked with clients to find the past roots of their current behaviors (2002, p. 46). Although as a therapist she was not a neutral, blank slate, being a coach allowed Wilder to be "freer to come forth" with a client, to challenge and question more directly, to focus on actions for the present and future, and to make specific requests for change that can be accepted, rejected, or negotiated. "In coaching, we don't need to unravel and reknit the client's life so thoroughly," she said. "Instead we figure out how to go from here to there, and 'there' is defined by the client right from the beginning of our relationship and reconfigured as we progress." Her leadership coaching is not for the faint of heart, she described, since "the qualities of being an excellent leader and of a good leadership coach are very similar. Being able to hold a sense of stability and success for my clients when they are under pressure from all sides is crucial, just as holding that for followers is important for a leader" (2002, p. 42).

The experience for a client of working with a coach feels quite different from working with a therapist or a consultant. Here's one way a client might conceptualize the difference:

Imagine you are learning to ride a bicycle for the first time, and you have a therapist, consultant, and coach ready to help you gain mastery. A therapist would be standing off to the side, closely observing your attempt to stay upright. She would be understanding and compassionate when you fell, make wise interpretations about why, ask some difficult and insightful questions to help you understand the origins of your lack of balance, and perhaps direct you as to how to get back on and do better, with this new set of insights. A therapist would want you to develop your own prowess about riding the bike over time, for you to notice how you keep getting your feet crossed, or turn the wheel wrong, and to understand what your history taught you to make you try to ride that way.

A consultant might be on a bike next to you, riding circles around you as a biking expert. He would note your current slow ability at riding, tell you exactly how and where you are doing it wrong, give you a detailed, step-by-step plan for doing it right, and then submit a report with all of the findings and suggestions, including suggestions for purchasing a state-of-the-art bike, and then ride off, to leave you to implement the suggestions on your own, in your own time frame.

A coach would climb on the seat right behind you and ask, "Where do you want to go today?"

Exercise: The Coaching Relationship

To understand the value and uniqueness of a coaching relationship, answer the following questions.

When, in the past, would it have helped you to have worked with a coach? Why?

_____

_____

_____

_____

How would working with a coach—not a therapist or a consultant— make a difference for you in your life or work today?

_____

_____

_____

_____

If you have been coached, what did you relish most about the coaching relationship? If you have not been coached, what would you most want from the relationship?

_____

_____

_____

_____

We have examined the distinctions among coaching, therapy, and consulting, and looked at the emerging knowledge base that defines the field of coaching. Now let's move on to the next item in positioning: your coaching competency. What core coaching abilities define a first-rate coach? The next chapter outlines the path to mastery in coaching.

CHAPTER 3

Becoming a Great Coach

Your reputation in a service-based business in large part is built and based on your competency and results. It may be obvious to state this, but all of the marketing strategies in the world will not sustain a coaching business if you can't deliver high-quality coaching services. Most of the new coaches we meet love being a coach, show innate talent, and feel naturally drawn to the profession. But a love of coaching alone doesn't connote skill-based excellence.

What determines greatness in coaching? We reviewed the coaching literature, ICF standards, and coach training curricula from a variety of schools, and interviewed both junior and senior coaches to contrast the core competencies of an average coach versus a great coach. What follows is a shortened interpretation of this information.

Robert Hargrove (2003) defined five basic competencies or "compass points" of coaching. An average coach with a minimum of training should be able to achieve Hargrove's five competencies at their most fundamental level:

- Partnership (work nonhierarchically in collaboration with a client)
- Future orientation (help a client set and achieve goals)
- Reinvention (assist client to make a change)
- Cognition (think clearly and strategically with clients)
- Expansion (encourage clients to get their needs and wants met)

But as Hargrove (2003) pointed out, a great coach goes beyond the basics in these categories. Masterful coaches go beyond the previous list of fundamentals to achieve the following in these five areas:

- Partnership (demonstrate total commitment to the client's success)
- Future orientation (create a culture of possibility)
- Reinvention (prompt personal transformation)
- Cognition (think "out of the box" and see the biggest picture)
- Expansion (encourage client to define and actualize a compelling vision)

Here are suggestions as to how you might include the advanced level of coaching, based on these five compass points, in your own coaching repertoire.

Partnership

An average coach understands the concept of partnership: You, the coach, are an informed, collaborative equal with your client. You stand on a level playing field with your client (not over him or under him, hierarchically). Your coaching relationship is not *mutual* because you are the one who is hired by the client and the sessions are to be about the client, not about you. But the relationship is structured so that the power differential is even.

Masterful coaches take the partnership model to a higher level. They take responsibility to be a fantastic partner, going above and beyond the coaching agreement to be highly attentive and really desire their client's success. Masterful coaches, according to Hargrove, listen for greatness. They listen with heightened focus and attention during the coaching session, and hear the full potential inside each client. A gifted coach who listens this carefully for greatness often senses a moment in the coaching session when a well-placed question or comment will lead toward a breakthrough for the client—where the client realizes something about herself, her work, or her life that she can change immediately to make life better. For an average coach, these breakthrough moments happen once in a while; with the great coach, they may happen in every coaching session.

Breakthroughs are possible when you listen on multiple levels. For example, you may be conducting a coaching conversation and listening to your client's story or narrative on one level. But on a deeper, meta-level, you may be listening for

- inherent strengths
- values

- what is said versus what is not said
- indications of hidden resourcefulness
- moments of unconscious brilliance on the part of the client
- repetition, stuckness, self-sabotage, unmet needs

"When I talk to my current coach," says the client of one gifted life coach, "each session leaves me feeling excited because I feel so supported by her and together, we see the choices and options I have in my life. My coach doesn't give me the answers to my challenges, but she is right there with me, asking good, hard questions. She really wants me to succeed in my job. She asks me, "What is blocking you from you making that phone call to the customer as soon as we are done with our session? Will you make it and e-mail me right back, and tell me that you got the sale?" She really wants to know that I am doing what I say I will. Or she asks, "What will you say no to this week so that you find one extra hour for exercising?" I had another coach, but she did not take so much notice of whether or not I followed through. This coach pushes me to really meet the goals I say I want. She makes me see what I need to do, and then she is the person I account to for making the change."

Future Orientation

An average coach is a competent strategist and can help a client set and achieve goals. The process of goal-setting becomes similar to problem-solving; it's a pragmatic, linear process of getting from here to there.

But great coaches find ways to make setting goals exciting for a client because they help a client see the rich options inherent in any given problem or situation. They infuse the present situation with hope, while pointing the way to a better future. Hargrove (2003) called this creating a culture of possibility and opportunity.

Sally, an executive coach, listened carefully to Bob's list of business complaints: his sales division had flat quarterly earnings; all of his people were stressed by earlier cutbacks; productivity was low, and morale lower. Sally made a big request. She asked if he would agree to double his expected sales goal for the next period. Bob scoffed and said this could not happen and asked how Sally thought he was supposed to do this. "Get real," he responded. Sally said she believed this vision was possible, based on three things. "I know that productivity, morale, and even sales results can and do shift and change all the time, and all three are directly influenced with the right brand of leadership. I can see you as being that kind of leader. Can you see that?"

Bob liked that self-image. Over the course of several coaching sessions, he proposed solutions, rejected others, and put a few into place. He was shocked at how easy it was to reengineer his sales department to begin to generate more sales calls and close more deals. All Sally had to do, as the coach, was hold the possibility of Bob as "that kind of leader" in the face of Bob's skepticism long enough for him to find a way to make it a reality. Great coaches help their clients see their future potential, even in the face of normal setbacks and uncertainties.

Reinvention

An average coach helps a client assess a current situation and make changes in his life and work, using a plan broken down into action steps, with incremental markers of achievement.

A great coach does this, too, but also can employ a nonlinear approach to prompt a process akin to evolution, where change happens more spontaneously. Hargrove (2003) stated that with a masterful coach, reinvention occurs as the coach stands outside the system and makes sure, by asking the client to make big and bold steps, that the client won't revert to old patterns and ways of behaving. With a masterful coach, personal transformation is lasting. The great coach is a willing and able catalyst for major change.

Some coaches prompt personal transformation using a process of paradox: asking a client to do the opposite of what is expected, which builds up some tension or internal struggle within the client. Things can "heat up" internally for the client, and then, suddenly, a behavioral transformation occurs.

Coach Carol Sommer (2002) described her use of the "never ready" paradox that helped her client Lisa, an amateur actress, transform herself from amateur to professional. Lisa studied acting and continually prepared for professional auditions, but never followed through. She didn't feel ready. She performed at amateur venues and got great reviews, but couldn't get herself to audition for a professional play. When she hired Carol as her coach, her goal was to complete a professional audition. Carol requested that Lisa target an upcoming audition, do her usual focused preparation, but then pass it up, not go to the audition. Lisa was shocked. She agreed to work hard and prepare, and then consciously not go to the theater to audition. She found that she was left with even more longing than ever to be ready to follow through.

The next chance for an audition was two weeks later, and again Carol requested the same process: seriously prepare, but not audition. Carol did add one condition, saying that if she was desperately, overwhelmingly tempted to go, she could. Carol reminded Lisa, "If by the fate of the gods you actually get the part, you can always decline it."

Lisa prepared, felt that she desperately wanted to go to the audition, did go, got the part, and accepted it joyfully. The paradox of the "not ready" strategy helped her to transform herself from amateur to professional in 4 short weeks.

Another use of coaching paradox: When experiencing writer's block in the process of writing her first book, the coauthor of the book you are now reading hired a coach. The author had many reasons why she felt she should write a book and outlined them all, without much conviction. The coach said, "I hear that you think this is a good career move, but I must say that I don't personally see a need for this book in the world. Until you can convince me and yourself that this book needs to exist, I suggest you don't try to write it." This intervention caused the author many weeks of angst. What was the need for her book in the world? Who would it really help? Why was it important? This one masterful paradoxical statement caused the author to reinvent her way of thinking about herself as a writer, and to reconsider the purpose behind the book she was writing. After a month of coaching and making some additional radical choices about what she wanted to do with her life, she finally found a reason to write. The block lifted and her work progressed. (This current book is her fourth in five years!)

Cognition

An average coach uses the coaching conversation to help a client to think more clearly and deliberately.

A great coach makes a coaching conversation a work of art, a lively dance that effortlessly generates changes in behavior for the client. The great coach does this by attending to what a client says as well as what is unspoken. Masterful coaches use their intuition to pick up on subtle hints or inklings, such as silences or certain word choices that a client makes, and then fearlessly asks a client to get to the truth of a situation. One coach often ends a problem-solving conversation with, "And now, tell me: What is the *real* truth about this? What are you not saying that we both need to hear?"

Executive coach Richard Leider (1997), who trains coaches, stated in a training session that the obvious question a coach first asks is: *What's the gap between where you are now and where you want to be?* The less obvious follow-up question that Leider then likes to ask his clients is: *How will you know when you get there?*

The right coaching questions can help clients feel suddenly empowered, confident, and eager to move forward with strong, decisive action. Hargrove (2003) suggested the following penetrating questions:

> *What unintended results are you getting now?*
> *How are you contributing to them?*
> *How do you need to shift your way of being, thinking, behaving?*

Great coaches frame their questions to cause a *leap*, to help a client jump over previous beliefs into new thinking. The best coaching questions can help a client face the truth of a current situation, have a fuller vision of what is possible, and recognize the precise steps that will motivate action. When coaching a manager who complained of being bored at work and doing things the easy way, even though his current project and coworkers suffered from his expedient attitude, a masterful coach confronted the client to ask the following questions:

> *If you are bored, what are you willing to do to change that?*
> *Can you hold yourself to a higher standard of being a manager?*
> *If you were to take yourself more seriously as a manager, how would you show it?*
> *What will it mean to your employees to work under a first-class manager?*
> *What might it mean to your boss and the team, when you are more engaged and committed to your project?*
> *How will you celebrate when you become a person who is no longer bored at work?*

Expansion

An average coach understands expansion to mean helping clients identify and meet their needs and wants.

A great coach takes the concept of expansion more literally and sees her mission as one to help a client define a big vision of the future and move toward it without fear. Margaret Wheatley, expert in organizational systems, wrote, "There is a new way of being in the world. It requires being in the world without fear, with play and creativity" (1996, p. 5). Adopting this expansive approach of being in the world requires the coach model to be fearless herself, especially during a coaching conversation. Great coaches boldly move a coaching conversation toward expansive concepts of legacy, abundance, accomplishment, flow, and happiness to help clients determine their "guiding principles," those attitudes that inform one's worldview. Many of the great coaches we interviewed had a set of guiding principles they used to formulate their coaching process.

The CoachU training program (2005), one of the most comprehensive in the industry, bases its coaching curriculum on nine guiding principles, a list of concepts about the human condition that lays the foundation for their entire coaching program. The coaches trained in the program can always check their strategies and coaching interventions against this list of principles to make sure that they are in line with the core program foundation. The list includes:

- People have something in common.
- People are inquisitive.
- People contribute.
- People grow from connection.
- People seek value.
- People act in their own interest.
- People live from their perception.
- People have choices.
- People define their own integrity.

Now that you have seen the CoachU list of guiding principles for coaching, create your own, based on the beliefs and principles that are true for you and your coaching.

Exercise: Your Guiding Principles

Fill in the following statements.

The three principles that guide my personal life:

1. _____

2. _____

3. _____

Exercise: Your Guiding Principles (continued)

I model these beliefs in the way I live by:

_____

_____

_____

The three principles that guide my coaching are:

1. _____

2. _____

3. _____

My coaching business and work with clients reflects these beliefs by:

_____

_____

_____

Advanced Skill Sets

To further hear what coaching competencies might contribute to a coach's business viability, we talked with an additional 30 coaches who earn a six-figure income and have been in the field for at least 10 years. We asked these senior coaches to list the competencies that helped them to build a successful business. The following skills seemed especially relevant for our inclusion. You can adopt and hone these skills regardless of your level of coaching experience.

Define and Close the Gap

Many of the 30 top-earning coaches we interviewed explained that they could get the coaching relationship with a new client off to a good start based on their ability to define and close the gap. They clarify the parameters of the "gap"—the empty space between where a client is right now and where the client wants to be in the future. Then they coach the client to close it, fast.

When defining the gap, the focus is on the space *in between* the two points (present and future), not the end point. Coaches talked about the size and even shape of the gap. If the gap is too big, a client gets discouraged. If the gap is too small, the coaching isn't exciting enough. If the gap is vague, the client feels confused. If it's too narrow, the client feels constrained. Just like Goldilocks, the coach and client seem to know when the gap is just right. The perfect-sized gap can become its own motivating force.

A wellness coach had an overweight client, Tim, who was the veteran of a dozen failed diets. Tim's goal for coaching was to lose weight sensibly. A too-small gap would be the space between Tim's present situation and an end goal of Tim learning to count calories. (Tim already knows how to do this on his own and it would not evidence any excitement.) A too-large gap is a goal of losing 50 pounds in 6 months. (For a serial dieter like Tim, this goal is too far away and the gap feels huge.) A too-narrow gap is to only focus on losing weight. (Although this is the object of Tim's coaching, more than weight loss needs to be factored in to make the gap compelling.) The right-size gap is to set a goal that feels just beyond the reach of Tim by himself, and yet broad enough that he can't wait to see the results of his life once he gets there. For Tim, the goal that worked was to lose 20 pounds in 3 months using diet and exercise, and to time it with a makeover for his apartment. He would paint his living room and add new "normal-sized" furniture that he could use for entertaining (his previous living room furniture consisted of one oversized La-Z-Boy chair.) Tim couldn't wait, and especially loved the idea of focusing on a new look for his home while he was dieting.

Sometimes, even a too-big gap can be managed with closely structured coaching. Ted, a career coach, was happy to begin working with Angela, who complained about her secure but dreary computer-tech job. Ted asked questions and listened intently to first help Angela define her current reality. "Here's my life," she said. "I have a boring, routine, unexciting job. I need to lose weight. I hate facing the weekends. I don't have much fun."

Together, they articulated her desired future: A great job. More fun with friends on weekends. Moments of joy in daily life. The gap between current reality and this desired future felt huge to Angela. Ted thought it might be too large, but Angela was unwilling to let any aspect of it be put on hold. Ted structured the coaching process into three smallish steps and one that was quite large; combined, they would all close the gap. The small steps sounded reasonable to Angela: joining a new health club and going four times each week, keeping a gratitude journal on the weekends, and signing up for a night course at the community college to improve her computer skills. The one big step scared her. Ted asked that Angela commit to finding a new and better-paying job within 6 months. He challenged her to create a plan and take the first serious step within 30 days.

Angela was shaken by this request and said that 6 months was crazy. Ted held firm to his request. He reminded her of her bigger vision several times. Angela finally agreed to commit to this goal, primarily because she remembered how much she loved the vision of a happier work life. At the end of 30 days she had a solid business plan to open her own data-processing company within 6 months.

With Ted's coaching, Angela followed through on every step: incorporating the business, creating a marketing plan, meeting potential clients, and, during the final 3 months, working full-time in both her new business and her day job. She slept little, kept exercising, and wrote in her gratitude journal. She was tired, but felt alive. "I am definitely not bored," she told Ted.

By the 6-month mark, she had three clients and several promising leads. She felt she needed 2 more months to firm up her new business contacts before she would be ready to quit her day job. Ted agreed to her new timeline wholeheartedly because they both could see how far Angela had moved and how close she was to meeting the goal. "Extending the goal was good judgment on her part, not a way to avoid the big step," he said. One year later, Angela says, "I wake up thrilled each day, living on the edge because I am in business for myself, but I am so happy and feel so proud. Without someone like Ted to take my complaints seriously, and ask me to really change, I could not have made this shift."

To close the gap, good coaches help clients put their emotion aside, so that the work and persistence required to meet a big goal or overcome a setback do not feel personally draining. A famous ice-skating coach says, "There is no room for emotions on the ice" and wants her athletes to spend the time in their sport "thinking, thinking, thinking."

Exercise: Define and Close Your Gap

Complete the following exercise to learn to use the size and shape of a gap as a motivating influence.

1. Think of a goal you deeply desire that does not exist in your present situation.
2. What is the smallest goal you could set? Pay attention to the size of the gap. Does the goal excite you?
3. What is the largest goal you could set? Pay attention to the size of the gap. Does the goal seem impossible?
4. What is the narrowest goal you could set? Pay attention to the size of the gap. Does the goal feel too controlled or constrained?
5. What goal would be just right and cause you to stretch just beyond your normal comfort level, but not put yourself into a state of resistance, stuckness, or terror? Define the specific goal that makes you feel excited and motivated. Notice the size and shape of the gap.
6. Develop a written action plan. Who will you be accountable to for your actions and progress?
7. Take the steps forward to close the gap and celebrate each win with a trusted friend, family member, or your coach.
8. What degree of energy, courage, resolve, and motivation do you need to stay with this goal? This is the same energy that your coaching clients will need to find, so make sure you know firsthand how it feels.

Move Clients Forward

The senior coaches we interviewed for this section of the book rely on their ability as motivators to keep clients engaged during the middle stages of a coaching relationship. Here are some of their suggestions regarding motivation.

- Assess whether a client is coachable. (When in doubt, review the well-tested Stages of Change model [Prochaska, Norcross, & DiClemente

1995], to determine who is ready for coaching, and who is not.) Clients who are not generally coachable fall into the the "precontemplation" stage (have no intention to make a change, just want to talk) or "contemplation" stage (a bit closer, may be ready to take action in 6 months). Coachable clients are generally in the "preparation" stage (have taken some small steps on their own toward their goal) or "action" stage (well into the process of changing overt behavior).

- Make requests at every session. The request is a powerful coaching tool. Be clear and firm with your request. Don't be shy about asking for behavioral change. There are three possible request responses from a client: yes, no, and a counteroffer. Learn to accept all three gracefully, and if you get a response other than a yes, get the client to clarify the objections or counteroffer, and make another request that the client can agree to.

- Use accountability. The best accountability agreements embody the SMART acronym (specific, measurable, attainable, realistic, and time oriented; Whitworth, Kinsey-House, & Sandahl, 1998). When clients are vague and unspecific about their goals, they can't move forward into action. A clear structure and weekly accountability (even with a gentle "How's it going?") can work wonders toward motivation.

- When a client is coachable and the coach makes requests and uses accountability and requests, but goals are still not getting met, some coaches say that it's time to take a look in the mirror. "Coaching begins at home," one of the senior coaches we interviewed explains. To get others moving forward, you must be a pro at moving forward yourself.

Betty, a life coach, hired us for mentor coaching to improve her coaching skills. Reviewing her caseload, she reported that six of her twelve clients were currently making little progress on their stated goals. She assessed all her clients as coachable, and they had achieved other goals before. We asked Betty what she was doing as a coach that contributed to this lack of motivation on the part of her clients. She thought about this and said that lately she didn't ask much of her clients because she was feeling personally overwhelmed and slow to make change herself. When her clients offered excuses or explanations about why they hadn't completed an action step, even one that they agreed to take and be accountable for, she as the coach rarely said anything. She accepted all explanations as valid, even when she realized that some of the explanations required more constructive coaching.

We asked Betty first to get motivated herself. She listed the items on her own to-do list that she was procrastinating about. Then we requested that she commit to achieving them within 30 days. She balked, saying she was much too busy this month, what with company coming, a sick cat to nurse, and a project to finish. We said, "Is this a no to our request?"

"It's not a no. It's what I go through in my mind and why I procrastinate. I want to comply with your request, but I am not sure I am up to it right now."

We held firm: "Okay. Let's make sure we are on the same page. We took you at your word when you said you really wanted to become a better coach. Did you mean it, or was that just an idle wish?" Betty laughed and got to work. One by one, she checked off accomplished items, and as she did this, she saw how firm and unforgiving she needed to be with herself. When she wavered on a goal, she used strong self-talk: "Come on, Betty. You can do this. Let's get going now. Just do it. No excuses." The power of the self-talk gave her a good understanding of how tentative she had been, verbally, with her slower clients.

Betty recognized that to become a better coach, she needed to add an additional "voice" to her repertoire. She had what she called her "church lady" voice—a sweet, tentative, caring voice—but she needed to have a "Nike (Just do it!)" voice as well, one that could hold herself and others accountable. A great coach needs to be able to be tough and have an edge, make large requests, and hold firm to the greater vision to move clients forward.

Exercise: Moving Forward

Complete the following exercise to experience your own degree of motivation.

1. This week, pick one goal you procrastinate about and take action to complete it.
2. Feel resistant and distracted? Push past your mental and emotional blocks.
3. Notice your self-talk. What role does it play in your motivational ability? Find a "Just do it" voice of your own, to help you stay focused. Notice where you might have gotten offtrack in the past. Keep going until the goal is achieved.
4. Identify the self-talk and other inner resources you rely on to accelerate your motivation.
5. Determine how will you use this inner motivational ability with your clients.

Stand in Abundance

The senior coaches said that another key to success with clients was their ability to *stand in abundance*, an optimistic viewpoint of seeing possibility within every situation. From this perspective, a coach sees that opportunity is plentiful and surplus continually circulates, so that it is possible to attract and procure the resources to meet future goals. Great coaches help their clients recognize an abundance of time, money, information, creativity, prospects, love, happiness, peace, and support. "Abundance is a game," one coach said, "where the mundane meets the divine."

Carol, a business coach, had been coaching her client Wilson, an accountant, for 2 months. Wilson's goal was to double the profitability of his business without working more hours and to generate more referrals, but he had no idea how. Carol asked Wilson to do some market research with each existing customer to hear about any unmet customer needs. After the tax season ended, Wilson sent out a survey to 60 customers asking about their personal and professional financial needs. Almost half responded and, at Carol's suggestion, he invited those who responded to lunch, one at a time, to talk more in depth about their answers to the survey.

As a result of the surveys and the lunches, Wilson now had a vivid picture of the bigger accounting needs of his clients, many of which he could categorize into four distinct areas. Now four new business options opened in front of him, including one that really excited him: teaching. His clients wanted to learn more about investment and tax incentives. Wilson marveled at the opportunities to teach group classes, to leverage his hourly rate, and to provide a new service. He also told Carol that he felt much more connected to his client base. Twenty-five existing clients now saw him as a caring professional, not just an accountant. As a result, referrals began to pick up. Abundance!

Having an abundance attitude doesn't mean that you live in a fantasy. A successful entrepreneur holds dual realities: you see life as it is, with its pragmatic limitations, and at the same time you see that opportunity is ever present. A reporter (Schulte, 2002) at a Young Entrepreneurs' Organization seminar in Washington, DC, attended by hundreds of CEOs who create businesses of all kinds that average $5 million in gross revenue, noted that the attendees shared one common notion: their unshakeable optimism about the vast opportunity they saw for themselves and others, even in the face of an unstable, unpredictable marketplace.

But with so much opportunity, what actions are best to take? Imagine you are standing on the bank of a swiftly flowing river. The river is full of business opportunities, potential clients, and collaborative possibilities rushing by. If you stand on the bank, the river seems to move fast and you only get a fleeting glance at the opportunities before they are gone. You are safe and dry, and wondering: How do I get into that flow without getting my feet too wet? Answer: You can't.

You will need to wade out, making some missteps along the way as you navigate the rocks and hidden pockets of silt and dirt, maybe falling down once or twice, holding a strong intention about the your ability to withstand the flow. As you finally learn to stand in the flow of the river comfortably, swaying gently with the currents, you can see close at hand all that goes by you, and decide when to make your move.

Exercise: Spotting Opportunities

Check off the following opportunities you want to pursue to create professional opportunities and to learn to stand in abundance.

- ❑ Partnering with others in new ways
- ❑ Brainstorming about new business
- ❑ Networking just for fun
- ❑ Thinking bigger and bolder
- ❑ Reorganizing what I already have or do
- ❑ Reconnecting with old friends or referral sources
- ❑ Modeling a successful strategy of someone else and following through to make it my own
- ❑ Spending money to make more money
- ❑ Trying something brand-new in my business, just because I want to
- ❑ Taking a bold risk that resonates with my vision
- ❑ Doing something that no one else I know has tried
- ❑ Doing something that everyone else I know has tried
- ❑ Taking a class or a workshop that stretches my skills
- ❑ Completing everything on my to-do list within 1 week
- ❑ Saying yes to things I would normally reject
- ❑ Doubling my goals in my prep form for the month and accomplishing them all
- ❑ Going into unfamiliar situations just to experience novelty
- ❑ Creating a project, budgeting for the project, and carrying it out to completion

Decide which opportunities to pursue this month and note the additional abundance that comes from taking action.

The Value of Training as a Coach

To train or not to train—that is the question for many new coaches when considering how to proceed in the business of coaching. According to the 2003 ICF survey we analyzed in Chapter 1, 70% of the coaches responding were graduates of a coach training program and the same number had been coached by a mentor coach. What could training offer you? Most coach training organizations offer:

- Coaching curriculum
- Information on coaching skills and marketing a coaching business
- Other resources (links to other organizations, reading material, licensing programs, assessments, additional courses once you have graduated)
- Certification within their program, which can be used as part of your future ICF certification
- A community of other coaches for professional support and business referrals
- A safe environment where you can practice your coaching, and get feedback, meet mentor coaches, and gain confidence.

When selling your coaching services, especially in the business world, your prior experience and track record probably matter more to potential clients than your certification in coach training (although a few corporations and organizations only want to hire ICF-certified coaches). To sustain a coaching practice and to see results with clients, however, your depth of training may become an essential factor.

Coach training can open up the coaching profession for you. Your training will put you in closer contact with senior coaches, give you skills and tools that you can use with clients, and teach you how to work with more than one type of client. Part of most coach training programs is that you, the coach trainee, can be coached by a mentor coach. If you have not yet worked with a great coach yourself, it is hard to understand truly the value of coaching. Coach training also encourages the need for self-regulation—taking responsibility for your own excellence by following the ethics and principles of accepted coaching today, working toward accreditation, and getting the peer supervision or mentoring you need to become and remain a great coach. In Part 4, "Profiles in Coaching," we profile 13 senior coaches who represent the most viable coaching specialties. The majority of them completed coach training early in their coaching careers. The few who didn't were able to develop a coaching practice by relying on their graduate degrees, additional professional certification, and prior work experience. Many of the coaches profiled are graduates of one of two coaching schools—CoachU and Coaches Training Institute (CTI). These coaches have been in practice for a decade or more; when they started their training, those two schools were among the few in operation.

Today, as the coaching industry explodes, so do the number of coach training schools. Some coach training programs have a course of study that takes 3 years to complete; others offer just a weekend. Some schools train you to coach a general population; others are more focused. Unfortunately, because schools vary widely in terms of curriculum, cost, time required, benefits, and trainers, and since most are privately held businesses, we could not find any published comparative review of the various coaching schools.

This means that you are on your own to investigate schools and compare tuition, course offerings, and overall benefits. We suggest that you train with those schools that are ICF-accredited (or pending accreditation). If you plan to get certified as a coach, training with an accredited school will be part of your certification application (see the Appendix regarding certification), so it is a wise investment to choose an approved school.

Some therapists, consultants, human resource managers, and organizational development specialists we have met question whether further coach training is really necessary before starting a coaching business. They may already have received similar training or demonstrated clear coaching ability in their prior work, already have clients who are eager to sign up for services, and don't want to commit the time and expense of further training. To evaluate your need for training, consider your current coaching experience as well as your specialty and your marketing niche (see Part 4 for a description of specialties and Chapter 5 to define your niche). At the very minimum, read on your own. See the Appendix for suggestions about books on coaching to help you assess your skill level and your need for further education. Remember, it's rare to embark in any profession without skill-based training.

Be a Model of Your Services

The senior coaches we interviewed embody what they sell. They are a model of their services. The partnership position of the coach-client relationship means that your clients will look to you as a real-life example. A coach is not a medical expert, or a boss who can tell others what to do without following one's own advice. If your life is not working well, it's going to be hard to sell your services as a life coach. If your business is in chaos, it will be hard to coach a business owner to success. If you don't pay attention to your exercise and eating habits, you will not have integrity as a wellness coach.

Lora, a leadership coach, went through her own hard-won experience as a leader. Prior to starting her coaching company, she worked for two corporations over the course of 12 years, jumping from promotion to promotion as she climbed the rungs of a steep executive ladder at a notoriously male-dominated corporate organization. After she left the corporate world, she built two small businesses and learned what it meant to be a CEO. She also pushed herself as an athlete, and co-led several hiking expeditions in Tibet, where she and a team of women volunteered to take small groups of inexperienced hikers through a walking tour of remote monasteries.

"I know firsthand the power and the pressure that leaders feel. I never ask an executive to take charge in any way I have not first asked of myself," Lora said. Because of her executive positions in management, prior business ownership, peak athletic performance, and toughness as a wilderness guide, her role as a leadership coach resonated with her clients.

Being a coach may require that you think about yourself as a standard-bearer. To have a successful coaching business, you ideally need to be:

- continually passionate about your work
- an articulate educator
- a skillful master of your methods
- highly collaborative
- interested in building a larger vision
- motivated and self-actualized
- grounded in your desire to serve others
- an entrepreneur who loves business
- confident about what you have to offer to the world
- self-aware, continuing to grow personally

Exercise: Becoming A Model of Your Services

Become congruent and model the services you offer. Check those items that apply and create a plan to accomplish each one.

❑ *I am on a strong financial track.* It's hard to be an effective coach when you are overly concerned about money. Get mentor coaching and financial advice so that your business prospers and you achieve financial independence.

*My plan:*_____

_____

❑ *I decorate my office space so that I love spending time there.* If you love to spend time in your office space, you will be happier when you are at work. Buy dependable equipment, upgrade your business systems, bring in fresh flowers, get comfortable furniture, and surround yourself with colors that make you feel good.

*My plan:*_____

_____

❑ *I find solutions for all the complaints I have regarding my work.* Correct all of the problem areas in your business so that you have no energy drains. Make your business a problem-free zone.

*My plan:*_____

_____

❑ *I get all my personal needs met outside of my practice.* Overworked coaches might have a business, but no life. Devote time to hobbies, self-care, and satisfying relationships outside of your work.

*My plan:*_____

_____

❑ *I have a supportive professional network and a mentor coach.* Get the support you need first, so that you can give to others from a full well, not an empty tank. Have a strong professional network that encourages your success.

*My plan:*_____

_____

The next step in the business model is to begin the process of differentiation, so that you understand your uniqueness as a coach and can manage competition by standing out from others. In the next chapter, we explore a process of self-exploration that will help you to determine your coaching specialty.

PART II

DIFFERENTIATION

CHAPTER 4

Four Questions to Your Perfect Fit

In Part I of this book, Positioning, you learned how to create relevance in your coaching by understanding more about the trends of coaching, the distinctions among coaching, therapy, and consulting, and the elements that create a masterful coach. In the chapters in this part, "Differentiation," we focus on how you define your uniqueness as a coach to showcase your distinct coaching services so you stand out in the marketplace, how you target a niche market, and the best strategies and approach for marketing your coaching business.

Finding your specialty as a coach is the first step in building a successful coaching business. Your coaching specialty is part business decision, part a decision of the heart. It's a contemplative process. Our process asks you to consider what you have experienced in your past that contributes to your coaching skills and what direction you would like your coaching to take in the future. When you take the time to answer all of the questions in this chapter thoughtfully, you will begin to see a direction emerging for your coaching, one based on who you are, what you have done, what you are proudest of, the skills and strengths you like to utilize, and your passions.

Deciding on your coaching specialty may be the most important step you take to differentiate yourself from the competition and, if done well, will also serve to connect you to the core of your coaching. Your specialty not only defines your scope of practice; it also helps you determine the marketing niche that will be your home base.

The questions we want you to contemplate and answer in this chapter function as markers that help coaches become successful in their selection of a specialty. These questions ensure that your practice will be reflective of your skills and your spirit, while also guiding you to evaluate what is most important to bring forward from past work and life experience. You will see that the gestalt that is created by thinking through each question carries over to the next and in total, can create a perfect fit between you and the focal point of your coaching services.

Question #1. What Are the Previous Work and Life Experiences that You Want Your Coaching Practice to Feature?

Coaches need credibility. Since coaching is a new profession, your credibility will be based, in part, on the prior work and life experience that informs and determines the nature of your coaching. Sometimes your prior experience is of such significance that it alone determines your coaching specialty and direction. In other cases, prior work and life experience needs to be examined and reintegrated to create a specialty that will be satisfying to the coach and valued in the community by others.

To determine how to utilize your prior work and life experience in your coaching specialty, begin by listing all past knowledge, expertise, and learning that feels important to your work as a coach. As you look at your list, underline or highlight those experiences that will or already do play a large part in your coaching. What experience in your past makes your coaching credible, reliable, and convincing today?

Note the jobs or careers you have had prior to coaching. Consider both paid and unpaid positions. Notice any overlap in duties or responsibilities as you create this list. What are the aspects of your work experience that make you the most proud, as you look back, or were the most personally satisfying? When did you feel best appreciated by others? Who did you help and how?

Look at your past life experience as well. What roles have you taken on in life? What challenges have you faced and overcome? What have you learned that informs how you coach others? What have you achieved in your relationships and your personal life that are part of the value you have to offer others in your coaching?

Here is how one coach integrated prior experience to determine his coaching specialty. Ned, a registered nurse for almost two decades, recently completed a 3-month coaching course and has two life coaching clients in his small coaching practice. He still works full-time as a nurse at a busy hospital. Ned had trouble, at first, responding to question #1 regarding prior experience. "I haven't really done much in terms of work other than nursing for the past seventeen years," he said. "I have worked at a large hospital on two units, working closely with patients who have chronic pain. I do like working with health issues, but I am not sure if I want that to be part of my coaching specialty."

We asked Ned to make a list of his previous work and life experience. Under work he listed nursing and bartending (an earlier job that helped pay his way through school). "That's about it for my work experience," he sighed.

"What about volunteer work?" we asked.

He added to his list, "Coach for a soccer team." Ned said he loved playing soccer in college and now, as father of two girls who only wanted to learn ballet, he volunteered as a coach for a county team. Ned saw a general list of available teams and one stood out. A "Special Olympics" team of moderately handicapped, preadolescent boys and girls was without a coach. None of the children had any experience playing soccer. Ned liked the challenge of working with these children and spent a lot of time teaching basic skills, breaking down the skills into manageable steps, complete with flash cards for the children to take home and review with their parents. Ned tried hard to make each practice structured. He also had fun. "I love coaching these kids, and it has been relevant to my work as a nurse, because many time the patients I see are quite physically limited and need a lot of motivation to move forward in their rehab programs. I really learned how to motivate the kids on the team with a mixture of work and play, and in turn used some of the methods with my patients, so that they can do more and keep going, even when it looks hopeless."

We asked him to list other life experiences. On this list were his obvious roles as "father, son, brother, husband" but also items that reflected his unique personal knowledge. He noted that he helped deliver his daughters during their births. He added his love of skiing and his time spent at ski schools in Vermont as a child, as well as the hours he devoted to teaching his two girls to ski. Ned looked at the list of his accomplishments and experiences, both in work and life and, in his understated way, said, "I think I am learning something about myself."

"What's that?"

"I didn't realize the patterns that run through my life: nursing, coaching, motivating kids, and competition. I am beginning to see that if I can combine most of these elements into a coaching practice, it will have compelling interest to me."

During the next 2 months, Ned attended a coaching conference. While networking with another coach, he spoke about his background in nursing and his passion for motivating handicapped kids using competitive sports. The coach put him in touch with a nonprofit foundation that sponsored a summer camp for handicapped children. Ned submitted a proposal and was hired as a peak performance coach by the foundation, to help train their camp counselors and staff using methods of motivation and coaching to spur the children to reach a higher level of competition and sportsmanship. Ned also began to offer services as a peak performance coach in his community and offered programs for several private schools who catered to handicapped and learning-disabled children.

Exercise: Work/Life Experience

Answer the following questions to better utilize your previous work and life experience in your coaching career.

What is the previous work experience that you want your coaching practice to feature?

_____

_____

What is the previous life experience that you want your coaching practice to feature?

_____

_____

What do you love to do in your spare time?

_____

_____

In what capacity do you volunteer your time?

_____

_____

What have you always wanted to do in your life or work that you don't get a chance to do now?

_____

_____

At the end of your life, what is the legacy you hope to leave?

_____

_____

What needs do you see in your local community or society at large that go unfilled?

_____

_____

Question #2. Where Have You Achieved Excellence in Your Life?

To become a great coach, you need to specialize in such a way as to showcase your excellence. When and how have you achieved merit on a personal and professional level? What are you proudest of in your life and work? What obstacles did you have to fight to overcome, and how did you rise to the occasion?

Susan Shevlin, a life coach from North Carolina, excels at helping others to find their life vision. She herself is blind—she lost her vision at age 16. But she came to recognize that vision is more than just seeing: "I transformed my physical blindness into insight. Today I practice what I call 'vision coaching.' In dealing with my blindness, I went through many shifts and changes during which I discovered my strengths and limitations. That passion later turned to a vision for assisting others to use and maximize their own strengths which, in turn, led me into the field of therapy and coaching" (2002, p. 115).

Peak performance coach Audrey Penn, from Maryland, was diagnosed at 4 years of age with juvenile rheumatoid arthritis. She studied ballet to overcome the muscle deterioration she suffered. She later used her understanding of physical therapy and mental toughness when developing a program of "alignment coaching" for athletes, showing them how to strengthen their natural abilities. Athletes visit her at her studio in Olney, Maryland, where she coaches professional athletes to perfect their sport. Her rigorous devotion to performance translated into a way to help athletes perform at their own levels of excellence.

Olivia Mellan (1994), a money coach in Washington, DC, told the story of her own shopaholic tendencies, hiding her new clothing purchases behind a chair, ashamed to admit that she was spending money even though she was earning it herself. She began to confront her money attitudes, and eventually developed a coaching practice that helps others deal with their money issues. Now a nationally known author, she writes a monthly column, "The Psychology of Advice," in *Dow Jones Investment Advisor* and speaks to national audiences about money psychology.

What have you learned to transform? What handicap or limitation have you overcome? Where do you shine in your life of work? Your accomplishments can be a signal of the gifts you have to offer to others. Incorporated into your coaching business. They can make your coaching business stand apart from the crowd.

Exercise: Excellence

Answer the following questions to define your excellence in life and work.

Where have you achieved excellence in your life?

_____

_____

_____

Where do you stand out from others in the work you do?

_____

_____

_____

What limitations or problems have you overcome in your life that inform your coaching today?

_____

_____

_____

What are you best known for among your friends and colleagues?

_____

_____

_____

What accomplishments or achievements come easiest to you in your life or work?

_____

_____

_____

What challenges do you enjoy the most?

_____

_____

_____

Question #3. What Skills and Strengths do You Possess that You Want to Use Every Day in Your Coaching?

Each coach relies on different skill sets and competencies in the process of coaching. Your list of personal and professional skills and talents may be broad or specific. Just because you are competent in an area doesn't mean you want to build a coaching practice around it.

One new coach, in assessing her work experience, noted a long prior career working as an addictions counselor within a prison setting. She was very skilled at anger management. She could calm an explosive situation, teach anger management skills, and show an inmate how to redirect anger in a more constructive way. But she told us that she didn't want to use that skill in her new career as a coach. "I have helped enough people to calm down for one lifetime," she said. Instead, for this question, she listed those skills and strengths that she had but did not use often, untapped talents that she said she would love to bring into play.

Christine, a human resources specialist working for a county government program, administered career assessments for unemployed workers and taught résumé writing. What she kept hidden was the fact that she herself wanted a new job. She liked the rare times she got to talk to the job seekers instead of just testing them. "I love the one-on-one time best," she said. "During that time, I really get to use the best of myself to help others. I have had some remarkable results, when I could just quietly talk to other people about what they really wanted in their work life and then help them create a plan for that. But it takes time that I don't often get to use in my regular work."

As she began to develop a business plan for a coaching business, we wondered with her how she would feel about having a job where she would need to use that skill every day. Christine's eyes lit up and she smiled. "If I could be the kind of coach who talked about vision, spiritual path, and finding what I call 'right work'—the kind of work I think we are all destined to do, each day, I would be thrilled to come to work." We asked her to get very specific about the skills and strengths that she would want to use in her new coaching business, so that she could bring the best of herself to her new career. We now ask you to do the same, in the following exercise.

Exercise: Skills and Strengths

Answer the following questions to define the skills and strengths you want to include in your coaching on a regular basis.

What skills and strengths do you possess that you want to use every day?

_____

_____

_____

What positive traits about yourself do you observe that keep repeating in various situations over time?

_____

_____

_____

What skills and strengths do you value, in their own right, regardless of recognition by others?

_____

_____

_____

As you rethink a recent goal that you accomplished, what natural skills and strengths did you use to achieve it?

_____

_____

_____

What social or intellectual skills have helped you to develop into the person you are today?

_____

_____

_____

Question #4. What are You Passionate About in Your Life and Work?

Coaches ask their clients to define their passions during coaching sessions because passion is a motivator and an inherent fuel for change. You need passion in your coaching business, too. Being passionate about your coaching specialty will help you in at least three ways:

- *Attraction:* Your passion and enthusiasm are your main calling cards for clients. When you are selling an intangible service, if you don't feel enthusiastic, it is much more difficult to interest or attract a potential client.
- *Congruence:* If you want to help others find their passion, you have to go first. You can't ask coaching clients to behave or attempt behaviors that you yourself shy away from. You must be passionate, open to new learning, and willing to take risks in order to inspire passion in others.
- *Pragmatics:* With enough passion, you won't mind all the marketing, administration, and other tedious tasks that owning and operating your own business require. Passion is the small business owner's daily fuel. Your day-to-day interest and excitement will help you through the normal ups and downs of building a coaching practice, year by year.

Joseph, an internist, set aside a few precious hours each week to attend coach training classes. He was curious about coaching and, while not wanting to leave medicine to become a coach, he wanted to incorporate coaching into his ongoing medical practice in some way. When we asked him to complete this question, he had no answer. Joseph had been a doctor for 23 years. It was satisfying, but not something he felt passionate about at this point in his career. He lived alone, was divorced, and was a quiet, thoughtful person. He finally answered, "I am not a passionate man. I am a conscientious doctor."

A month went by and he returned to the question of passion. "I would say I am an avid, enthusiastic reader. I actually live for the time, usually in the evening, when I am done with work and can sit in my large, leather reading chair and read about the Civil War. I have a secret fantasy that I have never divulged to anyone. I just love history. I wish I could make short documentaries about that war."

We stayed curious about the role of passion in Joseph's work and life, and continued to ask him to expand on this line of inquiry. Three weeks later, he said, "I realized I have a second passion. I love the *study* of medicine. It also involves reading. I love to do research in my field and have always done a lot of reading about difficult patient diagnoses." Another month, another insight: "I see through this coaching process, and through my coach training, that I must find a way to get reinspired in my field." And then, with a wink: "I may be quite a passionate man, after all, in my own way."

Joseph's inquiry about passion led him into a new and constructive way of understanding himself and integrating his coach training into his current work. He created a plan for adding more research into his medical practice by participating in an ongoing study with other doctors, one that was sponsored by the National Institute of Health (NIH). He saw variations in the results of patients in the study, and longed for a deeper understanding of what made treatment successful for some and not others. He developed a treatment protocol for working with patients in his own complex cases, and developed a short coaching conversation to have with certain patients, to gauge a patient's investment in treatment as an index of treatment success. Using his coaching training, he compiled a series of questions that clarified a patient's openness and willingness to fight for better health. The first question he asked each patient was: "What are you passionate about in life and work?"

Identifying, owning, and then embracing what you are passionate about is essential in your development as a person and as a coach. When you are contemplating a coaching specialty, don't discount the importance of passion in your decision. Sometimes we have to be temporarily grandiose to get to our deepest and most specific passions. These can often be plumbed if you ask yourself, "What kind of coaching can I do to change my little piece of the world?"

Exercise: Passion

Answer the following questions to explore your passion and apply it to your coaching.

What are you passionate about in your life?

_____

_____

What are you passionate about in your work?

_____

_____

(continued)

Exercise: Passion (continued)

What do you look forward to each day?

_____

_____

What inspires you or excites you to take action? If money were no object, how would you love to spend your time?

_____

_____

What is your description of a great day at work?

_____

_____

Putting It All Together

Now take some time to review your answers to all four previous exercises. Based on your prior experience, your excellence, your strengths and skills, and your passion, what is the coaching specialty that fits for you? In Part 4 of this book, "Profiles in Coaching," we define, examine, and give real-life examples of each of the following popular and financially viable coaching specialties:

- Executive coaching
- Leadership coaching
- Business coaching
- Skills coaching
- Career coaching
- Life coaching
- Wellness coaching
- Creativity coaching
- Relationship coaching
- Spiritual coaching

Must you pick a coaching specialty? Unlike other professions, where it is profitable to be a generalist, marketing as a coach is easiest when you specialize. Al and Laura Ries (2002) explained that specializing your services is the solution to an information-overwhelmed society. As a coach, you want to help your market remember who you are and what you do, and specializing does this by allowing people to associate you quickly with your services. From a marketing standpoint, good things can happen when you focus, rather than expand, your services.

In the next chapter, we look at exactly how you will make a shift from defining your specialty (what you do as a coach) to finding your niche (those particular clients that will purchase your services). Specialty and niche fit hand in glove: if no one wants what you have to offer as a coach, you have no clients. We want you to get grounded in a business reality and understand how to target your market so that you can generate a steady flow of clients.

CHAPTER 5

From Specialty to Niche

In the last chapter, we examined four questions to clarify the specialty and direction of your coaching skills and services. Now we want you to consider how your services will best fit into the ever-changing marketplace. It's time to define your coaching niche.

The concepts of *specialty* and *niche* are interconnected, but, like many marketing experts, we make a distinction between the two terms. Here's the difference: Your specialty is the precise *what* of your coaching practice—what you do and offer as a coach (your expertise, skills, methods, tools, information, advice, services, products). Your niche is the narrow *who* of your coaching practice—who you coach, the identified client base for your coaching services, the target market from which the majority of your clients and referrals will emerge. Sometimes what you do as a coach (build strong executive teams) dovetails with who you work with (executives), but other times your coaching skills may not immediately lead to a description of your market. For example, if you are a coach trained in the Authentic Happiness Coaching Program, and your purpose is to show clients how to become happier in their lives, how do you determine your target market?

The smartest way to build a full practice quickly is to target a market. Fairley and Stout (2004) made this point repeatedly: Success in the coaching business depends upon your ability to accurately identify the best, most highly niched market for your services. For most coaches, the ability to determine your niche, your specific market and audience, is the difference between business viability and business failure. Niching means getting specific about your market and narrowing the market parameters. Here are your first three steps:

- Target your market.
- Segment your market.
- Identify your ideal client.

Target Your Market

Some new coaches in business ask: Why do I have to narrow my audience rather than appealing to a broader market? What if by targeting my market I miss out on potential clients? It sounds counterintuitive to narrow your pool of clients just when you are desperate for clients, but targeting a market is actually the most effective way to build a coaching business because it helps you to conserve your energy, your costs, and your time. By targeting your market you will achieve three key marketing objectives:

- Focus
- Research
- Ownership

Let's look at these marketing goals one by one:

Focus

New coaches make the mistake of trying to be all things to all people. This is understandable, because when you are new and hungry for clients, you fear rejecting any potential business. It makes sense, in your urgency, to believe that anyone and everyone is a possible client.

But take a deep breath and think this through: even though you are new, you are building a coaching business to last, and you need to have a marketing plan that is effective over time to keep your marketing tasks manageable so you don't burn out. If you can get focused on one or two specific audiences, you will have a better chance to actually generate a steady flow of clients.

By focusing clearly on a niche, you can tailor your coaching message so that it has maximum impact. You won't spend time going to the wrong networking meetings that yield little in the way of results. You won't spend money unwisely, mailing announcements to uninterested recipients. Instead, you can anticipate where to get the biggest bang for your marketing buck, so that you only show up and promote your coaching business where it makes the most sense.

When a business owner takes a focused approach to marketing, the conversion rate of potential to actual clients goes way up. You increase your *return on investment* (ROI). When you focus, you can target people that are also focused—those potential clients who know what they want and need, and are looking for a coach just like you.

Research

To build a receptive audience for your services, you need to really know your clientele. Even though you may have some degree of knowledge or awareness of your market, do you know the coaching services they want? It's easier to figure out the needs of the market if you narrow your approach, because if your market is too broad, the market research (understanding who your coaching clients are and what they will pay for) is too vast and daunting.

Here is how to begin to research your market: Get out of your office and meet potential clients to find out what services they want. Ask what your potential clients read (magazines, journals, newspapers), the Internet sites they visit, where they shop, where they network, and who they turn to for similar referrals. Also interview those intermediaries who advise your potential clients.

Too often, we see coaches determine a specialty based on what they like to do, not on what is needed by their market. They quickly become frustrated when they find that the service they think is such a good idea is not one that is wanted.

Ronnie, an office manager, loved personal growth and had taken a year-long life coaching program by phone with a coach-training organization. She wondered if she could combine her love of adventure travel with her newly learned coaching skills and be a travel coach. Ronnie warmed to the idea of travel coaching as a specialty. As a travel coach she hoped to assess and advise elite travelers—those who traveled often and wanted unusual travel choices—about how to match their personalities and desires to their travel experience.

We asked her to do some informal market research to determine if travel coaching was a needed coaching service in her local community and professional marketplace. First, Ronnie created a profile of her ideal client: a single professional ages 30–55, who traveled to new destinations at least once a year. Ronnie, an extrovert who loved meeting people, decided to do some informal market research over several months in several ways:

- She rented a sales booth at a large "vacation expo"—a convention-center event sponsored by vendors of vacation and travel services, open to the public, to offer her brochures.

- She took a banner ad on a singles Internet site to direct people to her Web site.
- She joined a large local singles ski club that offered a host of other travel events, attended their meetings, networked, advertised in the club newsletters, and met members.
- She joined a group of women entrepreneurs and went to the networking luncheons to ask women about the need for her services.
- She offered everyone she met free coaching sessions as well as her brochure and her questionnaire.

We asked her to stay curious and detach from the results: this was an experiment in terms of testing the marketplace.

Ronnie tracked her results carefully: she kept records of how many people she talked to, with what outcome; how many introductory coaching sessions she booked, and how many of those became paying clients; what responses she got from which ads; what market approach yielded the most potential clients. After two months, she reported that, unfortunately, she could see next to no need for her proposed travel coaching services within the local and professional community.

"I met 130 new people at the six different events I attended. Not one booked a coaching session. I ran the ads. No one responded to those. I also did an extra piece of research and went to meet with agents from five well-known travel agencies. Of those, one person saw a possible alliance with me to do some public speaking about the single traveler, and felt that it might lead to some sort of consulting service, but he and I were pretty vague about the way it could go forward.

"I really stayed curious and asked questions of people and found that the kind of coaching service I want to offer is not really needed by those people I talked to. I am disappointed about this but very glad I didn't make an even bigger investment before I checked this out. The one need I did hear, over and over, came from the travel agents I met at the expo and the agencies. Every single one spoke of being incredibly stressed and burned out, with failing businesses, in need of time management skills, creative marketing ideas, and balance in their personal lives. They need life coaching, and some of them might be interested in my working with them as clients."

Ronnie learned an important lesson from this, and knew that her initial coaching idea, while fascinating to her, had little market relevance. She now had new information to evaluate, especially in light of the market need of travel agent burnout that might be a better niche.

Ownership

After you get focused and research the needs of your market, you are in a position to offer the right people the right services. If you target a narrow market, you can be a big fish in a little pond. Keep narrowing your audience. Research the needs of that market carefully so that you offer the right products, services, and information for that small, targeted audience. Do this well and the market will recognize you as a credible coach with needed expertise.

Say you are a business coach with a strong skill in sales, especially in closing a sale. Your market is people in business who want to learn to sell their products. This is a pretty broad market. To narrow your niche, define it further. Perhaps you have expertise with real estate agents. You live in Las Vegas and want to work locally. You have had special success with real estate agents who sell residential properties. In fact, several of your favorite coaching clients are the big sellers at their firms. You'd like to work with more clients just like them. Now we have narrowed your market: You are a business coach for real estate sales people who have earned over $1 million in the past year and sell primarily residential properties in Las Vegas, Nevada. With this more select market, it's possible to see how you might get better known and build a reputation much faster than if you stayed with a broad pool of possible clients.

Some coaches worry about competition in a narrow niche. If you research your market and in the process find out that there are other coaches working with your niche, don't get discouraged. Competition is often a good sign for the coach. It means that there is work available in that market. Don't let the fact that others are mining the same niche stop you from entering it. In fact, many marketing experts say that if there is no competition in a market, it's because others have already investigated that niche and determined it to be a total waste of time. Sometimes it's good to follow the crowd. Just figure out a way to stand out in that crowd.

Ben Dean, founder of MentorCoach (a coaching training organization for mental health professionals), suggested these additional considerations when targeting a coaching niche:

- *Burning need.* If there is an intense, perceived need for the niche in the minds of your prospects, the niche will respond to your efforts more quickly.
- *Underserved.* All things being equal, a coaching practice will grow faster in an underserved industry than in a highly developed one that has many vendors trying to meet the given need.

- *Precedent.* Are there already successful businesses operating in this niche? Some of the risk is reduced if you know there are others who are successfully targeting the niche on a local level.
- *Be first.* Take a successful coaching niche and narrow it further, to be seen as first in the field.
- *Discretionary income.* Can your prospective clients pay for your services? A professional niche or one that helps others to make money may be more viable, since the clients can consider coaching as a business expense.
- *Coherent group.* If members of your proposed niche feel they belong to a coherent group, you're more likely to have niche members forward your promotional material to others and generate word-of-mouth marketing.
- *Temporal dimensions.* Is the niche's need for your services short-term or enduring? It's far easier to serve existing clients than to have to continually acquire new ones. (Dean, 2000)

Exercise: Narrow Your Niche

Answer the following questions to gain clarity about your target market.

What is a precise and specific description of my target market? *(Answer in one sentence.)*

_____

_____

How can I narrow this even further?

_____

_____

What are the benefits and results I bring to this targeted clientele?

_____

_____

(continued)

Exercise: Narrow Your Niche (continued)

Who have I actually interviewed or spoken to who represents this clientele? What did I learn regarding their needs and wants in terms of coaching?

_____

_____

What organizations should I join that serve my targeted clientele? What print material and Internet sites appeal to them that I could be reading? What steps can I take to find out more about the interests, needs, and demands of this narrow market?

_____

_____

Do I think this market, as described, is small enough for me to build a reputation via public speaking, networking, and other marketing efforts over the next year?

_____

_____

If not, how can I narrow my description of this market further?

_____

_____

Do I have the right credentials, coaching materials, and programs or services to move into this market now? If not, what are my next steps in this regard?

_____

_____

Who is my current competition in this niche?

_____

_____

Segment Your Market

Segmenting is a marketing term that means to take what you know about your market, based on conducting interviews, talking to intermediaries, your own prior experience, and any other data that you may have purchased, collected, or developed, and analyze it to get a clearer understanding of who your coaching clients are and where to find them.

You may already use segmenting in your business marketing. If you bought a mailing list to send out a brochure or a flyer for direct mail, and if that list was based on a particular customer profile—gender, location, net worth, or profession—you used segmenting. If you joined the chamber of commerce and made choices about which committee to join based on who was already represented (type of business, age, nearness to your office), you used segmenting.

You have probably been on the receiving end of segmenting many times. If you ever visited an online buying site, such as www.Amazon.com to browse books, you might notice a section on the screen that states: "Customers who bought this book also bought" and then lists books that the data suggests you might want to buy. This is segmenting, trying to match your buying history against that of other like-minded customers, to try to interest you in more purchases. Here are some segmenting categories with examples:

- *Type* of client (example: professional, entrepreneur, creative, careerist, executive, CEO)
- *Size* of company or organization (example: small with 1–10 employees, midsize with 10–40, large with 40 or above)
- Financial *information* about earnings or net worth of individual or company (example: company earning revenue of $5 million or more, individual earning income of $100,000 or less)
- *Needs* or challenges of an organization (example: business in phase of start-up, turn-around, decline, culture change) or individual (example: person in career transition, postdivorce, retirement, new parent)
- Buying *habits* or *history* (example: single women who spend on average $5,000 annually on personal growth services, or midsize company that budgets $40,000 per year per executive for coaching)
- Personal *profile* including gender, age, ethnicity (example: single women over 60 who want to stay in good health)
- *Location* (example: freelance attorneys with billings of $1 million or more within 10 miles of your office)

As a coach, segmenting is only useful if it helps you to understand and interact with potential clients in a more congruent way. Here are two considerations to be aware of when segmenting your market:

1. *Even within a narrow targeted market, the buying patterns of clients are not always the same.* Let's say that you are a professional business coach, have some prior experience with entrepreneurs in start-up companies, and decide this is your targeted market. You get a list of start-ups in your community and begin to send marketing materials to all 100 start-up entrepreneurs. Here's the problem: since entrepreneurs represent so many different business and personality types and have such a vast degree of needs, unless you have a huge menu of services, only a small select group will actually need and buy your particular services.

   To avoid this problem, narrow your niche further. Your focus is too broad. Look at the segmented list and try to profile an ideal client in a more precise way. Be specific about exactly who your clients are and how your services match their needs. For example, instead of "entrepreneurs," narrow your description to "business owners of a start-up company with revenues of under $5 million who are new to business ownership and worried about sustaining rapid growth."

2. *You can segment on paper just fine, but can't find any actual clients to match your description.* Sometimes your best ideas about marketing needs are just that—ideas—and don't corroborate with your real world. Make sure to bolster any of the segmenting you do with real-life experience. Have conversations or interviews with real live people and organizations. Get out of your office and learn about your market. You need to understand who your potential clients are, but you also need to find them. Network with other coaches to see if your assessment of your target market seems to be on track. Spend an hour or two every day out of your office. Stay curious, and brainstorm with others.

Exercise: Segment Your Market

Analyze your niche by filling in thoughts about the following areas.

Define your target market in one sentence.

_____

_____

_____

(continued)

Exercise: Segment Your Market (continued)

Qualify or segment your target market by the following factors: type, size, buying habits, and any other information you may have.

_____

_____

_____

Further analyze your target market based on their needs, buying habits, or location.

_____

_____

_____

Does this target market purchase similar coaching services already? Are your services in line with what they normally pay? How much disposable income does your market have for self-improvement?

_____

_____

_____

Does this market have a lasting need for the services you offer, or will it be a one-time purchase?

_____

_____

_____

What are the best ways for you to reach this market (advertising, networking, word of mouth, speaking at conferences, writing articles)? Does location factor into reaching this market?

_____

_____

_____

Ideal Coaching Clients

An ideal client profile is another way to describe your market. Develop a one-sentence, conversational definition of the specific clients you coach, those who are best suited to your style, value, and skills. Your ideal client profile details your niche, and then explains additional qualities, desires, needs, and wants of those you coach best. A good ideal client profile helps you talk confidently about the kind of client you love to work with and can make it easier for a referral source to understand who to refer, or for a new client to understand what to expect when working with you in a coaching relationship.

One life coach who specializes in relationships profiled her ideal client: "I coach single and divorced women who are going through midlife self evaluation and have determined that what they want most is to find a beloved mate to grow old with. My ideal clients are often in their fifties and sixties. They are urban dwellers and live in the city where I have my office; they all have secure, stable careers, and have a deep interest in their own personal growth and in bettering the world around them. But they are lonely and not sure how to go about finding the perfect mate. They want to achieve this goal within a year, and they appreciate a structured approach and complete confidentiality as they move forward. That's where my coaching comes in."

An executive coach said: "My ideal clients are men, business owners in the high-tech industry in Northern California, who want to grow their businesses without sacrificing their family ties. They are usually in their thirties, really bright, self-made guys, most often with a working wife and young kids at home. They tend to be athletic, driven, and avid golf players; they constantly complain about their workload and frankly, they are candidates for an early heart attack. You know these guys—they miss out on a lot of family events due to work, they have dark circles under their eyes, they have no idea how to manage their time. With coaching, they figure out how to manage it better—a solid family life, big business goals, even golf—and they get their lives back in control."

Your ideal client description can be flexible and change to match your services, which may change over time. The client profile speaks to who you are as a coach as well as to those you would like to attract into your coaching practice. After you finish the following exercise that helps you define an ideal client profile, share it with your referrals sources to help them have a better sense of who to refer. Since ideal clients are not just born but also made, you can also share the ideal client profile with potential clients, to help them understand your approach and your expectations and let them know how to "get their money's worth" or increase the value they receive from their time in coaching.

Exercise: Identify Your Ideal Coaching Client

To understand the attributes of your ideal client, fill in these sentence stems:

My ideal client needs

_____

_____

My ideal client desires

_____

_____

My ideal client values

_____

_____

My ideal client expects

_____

_____

My ideal client agrees to

_____

_____

My conversational definition of my ideal client is:

_____

_____

Now check off every item that is true for you. Try to incorporate all of these into your practice over time.

❑ I can identify 10 ideal clients or 10 ideal organizations all within my target, segmented market at any given time.

❑ I can find an introduction to these clients, as well as contact information, so that I can communicate with them this month.

❑ These people or the organizations they represent have a strong need or desire for my product or service (which I know based on evidence other than my wishful thinking).

❑ The potential clients in this niche have the money to pay for what I'm offering and have purchased similar services in the past.

Planning for Business

Now that you have a better sense of what you do as a coach and who you offer services to, the next step in your business development is to create a business plan. Too often coaches avoid having a written business plan because it seems too cumbersome, especially for a small business. Research shows that success comes to those who do develop and use a written plan. We offer you a simplified process for an informal business plan that can see you through the first year. Because it is informal, you can revise and revisit your plan as often as needed. Use this plan to structure your current business, anticipate future challenges, budget for expenses, and determine your goals and action steps.

Consider this user-friendly business plan as an aid to promote more business comfort. Let it guide you any time you feel unsure of what to do next or feel overwhelmed. In this chapter we walk through the first three steps of your business plan. In Part 3, Entrepreneurship, we address the other aspects you need to consider regarding marketing, finances, and risk management.

Informal Business Plan

Your informal business plan consists of:

- *A business overview* (decisions to make regarding legal structure and business direction)
- *Your business identity* (a quick summary of your services, specialty, and niche)
- *Ten business goals* (a list of annual goals ranked according to priority and ease of implementation)

Business Overview

A business overview falls into two categories: your business structure and your business direction. By structure, we mean both the way you transition into coaching and the legal structure of your coaching practice. To understand the transition you are making or have made into coaching, consider that most coaches approach coaching as a second or third career. As a result, they set up a coaching business in one of the following three ways:

- *Integrate:* Professionals that *integrate* coaching use their coach training to enhance their existing career, without redefining themselves as coaches. They see coaching as a skill set, not a profession, and use coaching skills to offer an expanded set of services for a broader population. Psycho-therapists, doctors, managers within corporate settings, financial planners, attorneys, personal trainers, and others fall into this category in that they may take a coaching course, but decide not to change their current professional title or leave an existing career. These professionals incorporate a coaching style in their existing practice but do not define themselves as a coach on a business card or in any other professional materials. Integrating the skill set of coaching into an existing profession, without defining oneself as a coach, does not require any structural business change to an existing business.

- *Diversify:* Professionals that *diversify* have two careers and often two businesses, one a coaching business. They switch back and forth between professions, being a coach 1 day (or 1 hour) and a therapist, consultant, trainer, healer, the next. Some completely separate the two practices, working out of separate offices with two different business setups. Others have both practices under one roof. The ability to successfully diversify and shift roles back and forth relies on having clear boundaries and well-articulated services. This involvement in coaching may require incorporation, or a sole-proprietorship structure may suffice.

- *Reorient:* Professionals who *reorient* cease working at their previous job or career and transition to the role of coach. They drop any prior title and use "coach" as a professional title. They may work in-house as the resident coach in a corporation, work as a consultant or subcontractor for an organization, build their own coaching firm, or sell products that augment individual or group coaching. They may travel to coach clients, work from an office by phone, or work from home, but they self-identify as a coach rather than as a consultant or any other profession. This coaching involvement often requires a formal, highly protective legal structure, such as some form of incorporation.

The Right Structure

Based on your transition experience, you need to decide if you will be better served with a sole proprietorship, a limited liability corporation, or some form of incorporation. Some coaches, working alone in a small practice, are content with the structure of a sole proprietorship. This is the simplest (and most popular) form of business organization. You will be personally liable for all debts of your business to the full extent of your property. On the other hand, you have complete control of the business.

Other ways to structure a coaching business include: limited liability company (LLC); limited liability partnership (LLP)—a weaker form of an LLC; limited partnership (LP)—usually a passive investor; S-Corporation—incorporated, in which partners must disperse profits each year; and C-Corporation—incorporated, in which profits can be held within the company. Each structure has its pros and cons, taxwise and legally. Selecting the most appropriate structure is more an art than a science because advantages and disadvantages keep changing as the tax laws change (see chart on p. 92; Fleischman & Bryant, 2000).

The reasons to incorporate or use a structure other than a sole proprietorship usually have to do with protection and presentation for the business owner. In terms of protection, incorporation is thought to be the most protective structure for an individual in business, and a sole proprietorship has long been considered to offer few tax planning opportunities. This is changing based on current tax laws, and now a sole proprietorship has many of the tax advantages of other, more formal structures. Check with your lawyer and accountant for current information.

In terms of presentation, a sole proprietorship does not have the professional image as a business that incorporation offers. If you are going to market your coaching services to the corporate world, image matters. Consider incorporating or one of the other structures (LLC, LLP) if presentation is important to your business plan. If you file for incorporation, you most often need the services of a lawyer and it may cost between $500 to $2,000 to complete and file.

Vision, Purpose, and Mission Statement

The second aspect of your business structure—business direction—is usually established by taking the time to think through and write a vision, purpose, and mission (VPM) statement. As a coach, you may have asked your clients to develop a VPM statement, but have you done one recently to determine your own business direction? Since we are using an informal business plan, your VPM statement can be brief: The vision can be a sentence or two at most that sums up what you see as being possible for your coaching business in the next year. We like the purpose statement to address who you will need to become in order to make the vision happen. The mission statement specifies the actual steps that you must take to fulfill both your business vision and your purpose.

Most successful coaches operate in business with an up-to-date VPM statement. If you have been concerned with a lack of professional direction, if you feel like you don't know what is in store for you or your practice a

Chart of Liability of Owners Based on Entity Choice

Liability issue: Can lose personal investment in business

Sole Proprietor	General Proprietorship	LLC	LLP	LP	C-Corporation	S-Corporation
yes	yes	yes	yes	yes	yes	yes

Liability issue: Business entity's assets are exposed to satisfy debts, obligations, and lawsuits

Sole Proprietor	General Proprietorship	LLC	LLP	LP	C-Corporation	S-Corporation
yes	yes	yes	yes	yes	yes	yes

Liability issue: Owner's personal assets exposed to satisfy professional liability and other tort reforms against that owner

Sole Proprietor	General Proprietorship	LLC	LLP	LP	C-Corporation	S-Corporation
yes	yes	yes	yes	NA; usually just a passive investor	yes	yes

Liability issue: Owner's personal assets exposed to satisfy contract liability of entity (debt and obligations)

Sole Proprietor	General Proprietorship	LLC	LLP	LP	C-Corporation	S-Corporation
yes	yes	no	yes	no	no	no

C corporation, LLC, or sole proprietorship: What form is best for your business, Management Accounting Quarterly, Spring (2000), 14–21, by Gary M. Fleischman and Jeffrey J. Bryant. Copyright 2000 by Management Accounting Quarterly. Reprinted by permission of Management Accounting Quarterly via the Copyright Clearance Center.

---

year from now, if you feel bored with your current coaching business, you probably suffer from not having a coherent and compelling business VPM statement. Here is an example of an informal VPM statement from a creativity coach:

Vision: *My 1-year vision is to be coaching 10 to 15 ideal clients a week in my sole proprietorship. I will have completed the first draft of a book about my coaching with art and writing, and will be giving more presentations locally and nationally. I will have developed a stronger reputation as a creative force and coach within my community.*

Purpose: *I need to become a savvy public speaker. I need to become a stronger writer and commit to writing my coaching program in book form. I need to make time for my own creative artwork each week, to model my services. I need to reach out to others in the art community so I am not isolated in my work.*

Mission: *a) Take classes in public speaking. b) Join the National Speakers Association for support. c) Find opportunities for speaking locally and at conferences this year. d) Schedule 8 hours of writing time each week. e) Write a book proposal by the end of the year. f) Find three book agents to send my proposal to. g) Increase my marketing efforts to bring in more coaching clients.h) Keep time in my calendar for my own creative artwork. i) Connect with other community arts organizations and become a member of at least two.*

Exercise: Drafting a VPM

Complete these three statements using short, simple sentences.

Vision: *(What I see is possible for my coaching business in the next year or two)*

_____

_____

Purpose: *(Who I need to become to fulfill this vision, any changes I need to make on myself)*

_____

_____

Mission: *(The specific steps I will take to make my vision and purpose a reality)*

_____

_____

Business Identity

Now summarize and compile your thoughts and previous writing from earlier exercises to articulate your coaching specialty, niche, and services into one clear, short synopsis. (Review the exercises from earlier chapters to help you with this summary.)

Exercise: My Business Identity

Define the following aspects of your coaching.

My coaching specialty:

_____

_____

My niche market:

_____

_____

My coaching services:

_____

_____

How my services benefit my clients:

_____

_____

Recent coaching successes:

_____

_____

My ideal client profile:

_____

_____

The needs my coaching addresses within the local market:

_____

_____

What I contribute to society at large as a coach:

_____

_____

Business Goals

Now create a list of 10 annual goals for your coaching business. As coaches, we ask clients to set goals all the time. Setting goals is an art. Well-defined goals can give you the energy to motivate you to move forward, but the goals defined in the wrong way are a burden, so that you feel you are carrying around a heavy weight. Before setting your business goals, consider these criteria:

- First, *prioritize*: List ten big, visionary goals for the current year, according to their importance to you and to your business direction. (Example: *Double my client count; generate $90,000 of revenue; send out five proposals for a new business venture; find an agent and secure a book contract; move office away from home and into commercial space; hire new staff.*)
- Next, *analyze*: Do these goals add to your sense of motivation, or do you get tired just looking at the list? If it's the latter, change the goals or change the list so that it gives you a sense of urgency and energy.
- Finally, *categorize*: Relist the goals from easy to difficult, and commit this month to achieving the two *easiest* goals first. What support system do you have in place, or could you begin to put in place, to help you accomplish the goals on this list? How do you like to receive support when it comes to achieving goals?

Exercise: Ten Annual Goals

List the 10 goals that you want to achieve this year. Prioritize the list, from most to least important. Change or reword any that feel exhausting. Make your list energizing. Then rank them, from easiest to hardest:

1. _____

2. _____

3. _____

4. _____

5. _____

6. _____

7. _____

8. _____

9. _____

10. _____

Now that you have a better sense of your business structure, business identity, and top 10 working goals in place, it's time to begin the next step in differentiation: your plan for active marketing and attracting ideal clients. Since marketing is time- and energy-consuming, we want you to select the marketing strategies that actually work best for coaches, not those that work for other businesses. In the next chapter, we examine the top strategies that successful coaches report help them attract good clients. We also show you how to incorporate each one into your business.

CHAPTER 6

Attracting Ideal Clients

To be a coach in business, you need a steady source of paying clients. Since coaching is often short-term work, with clients staying for an average of 3–6 months, according to industry standards you will need to be marketing as a coach, in one way or another, on a regular basis. With marketing a given role for a coach in business, it's wise to consider how to leverage your marketing time.

Leveraging your marketing time means getting the most results in the least amount of time and effort. We propose that you take the guesswork out of marketing to save you from making marketing mistakes that can cost you time and energy. We know, for example, that marketing strategies that work well for other businesses don't necessarily yield clients for a coaching business. We want you to use the strategies that coaches have tested in the field and consider most effective.

Happily, we now have data to inform us of the marketing strategies that are working best for coaches. The 2003 ICF survey asked coaches to rank 20 methods of marketing according to their usefulness in bringing in new clients. In this chapter, we present the top eight strategies they reported as most useful, and then we offer ideas that will allow you to make the most of each one. We alert you to the strategies to avoid. We also suggest how to budget for your marketing, so that you know what to expect to spend in order to build a solid base of good clients.

But before we delve into these important strategies, let's first check your marketing mind-set: Are there any inner negative beliefs you hold about marketing your services as a coach that will block you from taking action? If so, let's address these first, before you get started with your marketing plan.

Marketing Mind-set

Selling yourself and selling your intangible coaching services can cause an otherwise confident and gifted coach to feel quite insecure. Selling is a challenging activity for many coaches. Coaches we talk to feel ambivalent or discouraged about the degree of marketing that a coaching business requires.

Since marketing is a necessity when building your coaching business, our goal is to help you feel comfortable and be articulate when educating others about your services, so you can deliver a compelling "basic message"—a verbal, eloquent introduction about who you are and what you do as a coach. Some coaches complain about the constant need to be both a public educator about coaching ("What is coaching, anyway?") and a salesperson for their particular services ("What do you do exactly?"). Our advice? Embrace both roles. This is a new profession, and all coaches are on the front lines as educators, helping to create the new market. Be patient with the public. New markets take time to build. Learn to speak about coaching with ease. As you accept the role of educator, you will become a much better marketer.

What are your particular concerns about marketing your business? Here are some common ones we hear:

I don't want to appear foolish or needy.
I can't think of what to say.
I hate to sound pushy or promotional.
I am so new at coaching that I really have little to communicate.
I am okay one-on-one with marketing, but I get tongue-tied when I need to introduce myself in front of groups of people.
I freeze when I even think of making cold calls.

Exercise: Resolve Your Concerns About Marketing

Complete the following exercise:

Write your five most common worries or negative beliefs about marketing.

1. _____

2. _____

3. _____

4. _____

5. _____

(continued)

Exercise: Resolve Your Concerns About Marketing (continued)

Now refute each statement. Refuting means that you use your cognitive ability to contest or counter the negative belief, which is often based on fear or anxiety. For example, if your negative statement is: "I am so new at coaching that I really have little to say," think this through and contest it, the same way a good defense lawyer would contest a statement by a prosecution witness. Is your statement always the case, or can you think of times when you've been new at some skill, but still found something constructive to say? Even if you haven't figured what to say up until now, could it change if you had the right script? A good refutation for the above statement might be: "It's true I am new, but I have one or two success stories I can talk about as well as my own prior professional or personal experience that is relevant to how and why I am coaching. I can relate all of that in a marketing conversation."
My refutations:

1. _____

2. _____

3. _____

4. _____

5. _____

Top Eight Marketing Strategies

Now let's review the top strategies that 6,000 coaches surveyed by the ICF in 2003 report to be most useful in attracting new clients. We will explain and explore each one to help you adopt it into your marketing plan. Here they are, ranked by the survey data in order of effectiveness.

1. Getting referrals from existing or past clients
2. Getting referrals from other professionals
3. Giving paid seminars, presentations, and workshops
4. Offering a free coaching session
5. Networking at local organizations
6. Writing and publishing a book or newsletter
7. Giving free talks
8. Having a Web site

Strategy #1. Getting Referrals from Existing or Past Clients

The best way to bring in a new client, according to the coaches surveyed, is to let satisfied clients spread the word about your coaching. Who doesn't love this kind of referral? But this strategy can make a coach feel passive. Referrals become a waiting game if you have to sit back and wait for your past or existing clients to tell others. Three proactive steps you can take to increase the likelihood of referrals from past or existing clients are knowing how to:

- Ask for referrals
- Offer evidence of results
- Encourage the buzz factor

Ask for Referrals

You need a way to communicate your legitimate business needs to others, such as your need for referrals (the lifeblood of our business) in a way that matches your sensibilities and ethics. The most straightforward way to ask for referrals is to formulate a simple declarative statement. Use it in conversation with referral sources and with existing clients, place it on your Web site, add it to the signature line of your e-mail, incorporate it within your brochure, and laminate it onto a sign and hang it in your office.

It is acceptable in coaching to communicate your needs regarding referrals directly with the public and with other professionals. Unlike some professions, such as psychotherapy and medicine, where the idea of soliciting clients via a direct request might be considered in bad taste, coaching adopts a forthright business model. In this business model, accepted referral requests can include the following:

"I prefer to fill any openings in my coaching business with referrals and welcome any recommendations you might make."

"My business is based on referrals. I appreciate any potential clients that you think I could assist."

"I only coach people who have been referred to me by someone I know and trust, and especially like to have this kind of referral relationship with existing and past clients."

Exercise: Referral Request

Compose a statement regarding your preference for attracting clients via referral that you can deliver conversationally to others or use in your printed materials. Write it here:

_____

_____

_____

_____

Offer Evidence of Results

Do you have easy ways for your existing clients to measure their improvement so that they see the value of coaching? By identifying and measuring results in an ongoing process, your coaching clients can chart their progress. It's easier for your clients to be enthusiastic about your services when they are clear about their results. Help your clients to articulate their gains. Use measures such as a pre- and post-test, or other assessments. Keep notes of your own with markers of improvement, so that you can help clients understand the effectiveness of your services and carry that message more easily to others.

Exercise: Measuring Gains

Pick one or more of the following strategies to help your clients articulate and measure the value of coaching.

1. At the end of sessions, leave time to debrief. "What was most important in our session today? How specifically might you make it count in your life this week? Was there anything that happened that you don't understand?"
2. Have a 3-month verbal progress update with clients to evaluate results and gains from that time period.
3. Have clients complete a written result survey or a post-test every few months.

Encourage the Buzz Factor

The current thinking about networking is changing. The old business maxim "It's not what you know, it's who you know" has changed to "It's not who you know, it's *how many* you know." Malcolm Gladwell (2002) looked at the business and social power that is inherent in the quantity, not quality, of relationships you can develop. The power comes not from the depth of your relationships, but from their sheer number. Using a series of studies, Gladwell showed that those individuals who know the most people, *especially superficially*, have a much greater chance to gain business success. The new definition of poverty is not deprivation, Gladwell concluded; it's isolation.

If you are isolated in your networking connections, then you may want to encourage your existing satisfied clients to help create a buzz about your services, and broaden your reach by carrying to others the message of what you do. How can you encourage the buzz factor?

Rob Walker (2004) looked at the recent phenomenon of ordinary citizens who voluntarily and enthusiastically offer their time and energy to market products for businesses via word of mouth. There is growth in marketing companies that harness unpaid citizens. One such company, BzzAgent, increases and monitors the buzz factor of products it represents by making sure that the volunteers who sign up to be word-of-mouth marketers have a list of talking points about the products they so actively promote to friends, families, and even strangers. With the talking points clearly articulated, and by giving volunteers pointed instruction about how and when to speak to others, BzzAgent can dramatically increase the sales of a newly published book, or the number of people who get interested in eating at a chain restaurant.

Walker (2004) found that the volunteers willingly and devotedly spread the word about products not for financial rewards, but for complex social reasons. Influencing others feels good and often gives purpose to one's everyday life, especially if that everyday life lacks sufficient meaning or excitement. The volunteers, when polled, said that they get a thrill out of being first, knowing about a product that they like before others in their social circles do, and becoming trendsetters.

The social science researchers who studied this phenomenon admit that most people engage in voluntary word-of-mouth buzz about books, movies, products, and restaurants as a part of normal social discourse. We call it making small talk, telling others about something we did, or bought, or saw that we liked. What is unique to BzzAgent and other such marketing companies is recognizing that this voluntary buzz can be structured and advanced as part of a formal marketing campaign.

How might a coach adapt this research for a coaching business? Some of the methods used by BzzAgent are far too promotional for a relational business such as coaching (example: instructing volunteers how to start conversations in supermarkets or on subways with strangers about targeted products), but one method is important for a coach to consider: in order to increase the natural buzz factor from satisfied clients about your coaching services, create talking points.

Talking points are the articulated benefits of your services, written by you and posted on your Web site and your printed materials. The benefits should spell out specifically how clients improve and what they tangibly accomplish from working with you. The talking points are the messages you want others to carry for you. To control that message, take time to craft your talking points. Then make sure the talking points are able to be seen.

To create the talking points, get some real-life feedback. Ask existing clients to tell you what they are getting out of coaching. Or get feedback in writing using evaluation forms. Find out what you deliver that is most valuable to others you coach. Then craft and abbreviate the feedback into short statements and use them as bulleted points in all of your materials.

Strategy #2. Getting Referrals from Other Professionals

The second favorite way that coaches attract good clients is through intermediaries. They develop strong ties to those professionals who are in a position to refer coaching clients. Depending on your coaching specialty and niche, this may become your primary marketing strategy. One leadership coach who works with CEOs of Fortune 100 firms tells us she never approaches individual clients directly. But she does market regularly to a select group of bankers, accountants, art dealers, and trust attorneys whose services these clients use; the intermediaries provide 75% of her referrals, and the other 25% comes from the CEOs she meets each month on the golf course.

To generate referrals from intermediaries and professionals, you need to know how to do four things well:

- Have a compelling introduction.
- Tell appropriate success stories.
- Network in professional circles.
- Develop a follow-up networking plan.

Have a Compelling Introduction

As a coach, you need to talk about your work with others in a lucid, positive, and energetic manner that invites conversation and builds a professional relationship. Being passionate about your work is the best way to become a great coach; knowing how to convey that passion through the spoken word is the best way to network.

Every coach marketing course encourages people to have an "elevator introduction," a 15-second verbal opening (one you can deliver between the lobby and first floor of an elevator ride) that engages a listener, so that instead of getting the usual bored or puzzled look, you hear your listener say "Tell me more" or "Give me your card. I have someone I want you to talk to." This is the first step to generating a referral effortlessly every time you say hello.

Here is an example of an elevator introduction that has generated referrals: "My name is Lynn Grodzki. I am a business coach for non-business-oriented professionals. Most of my clients are small business owners, therapists, and other types of healing professionals who are wonderfully giving and highly skilled at their craft, but naive when it comes to knowing how to build and manage a profitable business. I have a great time helping these talented professionals learn to make a lot more money, get highly organized, and, in the process, become successful entrepreneurs."

Here is one that bombs: "My name is Lynn Grodzki. I am a coach. I can see from your expression that you aren't sure what that is. Join the crowd! No one seems to understand the coaching profession these days. I help people overcome obstacles and set goals. It's hard to explain it completely. I do all kinds of coaching. I work with business owners. Actually, I work as a life coach, too. Sometimes I do a little executive coaching. I guess even career coaching. Oh, here's my floor."

As you can see, the first introduction targets a clear niche, identifies an ideal client type, adds in some passion of the coach, and sets up an introduction that can generate some further conversation and possibly an exchange of business cards between the coach and the listener. The second introduction is vague, unfocused, and defensive. It would leave a listener confused and unsure how to respond.

Exercise: Craft Your Elevator Introduction

Script a short introduction based on the following criteria:

1. *No more than three or four short sentences.* This is an introduction and you are going to memorize it, so keep it brief and easy to remember and hold in your mind at all times.

2. *No jargon or "glaze over" terms.* If you use coaching jargon or glaze-over terms (words that are confusing, technical, unspecific, or vague), your listener will get confused or lose focus. Let the introduction be specific and oriented to the real, tangible benefits of your coaching.

3. *Target only one aspect of your coaching.* You may have a diverse set of skills, and more than one niche or specialty, but this is a short introduction. You simply can't say it all. Target the aspect of your business that you want to build—an area where you want to generate referrals. Are you trying to fill a new coaching group or attract an ideal client type? You will have more impact if you let this introduction speak to just one component of what you do.

4. *Learn to love to say this introduction.* The most important part of this introduction is learning to love to say it. The words are just a vehicle to express your underlying feelings and enthusiasm. Passion is attractive.

Now write your elevator introduction:

_____

_____

_____

_____

_____

_____

_____

Tell Appropriate Success Stories

To explain the benefits of your coaching services, use a well-crafted success story that clearly explains the benefits of your services. A success story is a short synopsis of a successful coaching case, structured so that it doesn't violate client confidentiality. The focus is on the plot, not the character in the story. To create a success story, think about your five "best" cases. Omit all personal, identifying details and highlight the outcome. What tangible benefits did your client gain as a result of the coaching? Practice telling your success story out loud, so that you learn to use a conversational tone. Now you have another choice for a response when someone says, "Tell me more about what you do."

Network in Professional Circles

How do you meet intermediaries and professionals who may become referral sources? The easiest way is to join existing organizations. If you are a career coach and want to meet personnel or human resource directors who have employees to refer, find the professional associations that cater to these professionals and go to the meetings. If you are a life coach and want to meet alternative health professionals (nutritionists, chiropractors, acupuncturists), find the professional organizations that they attend. If you are an attention deficit disorder (ADD) coach and want to meet teachers who can refer students, attend parent teacher association (PTA) meetings at your local school. Use the Internet, ask for suggestions from the professionals you know, and keep an eye on the business pages of your local newspaper. Almost every profession has several societies or associations. Locate them, get on their mailing lists, and attend meetings regularly.

Develop a Follow-up Networking Plan

Building a professional network is a planned process, not a random event. Meeting someone once rarely generates a referral. You need continual contact with professionals in order to create referrals. It takes time for networking to yield results. If you give up too soon, you will not create a flow of business. Each time you meet someone, plan a follow-up campaign to help all your contacts become associates.

Exercise: Follow-up Networking Plan

Use the six-step process to have a system of follow up for networking.

1. Draw three circles on paper arranged in a bull's-eye pattern.
2. In the inner circle, write the names of professionals you already know personally, who currently refer clients to you.
3. In the middle circle, write the names of professionals you already know personally, who you wish referred to you, but currently don't.
4. In the outer circle, write the names of professionals you can identify but don't personally know, whom you would like to meet.
5. Inner and middle circles: Create a written plan to increase the contacts you have with people in both the inner and middle circles. Contacts can include: having lunch, sending a letter with an article that the professional might find interesting, making a phone call to say hello, sending an e-mail to check in, inviting the professional to a meeting or conference at your expense, inviting the professional to a social event. Plan to contact the inner and middle circle people on a regular basis and note the date and type of contact on a separate calendar. Minimum suggested contact is once every 6 months; maximum is once a quarter.
6. Outer circles: Find people who can arrange introductions for you to those in the outer circle. Once you meet the people in the outer circle, move their names to the middle circle and include them in your series of contacts.

Strategy #3. Giving Paid Seminars, Presentations, and Workshops

Getting sponsored and paid by an organization (educational entity, religious group, professional association, social club, business or corporation, nonprofit organization, large or small annual conference, local or national society, government or nongovernment agency) to deliver a seminar, presentation, or workshop is another well-regarded way to bring in coaching clients. You get visibility with immediate credibility by being sponsored to speak.

To interest a sponsoring organization in hiring you as a speaker, you may need to do some preparation and self-packaging. Research the organization and their membership so that you have a sense of the topics they want. Have a basic speaker packet prepared (a speaker sheet with your biography, picture of yourself, list of previous sponsoring organizations, popular topics of talks, and endorsements; an article you have published and reprinted; an outline of your proposed presentation; other promotional materials that establish your program).

Start by approaching the organizations and ask if they hire outside speakers. Decide if you will offer to deliver:

- a keynote speech (an opening speech that starts a meeting or conference and appeals to the whole membership),
- a breakout talk (a briefer talk given during the course of the conference, usually an hour long, on a topic that may not appeal to the broad population),
- a half-day presentation (3–4 hours), or
- a full day workshop (4–6 hours).

What can you charge for a presentation? Start by asking the organization what their budget is. The range for speaking varies greatly. Nonprofit organizations often have honorariums that of $500 and under for a keynote or hour-long address; larger associations pay from $500 to $4,000 for a keynote or 90-minute presentation; corporations generally pay in the $5,000 to $20,000 range for a workshop to keynote speech. You want to negotiate for additional expenses (travel, lodging, meals, transportation to the event), separate from the base fee.

To get repeat business from the sponsor, plant some seeds even before your speaking date to alert the meeting planner (your contact person at the organization) about other programs you have to offer. Make the meeting planner a hero for hiring you by tailoring your talk to be ideal for those attending. You can do this by informally interviewing attendees prior to your talk to make sure you are on right track, or spend time questioning the meeting planner about the needs of the audience. Offer your services and time to help promote your talk. Will you be available for an interview with the local paper or radio station? Will you offer the organization access to your mailing list? Will you do a Friday evening hour-long free preview before a paid weekend workshop? If so, let the meeting planner know. Ask for your own copy of the evaluations and if you can get the names of attendees for your mailing list. When the engagement is complete and if it goes well, don't hesitate to ask the sponsor for a testimonial letter.

To leverage your time, plan to target both specific organizations as well as the middlemen who book speakers—meeting planners and speakers bureaus. Bureaus work on a commission basis and find speakers for large organizations, sometimes charging as much as 25%. For this reason, most speakers bureaus will not work with a presenter unless the speaker charges at least $2,500 per engagement plus expenses (otherwise there is not enough profit for the bureau to be involved).

Exercise: Get Sponsored to Speak

Answer these questions in order to position yourself as a paid speaker:

What are the 10 sponsoring organizations I want to target?

1._____
2._____
3._____
4._____
5._____
6._____
7._____
8._____
9._____
10._____

Who can help me gain introduction to these organizations? How will I make my first contact—phone call, letter, face-to-face meeting? How will I follow up?

_____

_____

What are the titles of talks or presentations that I have successfully given in the past? Do the titles need to be revised to be more interesting or targeted to the organization? If so, what are my new titles?

_____

_____

(continued)

Exercise: Get Sponsored to Speak (continued)

Are my materials ready—speaker sheet with picture, biography, list of past presentations and sponsors, and selection of topics? Do my business card, brochure, and speaker sheet look professional and reflect my message?

_____

_____

Can I arrange with the sponsor to speak on a regular basis to their organization?

_____

_____

How will I capture the names and information of attendees for my mailing list?

_____

_____

hat is the smallest number of people I am willing to speak to? The largest? What is my ideal number?

_____

_____

What will I charge for this presentation? What is the minimum I will accept?

_____

_____

How might I help the sponsor to promote this talk?

_____

_____

Strategy #4. Offering a Free Coaching Session

The coaches surveyed agreed that offering a free session was an important strategy in bringing in new clients because potential clients get sold on coaching by being coached. Most coach training organizations promote this technique; as a result, it is a common practice. What is the retention rate of free sessions? Our informal poll of 50 coaches revealed a 50% retention rate from free sessions.

Free Coaching Session Format

We asked the coaches to share their methods of free sessions. We then developed a format, based on their responses and our own experience, that leads to the best retention rate and increases the chances of potential clients becoming paying clients. Here is the format, step by step:

First, prepare. Send out a form with some questions for your potential clients to fill out and return (no more than 10 questions) to help structure the session. The questions might include desired goals and important values. Not all potential clients like to fill out and send back information, so don't worry if this is not forthcoming.

Then, structure. Divide the actual coaching session time into three equal parts (for a 1-hour session, figure 20 minutes per part).

Spend the first part building rapport. Use any methods or skills you know to help potential clients feel comfortable. No matter what you talk about, your focus will be on building the relationship.

Spend the second 20 minutes coaching. Be a good listener, ask challenging questions, and try out a few coaching interventions with the clients. Be unconditionally constructive. To give the session some forward thrust, see if you can help clients develop a mini-vision of what they want from coaching. Be true to yourself, so that you can find out if potential clients are right for you, not just that you are pleasing to the clients.

Spend the final 20 minutes debriefing the session and planning for future sessions. Say: "Let's debrief for a little while. What we have done is similar to a coaching session. How was this for you?" Listen and reflect back what you hear. If you like the client, ask for the business. Say, "I liked the coaching conversation we just had. I feel that I can help you with the following goals and desires you express, and I'd be glad to work with you. Shall we go forward with coaching?" Take control at this point, don't be passive. Make clear suggestions about what you can offer. Then take a few minutes to clarify logistics. Review your fees, plan to send your client a policy sheet and a contract, get billing information, and schedule the next session.

Finally, future-pace. End each free session with a quick action plan for the client. Say: "What steps will you take between now and the next time we talk? I'll be looking forward to hearing about your progress."

Strategy #5. Networking at Local Organizations

Local business and professional organizations are a prime place for networking, and coaches surveyed found it another important marketing strategy for finding new clients. Some ideas for networking are covered in the earlier strategies we just explored, but let's look at others that can help you market best within local settings.

First, pick organizations that target your niche. While the Chamber of Commerce or Business Networking International (BNI) welcome all small-business owners, the general nature of these organizations makes getting a referral a hit-or-miss affair. Instead, try to join organizations that focus directly on the clientele you seek.

Targeting professional women as clients? Want to coach attorneys in small practices? Love to coach clients who are aspiring writers? Find those associations that cater directly to them. Then get on a committee, sit on a board, write for their magazines, speak at their conferences, become a delegate at their conventions, and use the time you spend in the organization to get better known within your niche.

Working the Room

Sometimes the hardest part of networking at an organization is walking into a crowded room, where you don't know a soul, and beginning to talk to others. If you find yourself at an association networking cocktail party, what's the best way to make connections? One coach who has built her résumé in a niche market solely through networking her way through a lot of membership cocktail parties offers this strategy:

Before the event, the coach finds out who in the organization is organizing the party. In this case it's Mary, the head of the membership committee. The coach calls Mary a day or two before the planned party, introduces herself (using her elevator speech), and states her goal: "I am a new to the organization and would like to meet ten members who have similar professional interests. Can you, Mary, help with me with some introductions at the party?" The coach offers to come early or to simply check in with the Mary during the party, so that Mary can perform some introductions or at least point out who the coach might want to meet.

The evening of the party, the coach shows up early, finds Mary, gets some vague pointers from Mary who is quite busy (Mary says, "See that gentleman over there? You should talk to him. He knows a lot of the key people in your market.") and begins to work the room. She approaches the gentleman, who is standing with two others. The coach walks up to the circle of men, puts a big smile on her face, waits for a break in the conversation, sticks her hand out for a handshake, and says, "Hi, my name is _____ and Mary suggested we should meet, because she thinks we could help each other professionally."

Then the coach launches into her elevator introduction and starts a conversation. She asks questions of others, tells a success story of her own, asks for business cards, offers hers, makes a little more small talk, and then excuses herself and goes back to Mary for the next pointer.

The next day she follows up. Every person whose business card she has gets a "Nice to meet you, let's have lunch" e-mail or phone call. Mary gets flowers!

The coach who told us this networking strategy is proof of its effectiveness. She went from being new in town and knowing a small handful of people to having a Rolodex of over 300 good referral sources at the end of a year, all from her willingness and skill at working a room.

Strategy #6. Writing and Publishing a Newsletter

Coaches also find that writing helps to attract new clients. Many coaches develop and produce newsletters, either for direct mail or e-mail. Writing a newsletter allows clients to know more about you and your coaching. Newsletters have more reach if they are not just promotional, but contain something of value for your readers.

Unsure about what to include in your newsletter? Keep it simple and nonpromotional. Have you read an important book or taken some training that is inspiring you in your work? Write about that. Are you finding a thematic topic that occurs in coaching sessions that fascinates you? Write about that. Your newsletter can be simple and still make an impact, if the writing is good. Remember, a newsletter is not a flyer advertising your services. It's a way to extend your reach and express the essence of who you are and what you do through the written word.

Exercise: Writing a Newsletter

Answer these questions to see if writing a newsletter or e-newsletter would be an effective marketing strategy for you.

Do I need to stay in touch with potential clients or referral sources on a regular basis?

❏ Yes

❏ No

Points to consider: If you have a mailing list that you ignore, a newsletter with a quarterly publication date will force you to stay

(continued)

Exercise: Writing a Newsletter (continued)

current. People seek coaching when they are ready. You can't rush another person's readiness for coaching, but you can stay in touch. Your newsletter is one way to help them feel connected to you and makes it easier for them to call when the time is right.

Do my referral sources or potential clients need an honest and open experience of me and my work?

❑ Yes

❑ No

Points to consider: Since coaching is unfamiliar, it's helpful to have a newsletter, instead of brochure, to let people know what you do. It offers you the opportunity to say more about your basic coaching message, in an attractive manner. Take people inside the heart of your coaching and let them "see" you in action, through your words.

Could I use some new opportunities?

❑ Yes

❑ No

Points to consider: Newsletters yield spin-off, just as books and articles do. Coaches report getting radio interviews, speaking engagements, and teaching positions as a result of their newsletters. You may find your e-newsletter articles being carried by other Internet sites and developing an international response.

Do I like to write and desire to be published?

❑ Yes

❑ No

Points to consider: Most of us need to grow into the writing process. Let yourself have a learning curve by publishing yourself via a newsletter. Start small and stay on track. E-mail newsletters may be the lowest cost of all to produce and send, allowing you to reach large groups of people without mailing costs of any kind. Edit your articles thoroughly and strive for brevity. Especially with e-mail newsletters, people at a computer like to scan, not read. Make sure that your content reflects your style and that it sounds like you.

Strategy #7. Giving Free Talks

Giving paid talks was high on the list of best marketing strategies, but coaches say that free talks can bring in clients, too. We have found that if you understand the process of *enrolling*, free talks work well as a method for attracting ideal clients.

Enrolling is a sales term that means getting people to buy your product or sign up for your services. For coaches, enrolling means influencing those in your audience to become paying clients. But the idea of influence can feel too promotional for some coaches, so here is a method of enrolling that is modified to reflect the ethics and sensibilities we think are representative of coaching. Our enrolling strategy is a much more subtle process than salespeople use, and it requires a specific coaching stance: building an authentic relationship *quickly*.

In this method of enrolling, you show up in your professional role, as a coach, from the start of the talk to the end of the talk. In your role as a coach, you focus on forming an honest relationship with members of the audience. Don't just say what coaching is; show it. Be a coach from the moment you say hello. Let the audience have an unvarnished experience of you in your role. Then build a bridge from the experience to the services you offer. If you do this well, members of your audience will feel connected to you and your coaching ability and have a clear understanding of how to hire you. Sound simple? It is, but not all simple things are straightforward, so let us break this down. Here is the format. Then we offer you an example of enrolling in action.

Enrolling Format

The three steps of enrolling are:

1. *Create an authentic relationship with your audience:* To enroll success-fully, you have to be willing and able to coach right from the point of contact. This is where most coaches go awry in public speaking. They are comfortable coaching in their offices or over the phone, but the moment they get in front of an audience they take on the role of a teacher, trainer, information provider, or facilitator—which are valid but more superficial roles. These roles will not yield the same results in terms of enrolling.

   Think about it this way: The primary motivation for people to hire a coach is because they have a gap between where they are right now and where they want to be. If you approach your presentation as a quick fix, you remove their primary motivation for hiring you and make the work of coaching seem superficial. But this is what many coaches do when they get in front of a room. They become anxiety-dispellers with a lot of suggestions and ideas to fix a significant challenge immediately. Be a coach. Take your audience seriously. Don't rush the solutions. Ask questions. Listen carefully. Be the same coach you are during a coaching session.

2. *Show what you do:* As you may have experienced in your life, the best coaches don't see it as their job to necessarily remove or reduce anxiety or fix anything in the first contact. That would be disrespectful to the client, the situation, the issue, and the relationship. Often, when you work with a great coach it heightens your initial anxiety because he or she must clarify the gap, frame stuck issues using a new perspective, or try to get to really know you. Great coaches offer the potential of something bigger than a quick fix for potential clients. They offer transformation, vision, and lasting change.

   Coach from the front of the room. To give people a chance to understand coaching, they need to see you coaching someone. Coach an individual, walk through the room and briefly coach several people, or bring a group of audience members forward and coach each one. Don't just lecture, teach, inform, or facilitate. Coach.

3. *Bridge from the experience you create to your services:* Don't be passive and assume that people will hire you if they like your talk. Be an active marketer. Ask for business in a way that feels appropriate for the setting. Help people in the audience understand how to take the next step in working with you. Say something like, "Some of you may have more questions than answers as I finish this talk, and that makes sense because coaching is a process of discovery and we did a little coaching here today. If you want to take the next step, all you need to do is come see me in front of the room after our talk, get my card, and give me yours. I will call you to schedule a coaching session."

Enrolling in Action

Vicki is a former human resources specialist, now an executive coach in a new coaching practice, who is asked to speak to a group of nonprofit executive directors at a local association meeting on the topic of leadership. Vicki is enthusiastic to talk to the directors because they constitute a prime target market for her as potential, individual coaching clients. She has 2 hours to speak and, since the talk is unpaid, she considers it to be a marketing event and wants to use the above enrolling format.

In her prior career as a human resource specialist for a large government agency, Vicki gave many talks and trainings for a wide group of managers. She knows how to be in front of the room as an instructor, trainer, and small-group facilitator. Since we know Vicki is a competent speaker in front of the room, we challenge her to let go of these former roles of teacher, trainer, and facilitator and stay firmly grounded in her role as a coach.

First Vicki talks to the meeting planner to do a quick needs assessment of the group she will be speaking to. Based on the discussion, she decides to narrow her presentation to motivational tactics, and writes up a brief description of the talk for the planner, with the title: "Leading with Influence: The Power of Ethical Persuasion." She then outlines the talk: she will use the first 45 minutes to establish a rapport with the audience by presenting many of the challenges faced by executive directors regarding leadership. The day of the talk, she allows for substantial give-and-take during this portion of the presentation, so that the concerns and problems of the audience are highlighted and opened up. She does not rush to fix any of the issues addressed, but makes important points from a coach's perspective, with careful listening and by asking provocative questions of each participant.

After 45 minutes, there is a slight tension in the room because the discussion is about what is not working well as leaders, and because Vicki has been pushing the discussion into a deeper level with her questions and comments. But at the same time, she senses that a level of sharing and support is building among the audience, as each person really explores the ideas and questions. Vicki sees that she has built a level of relationship with her audience and suggests a 10-minute break.

When the group comes back, she has rearranged the stage so that she has two stools at the front of the room and two mikes. Vicki takes 15 minutes to frame her points regarding motivation and ethical persuasion. Then she says, "In our first hour I heard several of you mention specific challenges you faced, and I would like to offer some coaching to help you move more comfortably to your goals." During the break, Vicki has preselected two people who have been very verbal in the earlier discussion and asked if they would be interested in being coached. Now she brings them up, one at a time, and coaches each one from the front of the room, weaving her talking points into her coaching, for about 15 minutes for each one. This is a complex demonstration of her topic, since she uses her own motivation and persuasive coaching style with each person she coaches, helps them get from a stated challenge to outlining their next steps, and does it with some humor and lightness that allows each person being coached to enjoy the experience. Vicki lets the group debrief her coaching, and continues to underline the points of her topic and the coaching process. The audience is quite fascinated by this demonstration, and many say that they had never seen coaching "up close and personal" and think that having a coach would be quite compelling.

The last 10 minutes of the talk, Vicki sums up her topic, reviews what she has done, and then bridges to her services. She says, "We only touched lightly on an important topic today. Some of you will want to explore this further, and I want to let you know that I am available as a resource for you to do just that. I work as an executive coach with clients just like yourselves, and from seeing the coaching today here in the presentation, you have an idea of what coaching is like in a one-on-one setting. If you want to take the next step and explore hiring me, all you need to do is come see me in front of the room after our talk, get my card and give me yours, and I will call you to schedule a coaching session. I also want you to know that I produce a free e-mail newsletter for executive directors on topics just like the one we covered today, and if you want to sign up, just leave me your e-mail address on this sheet of paper."

After the talk, several people approach Vicki for her card. The majority of the group sign up for the newsletter. A few want to continue the discussion with Vicki and ask for some quick advice on a problem that the talk touched upon, but Vicki deflects this kind of quick advice and simply says to each one that the question deserves more time than she can give to it right now, but she would be happy to schedule a session for such a discussion.

Debriefing with Vicki at the end of the talk finds that out of a group of 30 in the audience, she gathered 20 new names for the e-mail newsletter; she has five business cards to follow up with for coaching sessions; several other people asked about her range of services and mentioned interest at a later time. Vicki felt that this had been her most successful talk to date as a coach. "Coaching from the front of the room was scary," she said, "but I see how if I don't show people what I can do, they really don't understand my services. The thirty minutes of coaching and the debrief afterward was definitely the most exciting and compelling part of the presentation, and it would not have worked as well if I had tried to describe coaching, or just suggested people break into small groups to process the concepts. To make a strong connection with me as a coach, they really needed to see me in action."

Strategy #8. Having a Web Site

The Internet is the new yellow pages when it comes to reaching coaching clients. Coaching clients tend to be Internet savvy and you need to make sure that your Web site is designed to help you generate new business. Your Web site should be information rich (articles, tips, ideas, high-value reading), articulate (expresses your message well, clear sentences, no typos), and easy to navigate (links and pages that flow well). But above all, if it is a marketing tool, it needs to have *direction*.

Direction means that you have an objective in mind when designing your Web site. Having an objective for a Web site is similar to what a mystery writer needs to do: figure out the ending of the book first, and then work backward to the first sentence of the book, so that the story leads the reader in a desired way, to the right conclusion.

Having an objective for your Web site means knowing what you want your Web site readers to do, feel, or think before they leave your Web site. Possible objectives are: contact you; feel better informed; contact you for a coaching session; sign up for your teleclass; subscribe to your e-mail newsletter.

Pick one objective and design each page around it. An example of a Web site with an objective is Amazon.com, and how each page directs viewers to buy books. No matter where you are on the site, you are being pointed to the purchase button. If you know your end objective and start designing with it in mind, you can lead a viewer through the homepage, to other pages, to the desired goal, step by step.

Be transparent in your Web site (Godin, 2002). Make it easy to find all the essential information to hire you—how to contact you, what to expect from working with you, what you charge, and any other pertinent details. Don't be subtle or vague. Don't hide information. Put it out there and let your ideal clients self-select you as their coach.

Least Effective Strategies

Now that you have strategies for marketing that are based on evidence of proven techniques that work, take a look at the following strategies that coaches in the survey reported were not as effective. You may want to avoid these techniques altogether, or use them advisedly with lowered expectation.

The least effective marketing strategies include:

- Media publicity, including publishing articles or interviews in newspapers, journals, or e-zines

- Exhibiting with a booth at trade shows
- Advertising in magazines or newspapers
- Yellow pages listing
- Donations of coaching services (at auctions or other events)
- Producing tapes, CDs, or manuals of coaching
- Direct mail campaigns (letters, postcards, bulk e-mails)

Remember that marketing must be a proactive, ongoing process for a coach, not a passive, random, onetime activity. With any strategy you choose, you must plan, prepare, follow up, regroup and retry, and be comfortable in directly asking people to hire you as their coach. Now that you have a better idea of what is involved with marketing, we look at other aspects of entrepreneurship.

Your Marketing Plan

Now that you have a list of eight proven techniques and ideas for implementing each one, pick and choose from among them to custom design a marketing plan that fits with your preference.

Do you like to speak? Pick Strategies #3 and #7. Prefer writing? Focus on #6 and #8. Love to meet people one to one? Choose #2 and #5. Few coaches do all eight techniques. Find a few that work for you, and plan to repeat them often in order to see results. Think of your plan as an engine, a referral-generating engine, one that you can create and maintain with little stress, since the process will be repetitive and familiar.

Coaches in the ICF survey reported that they spend on average $100–$300 per month for marketing expenses. They also spent between 6 to 20 hours a month for marketing, administration, professional development, and research activities. You need to budget for marketing, in terms of money, time, and energy.

The biggest obstacle coaches face when marketing is that they don't take the time to create an actual written plan, with dates, times, a budget, a tickler or follow-up system, and external support. Using a plan makes marketing easier. A plan can make the difference between whether you will see marketing results or not. You need a blank page and your calendar. On the page, create a written plan for this month and next that includes the following points.

Exercise: 30-day Marketing Plan

Fill out the following questions.

What are my objectives?

_____

_____

_____

Who do I need to contact and in what way?

_____

_____

_____

Do I need to join an organization? How will I do that?

_____

_____

_____

What materials do I need to prepare?

_____

_____

_____

How often will I follow up with each person?

_____

_____

_____

What will I do each week and each day?

_____

_____

_____

(continued)

Exercise: 30-day Marketing Plan (continued)

What is my budget for the month?

_____

_____

_____

Do I need to budget more time, money, energy, or support to make this happen?

_____

_____

_____

Goals for my monthly plan:

1._____

2._____

3._____

4._____

5._____

6._____

7._____

8._____

9._____

10._____

In the next section, we focus on entrepreneurship: the mind-set and skill set every successful business owner needs to adopt. We will show you how to think and behave in business, while still holding firm to your sense of empathy, coaching ethics, and values. We examine why even good coaches can still go broke, and how you can avoid this to stay highly profitable. Finally, we will help you understand how to operate your coaching business safely, using the most ethical coaching behaviors to avoid putting yourself at risk, and how to evaluate your needs for liability insurance.

PART III

ENTREPRENEURSHIP

CHAPTER 7

The Coach as Entrepreneur

Our research finds that the majority of coaches are new to business owner-ship. Coaches complain that as "amateur entrepreneurs," they feel confused about what it really takes to be successful in the business of coaching. You may wonder about this as well. What makes one coach succeed in small business, whereas another coach—equally trained, personable, and just as talented—struggles? Is there a "business gene" that favors some coaches and eludes others? Is business success the result of nature or nurture?

Similar to the factors that allow you to thrive in your personal devel-opment, doing well in business is probably a combination of both. Having a business nature means that you have the innate personality for business. For example, some coaches are natural extroverts, self-identified "people persons." They tend to network spontaneously, and that instinctive drive to meet, make contacts, and explore opportunities with others creates a clear business advantage for them. They are self-starters and highly motivated to "make things happen." These coaches find the tasks of growing the business easy, although they may have challenges in other areas, such as attending to business details, getting organized, or follow-through.

Other coaches benefit from business nurturance. They learned a solid set of business skills at some point, from their family of origin, graduate degree, previous career experience, a strong mentoring relationship with a senior entrepreneur, or, even better, an entrepreneurial coach. Coaches who excel in business due to learned skills seem to make good, forward-thinking decisions about business direction with little effort. They have often been taught to be well-organized and strategic planners.

But what if you are a coach who is untested in business, with no natural inclination or skills, and an introvert to boot. Are you doomed to fail? We have hope for all non-business-oriented professionals. We have seen some formerly "clueless" small-business owners go on to build very strong and profitable businesses and achieve impressive business goals, just by having the right information, the coaching they needed to develop confidence, and, along the way, plenty of professional support. With time and practice, you can learn the behaviors of smart business ownership and the thinking and feeling attitudes that promote entrepreneurial excellence. In this chapter and the next, we want to coach you to do just that! To improve your entrepreneurial ability, you need three fundamentals:

- Strategic information about the business of coaching
- An entrepreneurial mind-set
- Professional and peer support

Strategic Information

Those who are successful in business seem to know a lot about their business or business in general. They know what steps to take to grow and expand, when to change course and when to hold firm on an established direction, how to attract and retain clients, and when a business strategy bears repeating or when to move on to try something else. We want to make sure that you have the information you need about the coaching business. Use the following checklist to find any gaps in your current business knowledge. Add up your scores and then see suggestions and ideas to help you become more strategic.

Exercise: Strategic Checklist

Check off only what is true for you today. Give yourself one point for each item. Each section has seven items for a total score of 42 points.

Start-up
To be successful in a coaching business you need to spend the time and money to make it highly professional, from the start.

❑ I make my office setting professional and businesslike, even if I coach from a home-based office. Coaching is a business, not a hobby for me.

❑ I have good phone equipment, a phone line and answering machine devoted solely to my business, and a good quality-headset (if I do a lot of coaching by phone). I check phone messages and read and respond to my e-mail at least twice each day.

(continued)

Exercise: Strategic Checklist (continued)

❑ I have decided on a business structure—incorporation, sole proprietorship, or partnership—and I can defend my choice.

❑ I have business cards that I am proud to distribute (I like the look and feel of my cards) and a brochure or printed information packet that is professional, lucid, and attractive that speaks to my basic message.

❑ I have a Web site that is well written, is visually attractive, and provides the essential information about my services that prospective clients need. It functions as both a calling card for those searching the Internet and a brochure for those who want to learn more about me and my services.

❑ I have a computer, printer, and fax machine that are in good working condition.

❑ I can accept credit cards as one form of payment from clients.

_____ total score

Raising Your Score: To understand more about your business structure, review Chapter 5 and see the section outlining an informal business plan (business overview, identity, and goals). To see a list of office equipment and expenditures, see Chapter 9, especially "Start-up Costs." To develop a message for your brochure and Web site, see Chapter 6.

Networking
A coach in business needs to have a positive outlook and a network of potential clients that will refer, as well as peers for professional support.

❑ I have created my current referral network and divided it into three levels: (a) colleagues who already refer to me; (b) colleagues who need to know me better in order to refer; (c) colleagues I have identified but not yet met, who I hope will refer to me in the future. I have a plan to move those in the second and third categories into the first level.

❑ I have a follow-up plan so that I stay in contact with those colleagues in the first and second levels (see above) every few months.

❑ I belong to a variety of professional associations and attend meetings and volunteer for committees, to further my connections to the community at large.

(continued)

Exercise: Strategic Checklist (continued)

❏ I surround myself with other successful entrepreneurial colleagues who want me to succeed, too, and give me ideas and tips to try.

❏ I have created my own advisory circle (read further in this chapter to see how to create this informal board of directors) so that I have professionals I can rely on for good business advice.

❏ I don't build my business in a vacuum. I ask for advice from others and find people (colleagues, mentor coach, friends, family) who I can be accountable to for achieving my business goals.

❏ I talk publicly about my coaching work when I meet people socially as well as in professional settings. I focus on the positive aspects of my work (my strengths, talents, and success stories). I do not keep my coaching a secret.

_____ total score

Raising Your Score: Chapter 6 addresses networking strategies for coaches, as well as the best marketing approaches to take and those to avoid. To build an advisory board, see "Advisory Circles" later in this chapter.

Business Planning
Your overall business vision brings meaning and direction to your coaching practice.

❏ I understand the concept of a building a business by design—that if I don't make choices for my business, circumstances will.

❏ I make the time each week to work "on" the business, not just "in" the business. My "CEO" time is noted in my calendar on a regular basis.

❏ I understand the trends in the coaching world, and can also spot trends that may impact my coaching business in the next year. I position my business to take advantage of these trends.

❏ I am a member of at least one coaching association and receive regular, up-to-date information about the coaching industry.

❏ I have a vision for my business: I can see where I want to be in the next two years, and I know what steps I need to take to get there.

❏ I have a list of ten business goals for the next year, and am moving forward on action steps related to these goals.

(continued)

Exercise: Strategic Checklist (continued)

❑ I have selected a specialty area of coaching that fits well for me. I am building a coaching business that plays to my strengths.

_____ total score

Raising Your Score: To plan for your business, review the exercises on vision and goal setting in Chapter 5. See the explanation of trends about coaching in Chapter 1. Answer the four questions to find your perfect fit for your coaching specialty in Chapter 4.

Marketing

At the heart of every healthy coaching business is a steady flow of new clients. Knowing how to market your services in an essential skill that will keep your practice viable.

❑ I have an articulated basic message that I use as a professional introduction.

❑ I can list the benefits of my services. I have written endorsements of my coaching program. I have success stories I can offer about my work as a coach, to help potential referral sources understand what I do.

❑ I ask for referrals in a manner that reflects the integrity of my coaching principles.

❑ I have a menu of services for new clients and have packaged my services in five different ways so that price need not be barrier to accessing my services.

❑ My promotional materials focus on the solutions I offer to others, in clear language that highlights what my clients really want.

❑ I have defined and segmented my target market. I know who my ideal clients are, where to find them, and how best to meet their needs.

❑ I know several marketing techniques that work well for coaches and can pick and choose the ones that are most comfortable for me to use at any given time.

_____ total score

Raising Your Score: Find the best marketing strategies for coaches, create your basic message, and learn to articulate a compelling success story by doing the exercises in Chapter 6. The interviews with

(continued)

Exercise: Strategic Checklist (continued)

successful coaches in Part 4 of this book give you many great examples of coaching success stories. Target and segment your market, and develop an ideal client profile in Chapter 5. Learn how to package your services in Chapter 9.

Money

A coaching business must make a profit. As the business owner, you need to attend to making money while doing the work you love.

❏ I have reconciled the difference between profit and service (see Chapter 9). I understand what I charge for my coaching services and why.

❏ I have developed a budget for my business for this year.

❏ I have a business plan that helps me to know what goals and actions I need to take each month, and how to judge what I am spending each month as I build the business.

❏ I have more than one profit center and revenue stream in my coaching business.

❏ I know the steps to building a six-figure business.

❏ I am very comfortable discussing my fees, how I handle missed sessions, cancellation policies, and other financial issues with my clients.

❏ I am building a coaching business to sell, not just to own.

_____ total score

Raising Your Score: Start creating your business plan in Chapter 5, and then continue with Chapter 6 for your marketing plan. In Chapter 9, see how to set fees and policies, develop a budget, identify multiple profit streams, learn how to package your coaching services, and plan to build a six-figure business to sell. See the Appendix for additional books about money, coaching, and business.

Ease

A successful entrepreneur finds that operating a business is not just work, but a personal pleasure.

❏ I know how to calm my anxieties and disappointments about my business.

(continued)

Exercise: Strategic Checklist (continued)

❑ I can relax knowing that I minimize risk in my business by using the best business practices and operating a highly ethical business.
❑ I maintain a balance among work, family time, and play.
❑ I set goals that energize me instead of draining me.
❑ I learn about and model the strategies of successful coaches.
❑ I collaborate and link with others to make operating my business more fun.
❑ My business operates from a model of abundance, not deprivation.

_____ total score

Raising Your Score: To be a model of the coaching services you offer to others, and understand more about abundance, review Chapter 3. To learn how to calm your anxiety and other difficult feelings, read Chapter 8. Minimize risk and follow ethical guidelines and best business practices in Chapter 10.

_____ Total score of all six sections

Scoring:
35–42 points: You have a strong sense of how to set up and maintain your coaching business, and you are a true entrepreneur. Use this book to validate your vision and to give yourself increased options.
27–34 points: You're definitely on your way to knowing how to build a viable coaching business. Use the chapters listed and other resources in the appendix to motivate yourself to take the important next steps.
19–26 points: Time to do some additional work on your business and on yourself, so that you can meet your goals and learn to enjoy the business of coaching. Each chapter can help you take steps in that direction.
0–18 points: You need to take some steps and implement strategies to build a profitable coaching business. Use this book to get started and see the additional business resources we list in the Appendix. Strengthen your business abilities by completing each exercise. Find professional support during your business-building process, to make it easier.

Develop an Entrepreneurial Mind-set

Developing a business mind-set means knowing how to think like a successful entrepreneur, by adopting an optimistic yet pragmatic attitude in order to make the right business decisions. Let's look more closely at how your mind works when it comes to minding your business. Are you a worrier—dwelling on worst-case scenarios, feeling down about your lack of success, rejecting possible ideas because you assume they won't work? Are you a planner—making mental lists of what to do next, staying focused and motivated? Are you overly optimistic—seeing many opportunities, not able to prioritize, needing direction? Are you a procrastinator—coming up with good ideas but never feeling ready to start?

How you think about your business influences your abilities and your actions. Negative beliefs and critical self-talk hamper your efforts, while constructive, optimistic yet pragmatic thinking helps you to take big steps. Developing an entrepreneurial mind-set—the combination of thinking, feeling, and sensing that is the hallmark of successful business owners—is the next step in your business education.

Coaches often have a part of this mind-set developed, but need to activate additional elements. For example, we are often very skilled at sensing, and can read subtle cues and unspoken signals. This is good and can be very helpful in business situations. But we must also learn to use the linear, unemotional thinking that is necessary in business. Successful entrepreneurs tend to display the following six qualities in their thinking:

- *Given a set of challenges, successful entrepreneurs see opportunities.* Coaches face particular challenges just from being in a profession that is not well understood by those who could benefit from its services. To deal with this, you need to see the opportunities inside each challenge and keep an optimistic yet pragmatic attitude. Can you see the opening in every rejection, the break in each obstacle?
- *Given a problem, successful entrepreneurs are both optimistic and pragmatic.* Being a successful entrepreneur means that you can balance dream with reality. Can you stay upbeat and at the same time assess the truth of a situation? Taking right action when you are in a challenging situation means that you have the skill of combining a confident stance with levelheaded expectations.
- *Successful entrepreneurs expect a lot from themselves and others.* They want a lot for themselves and others. Expecting a lot from others—those who work with you, be they staff or clients—means having clear boundaries

around your requests with clients or staff. Express your needs and wants directly. Expect those around you to come from the best in themselves, and hold yourself to this expectation as well. Wanting for others means that you can hold a big vision and goals for those around you. When one of your clients sets a goal, you will support the achievement of the goal by staying interested, by brainstorming, and by celebrating when it is met, but you don't demean the client by reminding or nagging about the goal. You are there as a very interested party for your clients to report to, but not for babysitting goals.

- *Successful entrepreneurs operate from a state of abundance.* When you, as an entrepreneur, begin to feel that there is a profusion of resources in your environment, it is easier to hold a big vision for your clients and yourself as well. You come to believe that there is enough in the world for each client you see to have a meaningful life, satisfying work, enough money to live well, love, and happiness.

- *Successful entrepreneurs are persistent.* Business is not for the faint-hearted. It takes effort to land a contract, set up a thriving coaching practice, identify and cultivate referral sources, fill a workshop, land a training contract, get a book deal. It's nothing personal when your goals take more effort than you thought they would. Can you find it within yourself to stay with your goal long enough to get results? If so, you have persistence.

- *Successful entrepreneurs enjoy making a profit.* As an entrepreneur, your developmental task is to develop an adult relationship with money. You need to understand that as a businessperson, making a profit from your coaching services is as much part of your job as being a coach.

Exercise: Develop Your Business Mind-set

Review the above list of six entrepreneurial qualities and answer the following questions:

Which of the six qualities do I currently possess?

_____

_____

How specifically do I demonstrate these qualities in my life and my business?

_____

_____

(continued)

Exercise: Develop Your Business Mind-set (continued)

Which of the six qualities do I need to develop?

_____

_____

What is my first step?

_____

_____

Professional and Peer Support

Having sufficient professional support is the cushion that makes owning and operating a business less of a burden on you, the business owner. Do you draw on professional support from others to help you weather the inevitable ups and downs of small business? If you operate in isolation, without input from colleagues who can listen and advise you, you are going about business the hard way. Instead, find others who can support you in constructively. Your professional support system will tend to fall into three areas:

1. *People you hire—staff, consultants, or coaches who help you to reach outcomes or accomplish specific tasks.* Hiring others is an easy way to feel supported when you feel overwhelmed, overworked, or under pressure. Sometimes you need to hire staff—a full- or part-time bookkeeper, secretary, receptionist, or others to delegate work to and ease the pressure. Most coaches in successful businesses delegate some aspects of billing, administration, public relations, Web site design, accounting, or promotion. Some also hire outside consultants—business coaches, financial planners, marketing experts—to assist with operational planning, goal setting, and future development. Hire people who know more than you do, or can do simple tasks more easily than you can. Whatever business problem you have, in today's service-oriented economy, you can probably find staff, subcontractors, consultants, a mentor coach, or other experts to help you resolve it. You will need to manage your staff, but it may be a workable trade-off for having additional support.

2. *People you attract—peers, colleagues, friends, or family members with whom you may or may not actually do business, but who offer support,*

advice, coaching, and brainstorming. Attracting people to your practice for collaboration can generate new opportunities and referrals for a practice. Join professional support groups (small peer groups you create and/or existing professional groups) to increase your connections in the community, especially if you are an introvert and tend to keep to yourself outside of working hours. Groups such as the chamber of commerce and other business-oriented groups for entrepreneurs can provide a lot of emotional support for you, as well as new business opportunities that you might never expect. As you attract others based on a similarity of goals or shared enthusiasm, you build a circle of encouragement for yourself. You may decide to pursue business endeavors with this circle of peers, or just use the time with them to mutually share support and ideas.

3. ***People you are attracted to****—those mentors and models of excellence who you seek out so you can shift to a higher level of accomplishment or awareness.* When you connect with mentors or those whom you admire, you can shift to a higher level of accomplishment or increased awareness. This might mean giving yourself permission to "hang out" with others who are much farther along the path than you are. There are many ways to do this: going to workshops, conferences, or seminars, getting supervision from the most senior, respected coaches you can find, reading books by your favorite mentors; or joining organizations where you will be in the same room with those you admire. Open yourself to feeling supported by any degree of contact, up close or at a distance.

Exercise: Identifying My Support System

Contemplate the following five aspects of support and fill in the sentence stems.

People I hire and why:

_____

_____

People I attract and why:

_____

_____

(continued)

Exercise: Identifying My Support System (continued)

People I am attracted to and why:

_____

_____

Do I need more support system right now?

_____

_____

Which areas do I need to increase and how will I do this?

_____

_____

Here are several additional ways to feel that you are part of the profession and get more support:

- Interview other coaches in your field.
- Read books about business and subscribe to business magazines.
- Join one of the many coaching associations.
- Ask a lot of questions at every opportunity.
- Model proven strategies of successful coaches.
- Hire a mentor coach who will coach you and make your process of building a coaching business easier.
- Attend business classes or business networking events.

Advisory Circles

If you've spent any time within a large corporation or nonprofit organization, you're probably aware of the important role of the advisory board. Ideally, a board functions as the brain trust of an organization. The CEO selects the best and brightest people from a variety of fields, from within and outside the organization, to provide advice and direction. In a perfect world, the board operates without any personal or political agenda, save one: they want what is best for the organization.

Create a formal advisory board to guide you on the direction of your coaching business. Ask the best and the brightest people you know to sit on your advisory board. Communicate with them on a regular schedule, individually or as a group, by phone call, memo, or in person. Let them advise you on your business direction, specific problems, business plan, marketing plan, or your vision, purpose, and mission statement. Let each member of your board offer expertise. Listen, make notes, follow through on the best suggestions, and express your open appreciation for the members of your brain trust. Add or subtract new members as your business develops.

Or take the brainstorming concept one step further and create an advisory circle, which is a blend of an advisory board and a brainstorming session. Here's how to proceed with an advisory circle:

Exercise: Advisory Circles

Follow this format to create your own advisory circle.

1. *Who:* Select four to six people for your advisory circle, including yourself. Who should be a member of the group? It will help if everyone is in business. You might include some coaches, but also consider having other types of professionals who are in business for themselves. Each person should be someone you respect, someone whose advice and experience will be relevant, and someone you would like to give your support to, in turn. When advising, everyone agrees to speak from a place of the highest good, without personal agenda. (For this reason, you may not want to have your spouse or close friends sit in on this professional support circle, unless you are sure you can both remain loving and objective for each other professionally.)

Who will be in my circle:

_____

_____

_____

_____

_____

2. *When:* If the group has six members, everyone agrees to meet once a week for a minimum of six weeks. Each meeting will take an hour.

When we will first meet:_____

Subsequent meetings: _____

(continued)

Exercise: Advisory Circles (continued)

3. *How:* The format of each meeting is simple—a different person takes center stage each time. One person takes 30 minutes to present one's professional situation and answers any questions other members may have; then the group gives their best advice for the remaining 30 minutes. During the advice-giving 30 minutes, the center-stage person must sit quietly, without defensiveness. The members of your circle will now give you advice, direction, and suggestions, based on wanting the best for you personally and professionally. They will talk about your situation among themselves, while you just listen.

Any changes to the suggested format that I need to make for my advisory group:

_____

_____

4. *Why:* The value of advice is hearing it cleanly, with detachment. You will hear many ideas that you may want to downplay or resist. Listen with an open mind and reject nothing at this time. Take notes. You are free to accept or reject whatever you like later, but first consider all the possibilities without excuses or explanations. When the time is over, thank your circle for their efforts. The next time you meet, it's somebody else's turn and you become part of their advisory circle.

How I will stay open and detached regarding the advice that is offered:

_____

_____

5. *How long:* Keep the circle meeting as long as it is useful to the group. Make time in each subsequent meetings for each person to briefly report on changes, action steps toward desired goals, and progress reports. Some coaches who formed these circles tell me that over time the circles shift and change structure, becoming less formalized and more like a support group, except that when one member faces a difficult situation they can revert to the process for giving clean advice (advice that is accepted openly by the listener, without resistance).

My plan:

_____

_____

Loving the Business

Your degree of enjoyment in the business of coaching is a leading indicator of your financial success. If you love business the same way you love coaching, you will spend more time and do more work to build an ideal coaching business. You may not have thought about what it would require to actually love your business, so we can help you along this path by suggesting that you adopt three simple premises. Premises are not necessarily truths, but rather strong suggestions about reality. We suggest you adopt these premises, as though they were true, in order to be successful in business by learning to love it. The premises are as follows:

1. *You are not your business.* You may be a sole proprietor and feel like you are the sum total of your business, but I strongly suggest you see your business as a separate entity. A major cause of hating business comes from overidentifying with your small business. Differentiate yourself. See your business as distinct from you, even if you built it, even if it only exists as a result of your actions. Think of it as a child you birthed who has a lot of you in it, but is not you. Your business has its own needs, its own nature, its own moods, and as a good parent or good business owner, it's your job to give your business what it requires to thrive. Don't get confused or feel resentful simply because your business needs what a business needs.

2. *Your business is an accurate reflection of your strengths and weaknesses.* Even though you are not your business, your business will mirror certain aspects of your personality accurately. For example, if you have strong boundaries regarding time, have always been a prompt person, and manage your time well, this will probably be reflected in your business: your sessions probably start and stop on time and your business calendar is clear and exact. If you are very disorganized and live with clutter and chaos, chances are your business mirrors your disorganization. Your paperwork is hard to find and file. Your treatment reports are late. Recognizing that your business is a good reflection of you means that when you want to make a change in your business, you may be able to effect this change more easily by making it in yourself first and then seeing it reflect in your business.

3. *All actions you take in business are fear-based or love-based.* You will need to take a lot of specific actions in order to make your business successful. Refusing to cross a room at a networking event to meet a potential referral source based on fear of rejection, or lowering your fee

because you fear that a client will leave if you don't, are examples of acting from fear. Every time you take a business action based on fear, you literally foreclose on your ability to feel affection and love for your business.

For example, you may need to make several marketing cold calls to potential referral sources. Doing this from a basis of fear means that you will make the calls from a basis of survival. You think, "If I don't make this call, my practice won't survive. If this doesn't go well, it will just prove that I am not a good marketer. I may have to give up on my business." Imagine the pressure that kind of thinking places on you as you try to develop professional relationships. Who could love a business that puts them into this kind of a spin? If you take action from a basis of love, you make the exact same call, but from a different perspective. You think, "I am calling this person to let him know how much I love being a coach. I will do this as a win-win venture and see what I can give, not just what I can get. Even if no results come from this call, I love to meet new people and learn about their needs, so I will just relax and enjoy the process." Same action, different basis, different experience of marketing, different feeling about the actions needed to keep a business operating. Every time you take action in regard to your practice, see if you can do it from a basis of love—love of self, love of others, love of your business, or love of the profession of coaching.

When you can give your business what it needs while not taking those needs personally, when you are willing to change yourself in order to make a change in your business, when you can take actions based strictly on having a positive regard for your business you will learn to enjoy the ride of business and be positioned for success.

Resilience

Let's face it. Business can be hard work. Creating and maintaining a highly successful coaching practice requires persistence and a healthy dose of resilience. You must be able to bounce back quickly from setbacks, ready to try again the next day. And the next. And the next.

Have client cancellations and caseload drop-offs got you worried? Are expenses mounting up without the increase in income to offset them? Is the added stress of difficult, unexpected life situations, combined with operating a small business, making life feel harder than usual? Rough sailing affects every business owner. If you feel as though your coaching business, or your life, is slightly out of control, you need to know how to stay calm, even in the face of turmoil. Resilience is a key business mind-set and behavior. Here are two strategies recommended by a sailor friend, which we offer as a metaphor for your business buoyancy:

1. *Become seaworthy:* When sailing in rough waters, our friend the sailor checks that gear is simple and uncluttered onboard. When you hit rough water, it's best to have less to attend to. Getting uncluttered mentally and physically in the face of business turmoil makes good common sense. Especially when you are under business stress, make space daily for mental downtime. Clear your brain. Relax with a hot bath. Take a walk. Schedule time for physical uncluttering, even in the face of deadlines. Get as organized and efficient as possible, to help you feel some internal degree of control. Clean out files; collect unpaid receivables; do your errands; make sure your office and workspace are uncluttered; clear your mind with meditation or long walks each day. Then you can attend to the important goals of each week, and not be concerned with the additional clutter or disorganization of mind, body, and space that can be so distracting.

2. *Heave to:* When our friend is sailing in very rough waters and the ride is getting uncomfortably bumpy, sometimes she sets the sailboat to a "heave to" position. This slows her boat down considerably, but keeps it moving forward. In this way, she holds a set course but allows for some natural drift to occur. The drift creates some turbulence on the water, and that disturbance counters the aggressiveness of the waves. The pounding felt when going upwind in strong seas almost miraculously disappears.

     We love this idea for those of us in small business. We take this to mean that when you are in the rough seas in business (or life), you slow down a bit, focus tightly on your goals, but anticipate and tolerate some drift. You will go off course and it may feel like you are wandering about, but as long as this drift is expected and you are still focused on your goals, you will be safely moving forward. The drift will help counter the problems in a small way and give you a more comfortable ride. Tracking this process is going to be key to knowing when you are moving forward, versus when you are dangerously off course. Here's what this looks like in a coaching business:

     Belinda, a business coach with several demanding clients, faced rough seas when her mother became ill and moved into Belinda's small home. Belinda's schedule suddenly became filled with getting her mother to the doctor, repeated emergency trips to the hospital, and much worry and concern as her mother's condition worsened. Belinda's energy level took a downturn and she missed a few important client meetings. One client threatened to fire her. She was concerned about her coaching business, especially because she felt too worn out to be really effective with her clients.

We asked Belinda to write a short-term statement that would set her direction. The statement was a way to set an immediate course and feel in control, to the degree she could. Her vision simply said, "I will calmly and logically take care of my mother and service my clients as best I can." She then listed weekly goals and made sure that they further the statement.

We also asked her to note the ways she drifted off course each week, as well as what progress she made toward completing her weekly goals. We reminded her that "small steps counted" when she would get frustrated about the slowness of her accomplishments. Week after week, we checked the integrity with which she held her statement as truth, brainstormed with her about her immediate goals, listened about the inevitable drift, and validated her slow but steady progress.

After 2 months, even Belinda could begin to see the forward movement. Because progress was slow and drift and distraction were unavoidable, without tracking her progress this closely she would have been discouraged and have felt like giving up. With careful tracking, she could see where she was at any given time, and with support she could begin to feel in charge of her life, despite those things that she could not control.

Exercise: Developing Resilience

Fill in the following sentence stems to help develop mental and behavioral resilience in your business.

To become more mentally seaworthy and clear my mind, I will take the following actions each day:

_____

_____

(continued)

Exercise: Developing Resilience (continued)

To become more physically seaworthy and clear my space, I will take the following steps:

_____

_____

To set course and hold my position despite rough waters, my statement of direction is:

_____

_____

My tracking mechanism to make sure I am on course will be:

_____

_____

Even after coaches begin to develop an entrepreneurial mind-set, they can be unexpectedly derailed by emotions and feelings owning a business elicits. How you handle the normal but difficult feelings that can emerge while you build your coaching business will factor greatly into your success. In the next chapter, we offer you the most effective strategies for developing emotional intelligence about business, so that you can continue to move forward and create a strong and viable coaching practice.

CHAPTER 8

Business and Your Emotional Intelligence

As you open and operate a coaching business, you may find it a much more emotionally challenging proposition than you had ever expected. Many coaches feel split—of two minds—about owning a coaching business: they are devoted to the practice of coaching, but less enamored about the business of coaching. In workshops we conduct around the country, we ask coaches in business to first describe how they feel about their chosen vocation of coaching. The word we hear most often is *love*. "I love the work I do. I love helping others change. I love being able to make a difference in someone's life and work."

Then we ask the same coaches to describe how they feel about owning and operating a coaching business, and the words we hear most often are *fear* and *hate*. "I hate the demands of my business. Marketing is so scary for me. I worry about money every single day. I fear that I could wake up one day and have all my clients leave. Do you ever get secure in this business? I hate how dumb I feel when it comes to making almost any business decision."

If you, like these other coaches, have mixed feelings between the *practice* of coaching and the *business* of coaching, and you don't find a way to reconcile the internal emotional battleground, you can sabotage even your best business efforts. But if you can learn to integrate these oppositional feelings, you and your business will both win. Some people say that there is no room for emotion in business. We disagree. All of your emotions regarding business are potentially important and need to be channeled into your emotional business intelligence. (Emotional intelligence refers to the concept of multiple forms of intelligence, as defined by researcher Daniel

Goleman [1997], that shows that our emotions are part of the necessary data we need for making good decisions.) You will need all of your emotional business intelligence in order to make sound decisions about the present and future of your coaching business.

An emotionally intelligent way to operate in a coaching business is to anticipate a range of normal (including negative) feelings that are natural for a business owner to experience. If you know what may occur emotionally, then you can prepare yourself so that when the emotions emerge, you can use them productively. You can learn to transform difficult and even upsetting feelings about business into opportunities for your personal and professional development. In this chapter, we will show you how to take good emotional care of yourself in the course of doing business, so that you get a chance to grow into a more competent coach and a more resilient businessperson. The first step is to reframe every emotional upset during the course of doing business as a potential AFGO (another freaking growth opportunity).

Letting Business Heal You

Sondra Ray (1980), personal growth guru from the 1970s and author of *Loving Relationships*, noted a difficult paradox about love. Although most people have an idealistic view of how love should be, Ray found that when one is actually in an intimate, loving relationship, the day-to-day process of love feels pretty muddled. Being in love feels wonderful and horrible because it brings to light all of one's unresolved issues and insecurities, all the unloving thoughts and feelings we have about ourselves and others. *Love brings up everything unlike itself, for the purpose of healing,* was a mantra Ray would repeat in her Loving Relationships workshops. That same paradox occurs to us when we talk to coaches about their feelings regarding business. The day-to-day process of closely relating to your business will bring up everything—irrational thoughts, deeply held negative beliefs, areas of your vulnerability—everything and anything unlike the cool, rational, businesslike attitude you would want to embody, for the purpose of *your* healing.

Small-business ownership is an intense learning environment. If you started your own business thinking it would offer you autonomy, a degree of self-esteem, and freedom, you are right, it will . . . except when it doesn't! In the course of building and operating a business, your business may also provoke a series of (sometimes irrational) feelings of anger, fear, disappointment, anxiety, constraint, and, occasionally, failure. On a spiritual level, you might understand the emotional process that small business ownership provokes as one of purification: like a boiling pot of water, your business will stir up any aspects of your personality that are immature and unresolved and bring them up to the surface of your conscious awareness for you to deal with. You get a choice when this happens. You can learn how to accept the difficult feelings and release them, like steam, for purification or renewal, or they can float on the surface, creating ambiguity inside you and clogging the daily workings of your business.

Being in business takes courage. It is not for the fainthearted. Business will allow you to mature psychologically and move forward, or it can emotionally bankrupt you. Sometimes we tell coaches that to let this maturing process of business play out, all they need to do is "stop working so hard on your business, and let the business do its work on you." What we mean by this is if you can accept and resolve the ways in which your fear, disappointment, or anxiety plays out as you go about the process of building your coaching business, you can use this heightened capacity to become a better entrepreneur.

To let the business work on you, start by noticing any business challenges you currently face and get curious about their deeper, emotional source. Here is a list of common business situations we have gathered from coaches we mentor, and the difficult emotion or negative belief that they say contributes to each challenge:

Business Challenges	*Emotional Source or Negative Belief*
Not enough clients	Fear of putting self forward
Invoices in disarray; slow to bill	Negative beliefs about money
Goes over the session hour; lateness	Poor personal boundaries
Charges under going rate	Low self-worth
Gossips about colleagues or clients	Envy and insecurity about self
Takes on too many volunteer projects	Not ready to get serious about vision
Business in constant crisis	Uses adrenaline as fuel
Business vision limited	Afraid to succeed

Exercise: Heal Your Business, Heal Yourself

Follow these steps to get to the source and solution of your current business problems.

1. Make a list of your business challenges and the emotional source or negative belief that contributes to the problem.

2. If you have trouble figuring out your source issues, brainstorm with others. Stay open to what you hear. Don't defend. Just see if the possible source resonates for you, and write it down.

3. Pick two internal source issues to address and correct this month. Heal the source issue, and often you will find that the business situation resolves much more easily. Let your business be a healing force in both your coaching business and your personal development.

Emotional Intelligence

Anticipating the normal, yet difficult emotions that occur in the course of business can help you build a stronger business, faster. The three most common emotions that cause coaches to get destabilized in the course of doing business—anger, disappointment, and anxiety—will sabotage your progress on a daily basis unless you get prepared to manage them. The strategies we look at next show you how to work with these emotions as they arise, so that you stay resourceful and proactive.

Anger

The stress of building a coaching business can certainly make a coach feel irritated. Some months, no matter how diligently you market, no new clients come in. Referral sources don't call back as promised. Someone else has taken the phenomenal Web site domain name you just dreamed up, before you could register it. Your teleclass doesn't fill. The clients you had scheduled cancel. The office space you lease is going up in price. Again. The proposal for a big executive coaching contract that you thought was a done deal is on hold. And you are starting to get steamed.

Anger in business can take many forms, including feelings of resentment (*How come that other coach has a waiting list and I don't?*), blame (*That HR director has never once given my proposals a fair chance*), and even self-pity (*Why can't I get a lucky break?*). When business gets you down, you can blame others and feel secretly sorry for yourself, *or* you be a savvy entrepreneur and reduce anger by *right action*, a Buddhist term that means taking constructive action in a particular way that is an antidote for anger.

Right Action

Eva, a wellness coach, worked out of a chiropractic office. She complained of being in a bad mood, week after week. She spent time, when not coaching clients, trying to network with physicians and health providers who could refer clients for her wellness coaching services. "But other doctors I meet are so limited in their understanding of coaching," she said. "I've tried to explain to them what I do and how I work with people, but they just don't get it. I don't even know why I bother with them. When they do send me a client, it's often someone who is uncoachable, someone depressed who really needs therapy, not coaching. I try to explain my ideal client profile, but they don't hear me. What's the point of this marketing, anyway?"

As mentor coaches, we asked Eva to become more aware of her bad mood and how it was affecting her business. She reported another probable result: lately, some of her clients were in bad moods, too. True, her clients often suffered from pain, which can make anyone irritable, and she made allowances for that. But Eva said that her clients were becoming less compliant about their coaching goals and, well, moodier. She wondered if her own anger about her coaching business was getting transferred to her clients.

The right action approach for managing business anger is twofold:

1) Address feelings of anger by taking constructive action.
2) Express gratitude daily.

To take constructive action, Eva created the following plan:

- List 10 doctors to call each month.
- Practice my marketing pitch.
- Follow up with clear written materials.
- Ask for referrals more directly and explicitly.
- Demonstrate my skills as a wellness coach in an informal way with every doctor I call, to show, not just tell, what coaching is about.
- Find 10 other referral sources besides doctors to contact this month, and call them.
- Recognize my role as educator about wellness when I am marketing my services.

To express gratitude daily, we suggested she keep a gratitude journal. Each day she recorded a statement of appreciation for herself and her efforts, and one for the doctors, for any and all of their efforts to support her (however minor or misguided those efforts might be, she added). After a while she could see that even when a doctor made an inappropriate referral, this was an act of kindness and support and she softened in her frustration. We asked Eva whether her clients were changing in their attitudes. Eva reported good news: her clients were once again making gains and several had begun to voice their appreciation of her as their coach. She also was pleased to tell us that she was feeling more confident in her role as educator about wellness coaching. As a result, within 3 months her practice began to fill with more clients from doctors.

Exercise: Taking Right Action

Go through the steps of this process to shift from anger to action.

1. Notice how often you are feeling frustration, self-doubt, self-pity, grandiosity, entitlement, blame, rejection, or resentment. Are you complaining about your coaching business on a daily or weekly basis to others? Identify whatever is making you angry.

2. Write down the angry thoughts and feelings, and the source of your anger. Make a constructive action plan to take steps to improve each situation starting now.

3. Write a daily journal of the gratitude and appreciation you feel for yourself and others.

Disappointment

Owning a small coaching business can be emotional roller-coaster ride. You can experience the highs of satisfaction and the lows of self-doubt, sometimes in the same day. If you take the ups and downs of business personally, you will feel weary and burned out. Even worse, you may make some business mistakes because you are not addressing your ambivalent, complicated, uncoachlike feelings.

When your best business ideas yield less than you hoped, when you face setbacks, when you are not recognized or valued as a coach in the ways you feel you deserve, you will of course feel disappointed. In business, if you are highly entrepreneurial, you will be very familiar with disappointment because you will try many things that won't yield much in the way of results. It can't be helped. In business, you have to stay busy with some degree of outreach, so entrepreneurs market, network, propose, and promote all the time. The ratio of marketing effort to clients yielded is always high on the marketing-efforts end of the equation. For example, a direct mail or e-mail campaign is considered successful if it yields a 1% return of actual services sold. You will expend energy, time, and resources as you build your coaching business and, over time, you will discover which are successful ways of generating new clients and which have less impact.

Building a full coaching practice takes most coaches several years. Your capacity to stay proactive, positive, and upbeat in the face of inevitable disappointment will be a bellwether of your entrepreneurial success.

If you can bear feelings of disappointment, you have a better chance of building a strong and lasting coaching business. Dealing with disappointment is difficult for some because of the sense of inner collapse: you feel that you have done your best, tried your hardest, and it still wasn't enough. Some coaches go into self-blame, or "awful-ize" the situation, because inside it feels like defeat. Keeping disappointment in perspective as an ordinary, expected feeling that results from trying to generate business is step number one.

Sometimes disappointment comes from the result of a single experience, but other times it is an accumulation of incidents that seem to grow with each additional letdown. One disappointment may trigger another, and you, as the coach, end up needing some strong talking-to so that you don't slide into a state of helplessness. The antidote for disappointment is optimism, and one good way to effect an optimistic state is by using entrepreneurial self-talk.

Entrepreneurial Self-talk

To recognize and contain your feelings of disappointment so that they don't snowball into helplessness, you need to have an internal business voice, a way of talking to yourself about business that is positive, clear, and logical. First, let your self-talk name the emotion you feel without exaggerating it. Say, "I was very *disappointed* about what happened" instead of "I am a failure" or using any one of a number of words that signal helplessness or hopelessness. Naming disappointment normalizes the feeling: everyone who is successful in business feels disappointed from time to time. Here are some other ways to reframe your language:

FROM: *"I don't have enough clients, which means I'm not a good enough coach."*

TO: *"I am disappointed in my client count so far, but I am willing to do a lot more to get additional business."*

FROM: *"The last three phone calls from potential clients didn't materialize because they said my fees were too high. This isn't going to work. I'll never be able to make a living wage."*

TO: *"Resistance due to pricing is normal in business. I am disappointed about the three calls, but it gives me a chance to rethink my pricing options and how I describe my coaching over the phone."*

FROM: *"I am so overwhelmed with the demands of my family and my clients that once again I didn't find any time to devote to my paperwork or filing. This is hopeless and I guess I have to live with a messy office."*

TO: *"I know I am busy, and it is disappointing that my paperwork got pushed to the bottom of my list of priorities again. This week I will structure some time to sort things out."*

Mary Anne, an executive coach and trainer in San Jose, California, had a narrow niche: she offered team-building seminars and leadership coaching for executives in the high-tech, dot-com industry. Her one-person business stayed full and profitable for a period of 5 years. She had a full client list and a contract with private and government companies, and often traveled to other cities, especially Washington, DC, where she delivered on-site seminars.

At year five of her business, Mary Anne made a decision to expand. She took out a bank loan, opened an office in Washington, DC, and hired administrative staff for both offices. Within 6 months, the high-tech industry suffered a major downturn, and both the government and private companies cut training and coaching programs from their budgets. Mary Anne saw her client base fall off in both cities and sadly realized that her dreams of expansion were over.

"I feel like a total failure," she said. "I am so stupid. I should have waited. I have lost thousands of dollars, had to lay off my own staff, and am back where I started, only poorer." Our first step was to help Mary Anne reframe her language of failure into the language of disappointment. Every time she began to blame herself and bemoan her situation, we asked her to replace her stinging self-rebukes with the simple statement: "I am so very disappointed."

Mary Anne found that this one basic intervention of reframing her self-talk made a noticeable shift. She stopped taking her situation personally. She wasn't stupid. She just got caught in a market shift that she hadn't foreseen. As she detached from the negative feelings, she could get to work on retooling and rebuilding her coaching and consulting business, to better adapt to the new market situation.

Every coach in business needs ego strength. Your ability to use positive, realistic self-talk can build ego strength and allow you to learn from your mistakes, instead of collapsing into negative beliefs about yourself or about your world (see exercise on p. 153). You will be better able to ride the normal ups and downs of business without doing damage to your sense of self.

Anxiety

Do you live with constant apprehension about your coaching business, independent of reality? For example, one coach says, "I feel like I am only one step away from being a bag lady on the street, even though my income is in the low six figures this year and I have plenty of money in savings. No amount of financial evidence completely eliminates this concern." Another complains, "When I take a day off, I find it hard to relax. I keep thinking I am forgetting something I need to do at work. I feel tethered to my e-mail and my phone, and get nervous when I leave the office for a whole day."

In psychology, when someone worries excessively they get diagnosed as having *generalized anxiety*. Generalized anxiety is an unspecific, vague worry; it feels like a dark cloud of uneasiness hangs above you, ready to rain down at any moment. As business coaches, we see a similar condition occur with some small business owners who also complain of ever-present worry. We have started calling this *generalized business anxiety* and the antidote is twofold:

1) Calm yourself.
2) Calm your business.

Calming Yourself

Jefferson, a program director at a nonprofit agency, hired a career coach to help him figure out a new career. After 6 months Jefferson decided that coaching was very helpful for him personally, and coaching was also a good choice for his future career. He got some coach training and made a plan

Exercise: Entrepreneurial Self-talk

Replace your negative self-talk with the following constructive statements to shift feelings of victimization to simple disappointment.

I can deal with anything bad that happens as long as I reframe the situation as *disappointing.*

The situation is not personal: it just happened.

I won't let difficult emotions knock me offtrack for very long.

No one has ever died from a bad feeling.

I have value, regardless of what situation I face.

My coaching expertise is good for the community.

I clear away the things that drain my energy.

I make a distinction between my personal and professional needs. I fulfill each in different ways.

I do not keep my services and expertise a secret from others.

I have symbolic and literal ways to tap into a wellspring of energy and love.

I feel gratitude every day.

I honor myself as a coach every day.

I take five action steps to move my business forward every day.

1. Now write a short two-paragraph description of a recent disappointment regarding your business and how you responded to it.

2. Rewrite the same event incorporating the positive self-talk examples from above. Remove self-blame, exaggeration, awful-izing, and victimized statements that make you sound hopeless or helpless.

3. Now notice if the positive self-talk makes a difference in how you feel and think about the event.

to transition after 1 year into his own coaching business. He reached his goal to transition in 9 months and left his job. The bad news? A constant state of worry.

"I never worried in my old job, but now that I am in business for myself and it's up to me to make an income, I can't sleep at night anymore. Mind you, nothing is wrong. I have a business plan and my business is growing. I am a good coach. I am taking all the steps I need to. But man, am I ever anxious," he told us. Jefferson had always worked as an employee. Now that he was the boss of his own business he was facing a degree of anxiety that was normal for a new business owner, but way beyond his normal comfort level.

"We want you to use your existing strengths and skills to find a way to calm yourself, while you continue to move ahead in your coaching business," we said.

"I would if I could," he said. "Got any ideas?"

Knowing that Jefferson was an avid hiker, we suggested a metaphor. "Imagine that you are on a long hike in some thick woods, alone, in unfamiliar territory. Nothing is wrong. These woods are safe, no real danger is present, but the forest is always somewhat unpredictable. Your goal is to stay on your established hiking route, stay safe, and above all, enjoy your journey. What will help you to best accomplish this?"

Jefferson had the answer immediately. "Well, to start, I need the right gear. I take care with the way I pack and carry my own backpack, and I have some great, lightweight rain gear. I need a map, so I can look around, stay alert, and stay on track. To enjoy myself, I always focus on my breathing easily so I don't get winded. I usually hum a little song to help me keep my walking pace even. Humming in my out-of-tune way even puts a smile on my face."

We asked him to translate the entire metaphor to his current journey of being in business.

"The gear is similar to the equipment I invested in for my coaching business," he said. "I have a good computer, phone line, and fax, but now that I think of it, I am missing something that I need to calm down. I need a software package to track my marketing contacts. I get anxious when I am disorganized, and it would help me if I could see who to call that week at a glance."

"What else can you translate that would help you stay calm and alert, but enjoy your business path?"

"Well, on my hike I have a map. I have a business plan, but I might need a more detailed one so that I am very clear about where I am going."

"Anything else?"

"The enjoyment piece—the breathing, pacing, and humming. I am not doing anything to help me enjoy the business process. I think I will find a way to do that. I need to think a little on what that might be, but I will find something that matches what I do when I hike, to help me go the distance in business."

"Remember," we cautioned, "in your metaphor, you needed to stay alert in the forest. As a hiker, you get used to walking with a certain degree of apprehension, to be safe. It keeps you attentive. So appreciate that anxiety plays a role in your business journey. Just bring it down to an acceptable level."

Exercise: Your Business Journey

Use the following exercise to develop a metaphor about following a path of your own making. Decipher it and then translate it to apply to your current business situation.

1. Close your eyes and imagine that you are taking a journey. It might be by foot, by horseback, or in a vehicle. You pick the terrain: on land, over water, in the mountains, through the forest, or across the desert. Imagine that you look forward to your journey; it is one of choice, a journey based on your desire to reach a great destination.

2. The journey is not dangerous, but it is challenging and you need to stay alert. Imagine how you use your existing strengths and inner resources to stay safe and enjoy the experience. What do you need to bring or have with you to make sure that you feel as calm and alert as possible? What is your mind-set? What helps you to take pleasure in the journey?

3. Now open your eyes and translate this imagery to your current business journey. For each item or resource in your imagined journey, find a correlation in your real business process. Use your imagination and creativity to generate resources that can make your business journey feel calmer and more enjoyable. Make a list of the resources currently at your disposal to smooth your journey.

4. What do you need to add to your life in terms of both tangible and intangible items to help you self-soothe and further reduce any generalized business anxiety? Create a plan for obtaining these items.

Calming Your Business

There are many aspects of a coaching business that can leave you feeling insecure. It's hard to predict the future of your client base, anticipate your exact annual earnings, or know whether your business is always on solid ground. While a degree of uncertainty is part of the package of owning and operating a coaching business, you, as the business owner, have more options than simply worrying and hoping. One place to start is to take steps to know how to have a secure client base. According to the 2003 ICF survey, the client retention norm for coaches is 1 year or less.

Coaches need to have a strategy in place to both retain existing clients and create a steady flow of new business. We offered you the most effective marketing strategies for generating new business in Chapter 6. Now we want to explore how to create a secure client base of existing clients by helping you to understand the aspects that create a strong connection between coach and client. This connection may be between you and an individual client, or you and clients within an organization with which you have a contract.

With a secure client connection, you can better weather the inevitable ups and downs, build a business that stays full with less effort, and above all, relax a little. You can become more flexible in the way you plan your work and your life. You can take a vacation and not worry about whether you will still have a practice to come back to; you can branch out and try new methods without fearing that your clients will leave; you can add new services, such as programs or workshops, and feel confident about filling them.

Retaining existing clients is, in large part, a factor of how effective you are as a coach. Your skills and style of work will determine how well and how long you work with existing clients. But it is also a business issue. From a business perspective, a secure client base means that you have a foundation of clients who:

- *stay with you* long enough to complete their coaching,
- *return to you* when they need further services, and
- *refer to you* based on their satisfaction with their experience.

A respected psychological theory—*attachment theory*—explains a universal human need to form close bonds with others. Healthy attachment signifies the reciprocity inherent in optimal human relationships. If you think of your client connection as a form of business attachment, it may be easier to understand how to develop relationships that work and last. Here are the three stages of healthy attachment that ideally occur within a coaching relationship during the first year, to promote a secure client base.

Stages of Client Connection

Stage #1: Loyalty—During the first 3 months, you help clients to establish an initial bond with you, so that they feel trusting, in good professional hands, as the process of coaching unfolds. They develop a degree of loyalty to you and to your coaching process, based on a combination of how you connect with them and the initial results of the coaching.

Stage #2: Advocacy—During the second 3 months, clients feel that you "have their back" and offer enough support to them and their goals that allows them to distance a bit. This stage requires a looser connection between coach and client, as you transfer the ownership of results to the client.

Stage #3: Enthusiasm—From 6 months to the end of coaching, clients differentiate further, recognize and generate their own goals and gains, and, in articulating these gains, want to share their positive experience about coaching with others.

Loyalty

In the first stage of client connection, loyalty, the client is often feeling most exposed, because the client has admitted to needing help. The coach must be available, reliable, and attentive, without being too anxious or overprotective. When a healthy connection is in place, the client bonds in a healthy way with the coach and develops a sense of loyalty to the coaching process (trust for the coach, reliance on the usefulness of the coaching sessions, appreciation of the accountability factor), which fosters initial client retention.

Lewis, Amini, and Lannon (2000) stated that the first step in healthy attachment is having someone with a keen ear catch your "melodic resonance." How do you catch the melodic resonance of a new client? As coaches, we are trained to be good listeners and to reflect back what we hear, to further our clients' personal growth. As a businessperson, your ability to hear and communicate what your clients want and need is essential to creating the first stage of client connection.

To enhance Stage #1: Stay open and curious about your client's requests and desires. Don't assume or prejudge what you hear. Don't rush in with ways to "fix" the client: nothing is broken. Instead, see if you can "make the client right," that is, if you can step inside the client's shoes and see the world from your client's perspective, to increase understanding and to better create an initial connection.

Advocacy

After working with a coach for a while, clients seek a more individuated level of connection. The client is less vulnerable or dependent and, while wanting support from the coach, needs to own the coaching process, to feel increasingly confident of new skills and behaviors imparted through the coaching relationship. Clients at this stage need to leave and return, either metaphorically (challenging the coach, disagreeing with strategy, generating more of their own ideas) or literally (taking a break). The coach who can anticipate and gracefully promote this stage of differentiation with a client is rewarded by the client's feelings of advocacy.

One executive coach who works within corporate settings put it this way: "At a certain point in my coaching contract, especially when I am working with a corporate client on a long-term project and coaching many levels of managers, things always get tricky. A program doesn't go as planned. Someone on the corporate team gets upset with me. The CEO wants me out, rather than make a necessary, big change. I always know it's going to come, it's a part of the process. It's hard on everyone, and the important thing is for me, as the coach, to stay calm in the midst of the storms that brew and help my client stay calm, too, by educating the client about the continued value of what I am doing for him and helping him understand why the storm is so intense and rough at the moment. He also needs to know that even if he tells me to leave, he can reconsider and hire me back again. As long as we have left each other well, I will be glad to come back in."

To enhance Stage #2: Prepare yourself and your client for the entire scope of coaching. Anticipate the experience together, so that there are no big surprises and everyone feels in partnership and informed. As differentiation occurs, celebrate it, and continue coaching with respect to the shift in client connection.

Enthusiasm

As coaching concludes the first year, the client connection shifts yet again. Clients are more autonomous. Many still desire a coaching connection, but of a slightly different nature. The coaching relationship becomes a home base—a place to leave (again metaphorically or literally) for periods of time, yet one to return to for welcome and consistency.

If the first stage of client connection responds to a client's reliance on or immediate need for help, and the second stage reflects the client's emerging self-sufficiency, you might understand this third stage as interdependence—a touch-and-go "dance" between client and coach. At this stage, you as the coach–business owner allow yourself to connect to your client the way a ballroom dancer might hold a seasoned partner: not too close, not too tight. You want to position yourself for more give-and-take with your client at this stage, to respect the maturity of the connection.

When this level of connection is working well, clients often become openly enthusiastic and endorsing of you and their coaching to others, and you may tend to feel equally appreciative of them. Coaching may continue after a year, with the client connection continuing to mature, if you can provide a rich environment for future client growth.

To enhance Stage #3: Make sure to add continual value to the coaching relationship, to help clients feel that the coaching environment is rich and ongoing. Added value in a coaching business includes the services you deliver that go above and beyond the initial coaching contract. What added-value services can you offer for your clients? Consider new program content, additional resources, and even your increased optimism, for a start. Adapt any and all new methods you may be learning, books you read, what you learn from your own mentor coaching, articles you write or collect, audiotapes, additional ideas, or even extra contact with you the coach.

The key to adding value is to use a plan. Add services gradually, perhaps one new service every 4–6 months. Adding too much too soon will diminish the importance of any single service, overwhelm you, and confuse your clients. Since adding value is an ongoing process, make it part of your overall business plan. Organize your offerings around a theme for the year. Add value that reflects your vision, purpose, and mission statement.

Exercise: Building a Client Connection

Answer the following questions to determine and enhance your client base.

1. The average length of time my individual coaching clients work with me in coaching is:

_____

_____

(continued)

Exercise: Building a Client Connection (continued)

2. If the answer to #1 is shorter than I wish, the average time I would like to retain clients in order to feel secure about my client base is:

_____

_____

3. In general, if my clients leave coaching prematurely, do they terminate during the loyalty (1–3 months), advocacy (3–6 months), or enthusiasm stage (6 months or longer)?

_____

_____

4. What is the reason that most clients give when they are terminating?

_____

_____

5. If the objection is money, how can I package my services (see Chapter 9) to overcome the objection?

_____

_____

6. If the objection is lack of value, how can I improve my skills (see Chapter 3) or articulate the benefits (see Chapter 6) to overcome the objection?

_____

_____

7. To build a stronger connection in the loyalty stage, I need clients to feel that our coaching relationship is reliable, boundaried, confidential, and collaborative. To retain clients at this stage, I will:

❑ make sure that the sessions are consistent and regular to establish good coaching boundaries
❑ add structure to the coaching so that clients can chart initial progress and see immediate results

(continued)

Exercise: Building a Client Connection (continued)

❑ be available by e-mail and phone to clients between sessions for questions or clarification

❑ stay open and curious about the client's needs and wants, while listening for my client's "greatness"

❑ try to see things from my client's perspective, to make sure I understand what the client is encountering

❑ other:

_____

_____

8. To build a stronger connection during the advocacy stage, I need clients to feel empowered, yet still supported by me as the coach. To retain clients at this stage, I will:

❑ ask more questions to encourage my clients to think for themselves

❑ allow the coaching to be a touchstone of support while my clients make big steps between sessions

❑ make larger, more consistent requests of my clients so that they stretch and accomplish more

❑ allow my clients to take a break from coaching if needed and then return when ready

❑ anticipate the sometimes bumpy road of coaching with clients so that there are no surprises

❑ regularly acknowledge client gains and progress

❑ keep clients challenged and focused on the next big goal

❑ other:

_____

_____

9. To build a stronger connection during the enthusiasm stage, I need to let my clients "dance" with me, so we move in tandem during a session and they feel a sense of ownership of their success and results. To retain clients at this stage I will:

❑ be honest and open with my clients in my feedback

❑ offer expansive topics for the client to think about and take action on, such as steps toward legacy, leadership, community, happiness, passion, and joy

(continued)

Exercise: Building a Client Connection (continued)

❑ take sufficient time to celebrate wins
❑ model enthusiasm for my client by making sure I am passionate about my work and life
❑ set a vision with my client for further coaching goals
❑ ask my clients to set their own agenda for each session, and hold them to high standards
❑ other:

_____

_____

Good Endings

Saying good-bye to clients can be another source of emotion in business. When the coaching is completed in a positive way, you will feel happy to see clients leave because it means they have accomplished their goals. But if you are honest, you may notice some feelings of loss when clients leave, especially if you felt a degree of honest affection for your clients and if the work was mutually gratifying. And if the coaching ends poorly, the process of ending can be confusing and upsetting for a coach.

Ideally, when clients finish their coaching, and the coaching went well, you want to leave the door open, so that when and if they desire to work with you again they can comfortably return. Businesses call this creating "lifetime" customers—customers who will stay with a company over the long term, repeatedly purchasing services and products, coming and going as need be.

You can consider clients lifetime clients, whether they are active clients (clients you currently see) or inactive (past clients who could return) if you can find ways to keep a line of communication open and hold a space for them in your heart and mind. The skill that is essential to developing lifetime clients is the ability to end coaching well, so that clients can easily return.

Helping clients to end well furthers the trust that is a goal of secure client connections. It can be hard to let go of clients gracefully when you don't think the work is completed, when each client represents a portion of your monthly income, or when you don't have a waiting list. Even when you have done everything right as a coach, not every client will leave well. But you can do your best to try to have good endings with those who are ready. Here's a checklist to help you put the steps in place.

Exercise: Creating Lifetime Clients

Check the items that are true for you. Circle the items that would help you to promote better endings with clients and encourage clients to return when appropriate. Then plan to incorporate the policies into your coaching business.

❑ I help clients leave coaching with an absence of guilt, embarrassment, or shame.

❑ In the first session with a new client I say, "I want you to know that one of my policies is to support all phases of your coaching. When you are ready to leave, I would like to help you to leave well. Here are my suggestions to make that happen."

❑ I have my policy of good endings explained in my client policy sheet.

❑ I educate clients about their role in making a good ending.

❑ Although a client has announced that the client is ready to leave, I take the time to anticipate with the client what the next piece of coaching might be, with me or another coach, if the client chooses to do more.

❑ When a client has decided to leave, I allow the coaching process to begin to wind down instead of trying to ramp it up.

❑ I spend the final session consolidating the client's gains—talking about how far the client has come, what the client got from coaching, and what didn't get accomplished this time. I allow time for both of us to express mutual appreciation, an important step in healthy closure.

❑ If I feel anxious about my finances when a client leaves, I practice all my calming techniques and get to work on my marketing plan.

❑ I consider appropriate ways to stay in contact with old clients in such ways as keeping them on my mailing list and sending them my periodic newsletter.

The next step on your entrepreneurial path is to make sure you know how to make money and stay profitable in your business. We want you to understand how to develop a budget, set and raise your fees, package your services, adopt multiple income streams, and build a coaching business, not just to own, but to sell.

CHAPTER 9

Why Good Coaches Go Broke

According to the data we now have about the coaching world, the majority of coaches are seriously underearning. The 2003 ICF survey reported that 70% of coaches earned less than $50,000 in annual gross revenue in 2002, and of those, half earned less than $10,000. This is far below a living wage for full-time work. In fact, only 10% reported earning $100,000 or more. The coaching profession was promoted to new coaches as a lucrative, easy-to-establish, high-paying career. But the reality is that many dedicated, talented coaches are going broke. Why is this happening and how can you make sure your coaching business earns a respectable income?

When you remember that any new business ownership is a risky venture (nationwide, one-third of all new businesses fail within the first 4 years), you can see that the coaching profession was oversold and gave coaches unrealistic expectations. Most new businesses take 3 years before they show a profit. Using the data from the survey, it now seems that a coaching business is similarly slow to build and become profitable.

Here's the good news: If a coaching business follows the pattern of other small service businesses in terms of business earnings and growth, then everything you can do to become more entrepreneurial and smarter about business in general will help. But as we show throughout this book, you also need to adapt general business strategies to make sure that they fit the specifics of a coaching business.

In this chapter we help you to understand the best financial strategies for a coaching business. We want you to know how to set and raise your fees, budget your resources, select packaging options, and diversify your revenue stream. We will also explore the key principles to creating a six-figure coaching business, and look at how you can build a business not just to own, but one that can be sold when you are ready to retire.

But first things first. Before we look at these strategies, let's check your money mind-set. Just as with marketing, if you have concerns or negative beliefs about money, you will sabotage your strategic efforts when working to make a profit. Most people have a love-hate relationship with money; it is often one of the most emotional issues in business. One coach calls her issues about money her "business shame," a sense of inadequacy or failure because her mind freezes when it comes to discussions of profit, budgets, financial planning, and setting her fees. We want you to have an adult, healthy relationship to your earning ability. Two immediate steps you can take are:

1) Reconcile profit and service.
2) Think rationally about money.

Reconcile Profit and Service

If you are a coach, your purpose is to help your clients. If you are in business, your purpose is to make a profit. In effect, you must profit from those you help. This is the dilemma for some coaches, the close connection between service (helping, assisting, aiding, benefiting) and profit (taking advantage, making money, achieving financial gain). In order to have a successful coaching business, you must do both *equally well*.

For some coaches, service is the "better" of the two concepts. You may think: How can I be a person who cares about and helps others and, at the same time, takes money from them? What if their resources are low? If the coaching I offer is critical to their success in life or work, how can I withhold it due to cost? Maybe I should coach for free? But then how do I survive? This internal dialogue can become a personal, internal battle, unless you can comfortably reconcile profit and service.

There is no one exact way to unite these two concepts. It's different for each coach in business. But you need to have a way that makes sense to you, in your heart and your mind. Possible ways to reconcile these concepts are:

- Separate the caring and affection you may have for your coaching clients from your skills, recognizing that you charge for the skills, not the caring.

- Sell specific, concrete coaching services with measurable results, not intangible or invisible services (such as long-term coaching conversations without ways to evaluate direct outcomes).
- Think in terms of the time and value you provide that keeps working even when the coaching stops.
- Be mindful of the viability of your business (if your business doesn't make a profit you will no longer be able to provide services to anyone).

Money Maturity

You also need to check and see whether you have any unconscious, negative belief systems that may cloud your ability to think rationally about money. You may be mature in most areas of your life, but undeveloped when it comes to thinking and behaving well around money. If so, it's time to grow up and develop an adult relationship with your money. The first step is for you to inventory your current money attitudes and identify any negative beliefs that may play out in your coaching business.

Exercise: My Negative Money Attitudes

Check the following three negative attitudes or beliefs that apply to you, as well as the ways that they play out in your practice. Use the blank spaces to add in additional comments.

1. *Deprived Attitude:* Maybe you grew up with money deprivation. There was never enough money for your basic needs as a child. Or you have struggled throughout your early career. You still believe money is in short supply and watch every penny, reluctant to spend on anything "unnecessary." As a result, you fail to give your business the resources it needs to flourish.

　You believe:

❏　I can't make money.

❏　I am just one step away from being on the street.

❏　I can't charge what I am worth because no one will pay my full fee.

❏　Money doesn't grow on trees.

❏　Other:_____

(continued)

Exercise: My Negative Money Attitudes (continued)

How your belief plays out in your business:

❑ I won't get additional training or mentor coaching to develop my skills because it costs too much.

❑ I don't join associations because it's not cost-effective; who needs it?

❑ I fail to give my business the equipment, advertising, and other resources it needs to flourish.

❑ I miss networking opportunities that could benefit my connections unless they are free.

❑ Other:_____

Resolving your deprivation attitude: Heighten your awareness. Recognize any childhood money-related beliefs you still have. Give your coaching business a chance by spending money on resources it needs to thrive. Get a second opinion on your budget operating expenses, to make sure it is substantial enough for your business to grow.

2. *Dissociated Attitude:* Maybe you grew up believing that money was mysterious because no one in your family understood how to make it or save it. Money may not feel important, as a result, because it has never made sense to you. You ride an emotional money roller coaster: You are surprised or happy and high when you have it, and confused or devastated when you don't. When your coaching business goes through a slow time, you are down and self-critical; when it's up you feel great. You may feel that outside forces control your money flow—unseen energy sources or your personal karma. Mostly you are perplexed because there is so much about money you don't comprehend.

You believe:

❑ Nice people don't talk about money.

❑ I only care about helping others.

❑ If I don't pay attention to money, it always comes when I really need it.

❑ Keeping track of my money leaves me depressed and confused.

❑ Other:_____

How your belief plays out in your business:

❑ I hate to discuss my fees with clients.

(continued)

Exercise: My Negative Money Attitudes (continued)

❏ I don't bill on time and carry the debt of uncollected accounts when I do bill.

❏ I don't know what I make or what I owe.

❏ My business constantly swings from positive to negative cash flow.

❏ Other:_____

Resolving your dissociated attitude: Don't hide your money issues. Discuss your finances with your mentor coach, peer support group, or others in your advisory circle. Have a good tracking system for your money and look at your bottom line often. Get to know your finances personally and spend time thinking about money.

3. *Demonized Attitude:* Maybe you believe money is inherently wicked. You watched anxiety on your parents' faces when they talked about money, so you feel scared or impure when you have to deal with it, too. You are reluctant to raise your rates, negotiate, or hold your boundaries about your established financial policies. You find all aspects regarding money unpleasant and suspect.

   You believe:

❏ Money is the root of all evil.

❏ I can't have money and have integrity, too.

❏ Only greedy people think about money all the time.

❏ Money is dirty and corrupting.

❏ Other:_____

   How your belief plays out in your business:

❏ My fee for services is lower than anyone else's I know.

❏ I don't hold my boundaries about my established policies.

❏ Clients take advantage of me.

❏ I sacrifice my time (bartering, sliding scale, pro bono) so that I don't have to think or talk about money.

❏ Other:_____

Resolving your demonized attitude: If all of your coaching clients are on a sliding scale, pro bono, or barter basis, get some business coaching so that you determine a plan to raise your fees, and charge a full fee to all new clients. Read some of the books on money mentioned in the Appendix, to help you shift your negative mind-set and see that money is neither good nor bad: it is a neutral exchange.

Budgeting for Your Business

Let's get pragmatic about money. Your coaching business needs to operate with a budget. You must have a way to collect and analyze information about your business financially, track your current income and expenses, and project your future money flow and resources. Here are some basic business terms we will be using as we discuss your budget:

Gross income or *revenue*—all of the money that you earn in your practice.

Expenses—the costs you incur from doing business. There are two types of expenses:

- *Direct expenses*—the essentials that must be in place to allow you to run your business (office space rental, utilities, telephone, billing, accounting, postage, supplies, Web site, office equipment, advertising, marketing, professional dues, training, self-employment tax if you are a sole proprietor, liability insurance;
- *Indirect expenses*—those expenses that you may write off to the business that are nonessential, but helpful (publications, office decoration, meetings, travel to conferences).

Some coaches have low direct expenses (they work out of their home by phone, employ no staff, don't advertise, have few equipment needs), whereas others have more overhead (high rent and utilities, multiple offices, constant marketing and advertising costs, direct-mail campaign, Web site upgrades and hosting, support staff, billing service, print materials, coaching associates or subcontractors, additional equipment, licensure fee for assessments, unpaid travel costs including entertainment to solicit new clients).

Net income or *profit*—what's left of your revenue after you pay your direct and indirect expenses.

Now an important point for you to understand: Any service business where the product you bill for is based primarily on your time (such as a coaching, consulting, or therapy business) is an *expensive* business to operate. If your coaching business sells time—your time with clients—your business has a built-in income limitation that affects profitability. Your time is considered "active income," and a limited resource: you only have so much time in a given week, or so many client sessions you can conduct each week, and that means your expenses, as a percentage of your gross income, will stay high.

A business whose product is based on time can't match the profit ratios of a manufacturing business, whose income is based on other means of production. At a manufacturing plant, machines can run all night. You may only be able to work 25 hours a week. You simply can't produce as much as a manufacturing company, to offset the expenses of operating the business. Whether you are a sole proprietor or part of a larger coaching-consulting group, whether you work from home or out of a fancy downtown office, your business expenses will be a substantial percentage (most often 40–50% when you include the self-employment tax) of your gross income, and that makes a coaching business a relatively expensive business to run.

Even though we will suggest ways that you can boost your income by leveraging your time or diversifying your coaching services, if your primary revenue stream is generated by delivering hourly coaching sessions, your profit potential will always be capped. Since you have some set expenses that must be in place in order to operate, your ratio of expenses to profit will always be relatively substantial. In order to be as highly profitable as possible, you need to carefully consider additional strategies, such as passive income streams, keeping a tight budget, and setting your fees correctly. Let's start with the initial expense of a coaching business: your start-up costs.

Start-up Costs

New coaches have many questions about the cost of start-up: What do I need to spend? How do I allocate money to take my business to the next level? What resources should I purchase, and when?

Here is a list of common start-up expenses for the first 12 months of a sole proprietorship. (We have noted the budget items in terms of *both* money and time, since both may be in short supply.) Based on your specific situation, your actual spending may be above or below what we list, but you can use this as baseline for planning and thinking about what you are spending. For a more detailed explanation about budget allocation, we recommend *Getting Started in Personal and Executive Coaching* by Fairley and Stout (2004), which offers an excellent comparison among the necessary expenditures for a $2,000 startup, all the way to a $20,000 start-up. Our projected costs for the following annual budget come in at the midway mark, between $5,000 and $10,000.

Chart of Projected Start-up Annual Costs for a Sole Proprietorship

A budget of annual expenses coaches may expect to incur during the first 12 months of business.

AFFILIATION.

Join the one of the national coaching associations to give you immediate affiliation with the industry.

Projected annual cost: $175

Your time: 15 minutes to sign up online, open-ended amount of time to attend local chapter meetings.

TRAINING

Training costs can included time-limited workshops or ongoing courses. Because costs of training vary widely, this is an average *annual estimate.*

Projected annual cost: minimum $200; maximum $4,500

Your time: minimum—15 hours; maximum—250 hours

MENTOR COACHING

The majority of new coaches receive mentor coaching to improve their skills.

Projected annual cost: $2,400 ($300/month for 6 months)

Your time: 24 hours

BUSINESS IDENTITY

You need professionally printed business cards, letterhead, and envelopes.

Projected annual cost: $400

Your time: 1–5 hours to compose and design; additional time to get printed

BILLING

Use a computerized system that tracks your billing with clients and produces invoices, or hire administrative help. Talk to your bank about becoming a merchant account holder to be able to accept credit card payment from clients, or see the Appendix for listing of practicepaysolutions.com, a popular credit card billing company for coaches.

Projected annual cost: $350–$500 (discount costs for credit card merchant account vary from 2% and up, plus administrative fees)

Your time: 2.5 hours a week to invoice, reconcile, pay bills

WEB SITE

Use do-it-yourself software or hire a designer, find a hosting service, and get a domain name registered.

Projected annual cost: $250–$2,500 to design and $500 to host-domain name

(continued)

Chart of Projected Start-up Annual Costs for a Sole Proprietorship
(continued)

Your time: 2 weeks to 1 month of time to write; several more weeks to approve the design and reedit changes.

OFFICE EXPENSE AND EQUIPMENT
If you work from a home office you need a dedicated phone line, phone machine with voice mail, fax, computer, printer, and Internet connection. If you work from an office, add expenses of rent, utilities, parking, and administration. Price varies based on equipment costs.

Home office projected annual cost: $2,500

Outside office projected annual office cost: $15,000

Your time: 1 week to 1 month to purchase equipment, set up office

NETWORKING
Costs for networking, including meeting with others, meals at your expense, professional dues, conferences, and event fees.

Projected annual cost: $250–$1,000

Your time: Figure 5 hours a week the first year to contact, follow up, and meet with your network

PRINTED MATERIALS
You need additional business identity materials for networking and speaking opportunities, which may include a brochure, reprints of articles you have written, white papers, your CV or biography, professional photo, packaging folder.

Projected annual cost: $500 on home printer, $2,000 professional printing in small quantities

Your time: 2 weeks to 2 months

Sample Budget

Here is a sample budget of a coach in business her first year. She is a sole proprietor, with no staff or employees, and she has a small home office. Her fee for individual coaching is $125 per hour. She has a few additional services that include speaking and selling a self-help book she wrote and self-published. She has additional fees from a small corporate consulting project, and offers a daylong workshop twice a year to a local nonprofit foundation. Her expenses include most of those listed in the projected annual budget.

Chart of Sample Revenue and Expenses

Revenue

Total coaching hours (10 clients at $125 per hour)	$30,000
Total coaching products (books, tapes, manuals)	8,500
Additional services:	
Consulting	11,500
Training	0
Workshops	2,750
Total additional services	13,250
Total gross revenue	$52,750

Expenses

Direct expenses (equipment, Web site, training, phone, dues)	$8,200
Indirect expenses (training, travel, books)	7,300
Taxes (self-employment tax)	8,000
Total expenses	$23,500
Net profit (Revenue minus Expenses)	$29,250 (55% of income)

Analysis: Even though this profit of more than 50% may look like a lot, the coach has yet to deduct any salary or money to pay herself. She is also liable for additional state, local, and federal taxes beyond the self-employment tax. If all of these were deducted, this business might not show much profit this year, just expenses, taxes, and a small salary. But she still made a profit and in her second year, this coach secured a larger corporate contract for training, added five clients, increased her expenses in the following areas, and kept her net profit picture the same at roughly 50%. Her additional expenses for the second year included:

Administration: Part-time administrative help for billing, scheduling, marketing, receiving or returning phone calls.

Liability insurance: Annual coaching insurance to protect against liability. (See Chapter 10 for a discussion about purchasing this insurance.)

Marketing: Increased amounts for networking and advertising budget the second year by 100% to include consultation from marketing coach and attendance at a marketing workshop.

Advanced printed materials: Additional business cards, professionally printed letterhead, speaker packet, color brochures.

Advanced Web site services: Added capacity to send out e-mail newsletter using Web services to design and broadcast.

Training and travel: Attended two coaching conferences sponsored by large coaching associations to train and connect with other professionals.

Analyzing Your Budget Further

Your budget as a sole proprietor can be analyzed in three, equally important ways: First, your budget is a profit statement of your income, minus your expenses. Tracking your income is important, but you can be making a net profit while still being in trouble financially. This one analysis won't alert you to whether or not you are actually able to put money into your bank account, or whether your debt is increasing at the same time your income is going up.

Second, to understand the actual money you retain from doing business, you also need to look at cash flow. Cash flow can be traced by looking at the following items on your budget:

- Beginning cash on hand (in your bank account)
- Plus collections from clients
- Plus income paid from other coaching services (those you have collected)
- Minus expenses paid
- Minus interest on loans
- Minus taxes

(which equals your ending cash on hand)

Things to notice: the increase (or decrease) in cash from the start of the month or year to the end of the month. This analysis does not take into account money owed to you, just the actual cash you have been paid to date.

Chuck Kremer explained in his book, *Managing by the Numbers*, that your operating cash flow (the money that actually flows in and out of your coaching business) is critical to track because it shows the real-life of your business, not just the theoretical accounting picture. If your cash flow is

Exercise: Your Annual Budget

Fill in the blanks to create your projected financial budget for this year and next, using the broad categories of the following table.

Item	Current year	Next year
Revenue:		
Individual coaching services		
Coaching products		
Consulting		
Training		
Workshops or classes		
Other services		
Total revenue		
Expenses:		
Affiliation		
Training		
Mentor coaching		
Business identity materials		
Billing		
Web site		
Office expense		
Office equipment		
Networking		
Printed materials		
Liability insurance		
Travel		
Marketing		
Professional development		
Self-employment tax		
Other expenses		
Total expenses		
Additional taxes		
Net Profit (includes your "salary")		
Cash flow		
ROA		

continuously positive, you know you are generating enough money to keep your coaching business going. If your cash flow is negative, it may be drained by business credit card debt, other loans, interest payments, or lack of payment from clients. This means that no matter how much you show your coaching business earns on paper, in real life it is not yet viable.

Third, analyze what accountants call your ROA (return on assets). To find your ROA, take your net profit (the last line on the sample budget we give you) and then divide it by your business assets. Your assets include:

- Cash on hand or its equivalents
- Inventory (products, books, tapes, manuals)
- Receivables (money owed to you from clients and contracts)
- Fixed assets (office equipment and office furniture less depreciation)
- Other business investments (real estate, etc.)

To find your assets for any given time period, take the beginning assets at the start of the year, those at the end, and divide by 2. You ROA is useful because it includes your net profit as well as how you manage your assets. It takes into account the small size of your business and your profit, given the scope of your assets.

When you look at all three bottom lines—net profit, cash flow, and ROA—you will have a more complete picture of your finances and budget than what is shown through any one of these analyses. Your business must show a profit, generate cash, and have a return on investment. As Kremer explained, your business can look good in terms of net income on paper, but when you try to find the cash to attend a workshop, you find you are cash-poor. Or you may have a strong ROA, but your income is dropping because of a slow-down in clients. You really need to keep an eye on all three to be sure your coaching business stays in good shape.

Your Coaching Fee

What do coaches charge for individual sessions? According to the 2003 ICF survey, the average fee charged by all coaches is in the range of $100–$200 per hour. In Part 4 of this book, "Profiles in Coaching," you will see the specific fees for each of the top coaching specialties.

Individual coaching fees vary widely. Take three existing executive coaching companies: On the high end, there is a coaching firm called

Atticus, which specializes in offering business coaching services to legal firms. Atticus's associate coaches report that they charge clients a retainer of $3,000 at the time of signing a coaching contract, and then a fee of $850 per month for 2–2.5 hours per month of coaching time and assessment tools. Over a year's time, this averages at $430 per coaching hour.

In the midrange level is the College of Executive Coaching, offering executive coaching at a rate of $1,200 per month for four 45-minute sessions with fax and e-mail additional support, which is about $300 per hour (as stated on their Web site).

On the lower end is the Coach Connection, a coaching firm that charges $350 for three executive coaching sessions per month, or $120 per hour (according to their Web site).

Location of the coaching company affects fees as well. Executive coaches' hourly fees range lower in Canada than in the United States. We found that U.S. executive coaches generally charge between $120 and $400 per hour, but a review of coaching fees done by the British Columbia Leadership center cites Canadian executive coaches charging $90–$300 per hour. In the UK, fees for executive coaches average around £2,000 per day, according to the UK Institute for Employment Studies (Carter, 2001).

Coaching fees also vary depending on specialty. Personal coaching fees (life coaching, wellness coaching, creativity coaching) traditionally charge lower fees than executive or business-related coaching. Fairly and Stout (2004) noted that personal coaches charge an average of $130 per hour. Executive coaches average $198 an hour. Our informal Web site survey of 50 life coaches chosen at random across the United States and Canada showed fees ranging from $75 to $165 per hour. In contrast, 50 executive coaching sites listed fees of $125 to $375 per hour.

Your profitability in business depends in large part on how you charge for your services. With such a wide range in fees, your fee for coaching services should reflect three criteria:

- Your business plan (make sure that your coaching fee is geared to your business vision and goals for the year, so it is grounded in your best projective thinking)
- Current market information (know who is charging what and why, so that your fees are in line with other coaches who offer similar services or products)
- The perceived value of your services (know what coaching services are highly valued by your target market and why, so that you can raise the perceived value of what you have to offer)

Exercise: Setting Your Fee

Use the following criteria to determine the fee you will charge clients.

Business Plan: I want to earn a revenue of $_____ this year, and this translates into the following hourly fee for services:

_____

Market Forces: My competitors (those offering similar services in my area of expertise) charge the following fee for services:

_____

Perceived Value: My reputation, unique services, or market demand affects my fee in the following way:

_____

_____

_____

Based on this, the best fee for my services is:

_____ for individual coaching sessions

_____ for group coaching classes

_____ for half-day coaching on-site,

_____ for full-day coaching on-site.

Other fees for my services include:

_____

_____

_____

Raising Your Fee

If you are undercharging as a coach and need to raise your fee, you probably have a fee in mind. How do you communicate the fee increase to individual coaching clients in a way that will preserve the coaching relationship? We suggest you follow the following checklist to develop a policy regarding fee increases.

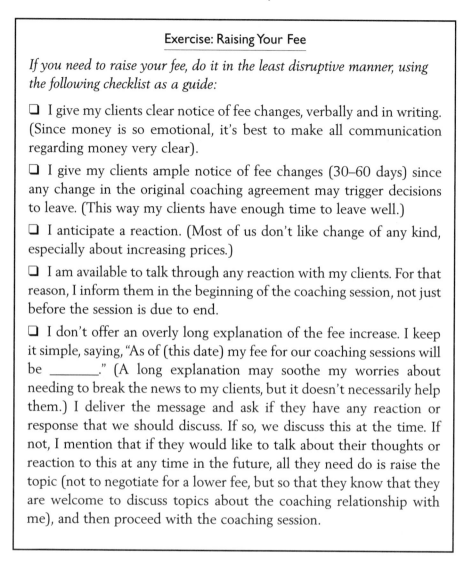

Exercise: Raising Your Fee

If you need to raise your fee, do it in the least disruptive manner, using the following checklist as a guide:

❑ I give my clients clear notice of fee changes, verbally and in writing. (Since money is so emotional, it's best to make all communication regarding money very clear).

❑ I give my clients ample notice of fee changes (30–60 days) since any change in the original coaching agreement may trigger decisions to leave. (This way my clients have enough time to leave well.)

❑ I anticipate a reaction. (Most of us don't like change of any kind, especially about increasing prices.)

❑ I am available to talk through any reaction with my clients. For that reason, I inform them in the beginning of the coaching session, not just before the session is due to end.

❑ I don't offer an overly long explanation of the fee increase. I keep it simple, saying, "As of (this date) my fee for our coaching sessions will be _____." (A long explanation may soothe my worries about needing to break the news to my clients, but it doesn't necessarily help them.) I deliver the message and ask if they have any reaction or response that we should discuss. If so, we discuss this at the time. If not, I mention that if they would like to talk about their thoughts or reaction to this at any time in the future, all they need do is raise the topic (not to negotiate for a lower fee, but so that they know that they are welcome to discuss topics about the coaching relationship with me), and then proceed with the coaching session.

Revenue Streams

Very few coaches can make a six-figure income from individual sessions alone. A good strategy for your coaching business is to diversify with more than one service, so that you have multiple revenue streams feeding your business. Diversifying your business benefits you in three ways:

- It can eliminate the financial ups and downs. When coaching sessions are not selling well, your other services may be in demand, leveling the profit picture.

- It offers your clients choices. Our consumer-oriented culture is accustomed to choice. When you go to a restaurant, you expect to be able to choose from a menu of items. Your clients may appreciate some choice within your offerings, too.
- You develop additional "business muscles." Years ago, health fitness experts realized the value in cross training—incorporating more than one form of exercise into a workout to keep an athlete in peak condition. Just like an athlete, it's good for coaches to become cross-trainers and diversify, to become more flexible, versatile, and well balanced.

Here's an example of the multiple revenue streams of one entrepreneurial coach, Ernest Oriente, who specializes in sales and marketing strategies for real estate agents and property managers. He detailed his revenue streams on the CoachVille.com Web site (2001):

- private coaching, working one on one, by telephone
- group coaching for those within a company
- group coaching within a profession or industry
- sales assessments, testing, and benchmarking for hiring or building dynamic teams (Oriente said that this service alone generated passive income in the amount of $700,000 for his coaching company in 2001.)
- rental of telephone conference lines
- recruiting services for the placement of high-level executive positions
- business valuations (consultation and report to determine the value of a business and for planning the sale of a company)
- presentations, speaking, and writing books

Exercise: Develop Multiple Profit Centers

Check the services you already offer or want to add to your coaching business. The goal of each service is to generate additional income for your practice.

❑ individual coaching sessions
❑ workshops
❑ classes or telephone groups
❑ e-mail consultations

(continued)

Exercise: Develop Multiple Profit Centers (continued)

❏ on-site consulting for corporations and organizations
❏ organizational development (team-building, mediation, leadership training)
❏ conducting assessments or supplying testing materials
❏ publishing or self-publishing and distributing books, manuals, or pamphlets
❏ audiotapes or CDs
❏ videotapes
❏ additional complimentary product sales
❏ writing articles for publication
❏ radio or television appearances
❏ public speaking engagements
❏ other training or teaching endeavors
❏ program development for yourself or others
❏ licensing your programs to others
❏ Web site or e-mail newsletter with membership fee

Revenue Stream Tip: Add services in a planned, not random manner. Set aside the resources, space, and budget to finance the additional profit center. Treat it like a separate yet valuable part of your existing practice. Track the income separately and the time involved. Note the cross-referrals it gives you. When it is well established, consider adding another one. If you add one additional profit center each year, you will have a full, diversified business within 5 years.

Packaging Your Services

Successful coaches package or group their services to create a menu of payment options for clients. Packaging creates choice and gives clients a sense of control regarding how they spend their coaching dollars, a strong business selling point. By mixing and matching services and their price points, you can custom-design an optimum coaching package for every client. One way to present these packages is to name them, price them, and then list them in all of your marketing materials and on your Web site. Here's an examples of how one coach packages her services:

Sandy Forster (2002), a money coach from Queensland, Australia, offered the following diversified services to help her clients have greater levels of prosperity: individual coaching, telephone classes, audiotapes of a money-based program, and workshops. She packaged these services into three combinations, and named the packages: Gold, Deluxe, and Elite:

- The Gold package includes 10 weeks of group coaching with daily e-mail support and is priced at $295. This package is designed for those who want the most economical coaching.
- The Deluxe package includes the services of the Gold package, plus a one-on-one prosperity coaching session with Forster and is priced at $495. This is designed for those who prefer additional focus and support.
- The Elite package adds these services plus a CD set, a workbook, and a series of six one-on-one prosperity coaching sessions with Forster, for a fee of $1,400. This package is geared to those individuals who want the added focus of private coaching sessions as well as tools to use repeatedly.

Forster said that she finds having various pricing options and package inclusions means that she has something for everyone. She is able to attract clients from both ends of the economic scale, to assist them to bring more prosperity into their lives.

Even if you offer only one service, you can create a menu and a pricing package. Let's say that your only service is individual coaching sessions. The variables we will use for your menu and package of services will be time and frequency.

Here are your two menu items:

1) individual coaching sessions, 1 hour
2) individual coaching sessions, 30 minutes

Based on these two menu items, here are three packages from which a client can choose. Each one has been given a name, a description, and a price point:

- Package #1: *Action Coaching:* Ideal for someone who is ready to make a big change and needs support, motivation, accountability, and a big push to meet a major goal. Four hours per month, one session a week. Price: $400 per month.

- Package #2: *Continuance Coaching:* A chance to consolidate gains, feel supported, set new goals, and continue to build momentum. One hourly session twice a month, every other week. Price: $200.
- Package #3: *Steady Coaching:* Supportive coaching for checking in and staying on a steady track. One 30-minute session twice per month, $100 per month.

Exercise: Packaging My Services

Follow the directions to package your services by combining, naming, giving definition, and pricing the packages.

1. List your current services.
2. Combine them into three distinct packages.
3. Name each package.
4. Give each a rationale and description.
5. Price each package.

The Six-Figure Business

Although only 10% of the coaches in the 2003 ICF survey reported making $100,000 or above, most coaches in business aim for this level of earning. What does it take to make six figures? We have analyzed the businesses of over two dozen successful coaches and see a pattern of indicators. Here are seven suggestions for what you can do that will lead you in the direction of a six-figure coaching business:

- *Pick a lucrative specialty:* Coaches who specialize in professional services, such as executive, leadership, or business coaching, regularly charge and receive the highest fees. If your coaching helps others or organizations increase their own net worth, you can charge at the highest rates.
- *Build a reputation in your niche:* If you target your market and narrow your niche, you can more quickly build a reputation in your field. Your reputation leads to visibility, and you can then position yourself as an expert about your market. When you are in touch with the needs and wants of your ideal coaching clients, you can charge at the top of the fee scale.

- *Create a platform to stand on:* Every coach who makes six figures that we met and interviewed had a platform to stand on, beyond just individual coaching services. The platform for top-earning coaches often includes multiple revenue streams and lots of outreach activities such as speaking and writing, books, trademarked programs, and teaching positions at universities or within coaching organizations, which all confer expertise. Having a platform translates into paid speaking opportunities, a national reputation as a coach, and many more opportunities for linking or affiliating with others. Having a platform leverages a coach's marketing time and effort, since word of mouth grows and clients begin to find you instead of you needing to find them.

- *Market consistently:* Coaches who earn six figures are always marketing, although many would say that they don't. But when we asked specifically how they spent their time, they all included a high amount of outreach activities—local and national networking, public speaking, teaching, writing, sitting on boards, and attending conferences and conventions. In summary, all coaches in high earning levels are out of their offices and in the market, meeting others, all the time.

- *Model a winner:* Coaches who earn high fees don't reinvent the wheel. They borrow and adapt successful business models of others for their own coaching businesses. To do this for yourself, find successful mentors and adopt their businesslike, highly profitable strategies and business behaviors to use in your own business.

- *Package your services:* The high-earning coaches have several services, all packaged more than one way. The added flexibility means that they retain more clients because they offer more choice.

Building a Business to Sell

Your long-term financial status as a coach is important to consider. Why not build a coaching business not just to own, but one that you can eventually sell when you are ready to retire from coaching? Is it possible to sell a coaching business? Yes, but you will need to start positioning it today. In order for your coaching business to be attractive to buyers, it needs to have multiple transferable assets.

Too often, a small, solely owned coaching business has only one asset and it's a nontransferable one—the coach's relationship to the clients. Even though you are the star attraction of your business, your cachet can't be easily transferred to a potential buyer. Can your clients be transferred to the new owner? That depends upon whether your clients perceive that their main attachment is to you, or to you as the purveyor of the programs and services you offer.

One executive coach had a long career as a senior manager in an information technology firm. After retirement from that firm, he developed a coaching company consisting of one person, himself, to do as a coach-consultant what he had done as a manager: coach senior managers in the information technology field in areas of business management and leadership.

Even though his was a tiny firm, he conducted business and set up procedures to mirror those of a larger company. He developed a professional, glossy packet of printed materials for marketing that clearly outlined his services. He kept a file of endorsements of past and existing clients. He maintained an active mailing list for both direct and e-mail communication. He kept exacting written records of all outcomes and processes of each coaching contract, including financial transactions and billing.

He wrote two handbooks for a new owner, one describing his marketing approach and the other a "train-the-trainer" manual for delivering his programs and services. The marketing handbook succinctly explained how he made the first contact with a potential client, the formulas he used for pricing, three possible formats for proposals, written examples of signed client agreements, and all his business policies. The second one gave a new owner the ability to match his coaching results.

He kept records of his profit-and-loss records for each year he was in business. After 5 years in business, he could show a total revenue of $430,000, with the bulk of revenue coming from the last 2 years and with an average 38% profit for those years. He used a business valuation company to provide him with an estimate of selling price: based on the systems in place, the transferable nature of his services, his careful documentation, solid client reputation, and the strong balance sheet, he was able to sell the practice for $185,000 with an agreement to take 6 months at a small salary to help hand off clients to the new buyer.

What price can you expect to get for your business? While a manufacturing company might be sold for five times annual earnings because it has a product, plant, staff, and system in place, a coaching business *without* all of the above elements in place might not be saleable, or sell at one times annual earnings. You can add to this ratio, to sell at two times earnings or more, by having as many additional tangible assets as possible.

Tangible Value

Create tangible value that is transferable. Turn your ideas into programs, document those programs, and establish your methods in writing and on video. Create as much product as possible. Write, research, and publish to validate your methods. Begin to train others in your methods, so that you have a pool of potential buyers when you are ready to retire. Document everything you do that is successful in earning revenue. Apart from the programs and services that you deliver—which also need to be created in tangible form—here's a list of six tangible assets that can add to the selling price of your coaching business.

1. *Brand name:* If you can name your type of services in a recognizable way as separate from your identity, you have a salable asset. You can more easily sell your methods than sell yourself.
   How to: Look at your professional field for examples of this. You will find programs and methods that are trademarked. Read Tom Peters's (1997) classic article "The Brand Called You." Go to the United States Post Office Trademark Office Web site (http://www.uspto.gov) for complete information on how to trademark a brand name. Brand names carry value, since they have a separate identity, apart from their developers.

2. *Mail list:* Build a large, opt-in direct-mail or e-mail list for your practice of clients and referral sources. A practice with an e-mail or direct-mail list of 5,000 current names can significantly add to the value of a business.
   How to: Use your advertising and speaking engagements to build your mailing list, not only to generate referrals. Keep a good database. Rent e-mail or direct-mail lists from colleagues or other organizations who support your work. Get permission from those on your list to transfer their names to the new ownership; be ethically correct by only trans- ferring the names of those who have given their permission. See Godin (1999) for ideas of how to achieve this goal.

3. *Promotional materials:* Develop brand-name recognition via your promotional materials now, with brochures that highlight the method or the program name more than your name.
   How to: Take the time and effort to create a professional package of materials. Keep a portfolio of your winning advertisements, brochures, and marketing materials that have generated good results for your busi- ness, along with the details of those results. This is part of the assets you can offer someone who wants to reproduce your results.

4. *Measures:* Have a system of tracking your effectiveness over time.
   How to: If you develop a great survey for clients that measures their satisfaction and you have used this not only to boost client satisfaction, but also as part of your promotion, this transferable measure is a definite asset for a potential buyer. Keep good files recording all the diagnostic tests and surveys you use. Keep a file of endorsements and evaluations.

5. *Ancillary products:* Develop a product line of materials to sell— programs, assessments, pamphlets, manuals, audio- or videotapes, training materials, books. Even if you have not promoted your product line sufficiently during your owning of the business, it doesn't lessen its potential value to another buyer.
   How to: Get legal advice regarding licensing agreements for all written and recorded products. Keep thorough records and originals of all scripts, tapes, videos, and manuscripts. Make sure the packaging reflects your quality and matches your brand.

6. *Business management:* If you have created a thriving business with easy-to-understand administrative systems in place, you have an additional asset.
   How to: Find systems to put in place that are easy to explain and transfer to others. Document your systems in a written manual— staffing procedures, outside contractors, maintenance services, written agreements, marketing, networking, program development process that you use. Present a potential buyer with your clear, complete business management program.
   Create a plan for the legacy and long-term financial health of your business by positioning it as a business that can be sold when you are ready to retire. Consider which of the above transferable assets already exist in your practice and which you need to develop.

Now let's look at a final, important aspect of your coaching business success: how to stay risk-free, safe, and secure. In the next chapter we look at the complexities of confidentiality, dual relationships, coaching agreements, ethics, and how to evaluate the benefits and costs of liability insurance.

CHAPTER 10

Staying Safe and Legal

Owning a coaching business can be a great career move: you get to make a difference in the lives of your clients and work within a setting that you control, one that suits you best. But despite what you may think, it is not risk-free. We live in a litigious society, and anytime that you offer a fee-based service to clients, there is a possibility of your clients being unhappy and refusing to pay, or worse, suing you. Even though your coaching services may be intangible, you are at risk for paying concrete, tangible damages.

Some coaches say, "I can't be held responsible for my clients' results because I never represent myself as an expert or a problem solver; I'm just there to listen and ask probing questions." Wrong. Even though you may try your best to set up a partnership model with clients, the fact that you are the coach and being paid by the hour for your ideas, suggestions, counsel, mentoring, or advice regarding professional and personal goals means that your client can try to hold you liable in court for bad results, pain, or suffering based on the coaching you offered.

Coaching clients are just like any other consumers: expectations are high in the beginning of coaching, and not always met by the termination of the business relationship. But you are not without protective options. In this chapter, we will show you the steps you can and should take to create client satisfaction and prevent misunderstandings or lawsuits. (Lawsuits against coaches have already been filed, according to legal experts.) Managing your risk as a coach in business means that you need to be smart and principled about how you operate. To work legally and safely, we will examine the following aspects of risk management:

- Best business practices
- Ethical standards
- Problems of dual relationships
- Complications of confidentiality
- Your coaching agreement
- Resources for liability insurance

Best Business Practices

Your first defense against client dissatisfaction begins with the way you conduct your coaching business, starting with your initial contact with a client. As the business owner, it is your job to create clear guidelines around your coaching so that potential clients can easily understand what to expect when they hire you. Your clients need to know, ahead of time, what coaching is and is not; how to get their money's worth from the coaching experience; and all the rules and policies that make for an optimal coaching experience. Here are four guidelines for best business practices:

Don't Overpromise Results

Unfortunately, coaching has attracted a lot of hype because some coaches promise miracles. We spent several hours conducting an Internet search of coaching Web sites and saw evidence of some coaches promising outcomes that can't be guaranteed. Because these promises are in print on the Web sites, it can invite a lawsuit if a client hires the coach and feels the promises are not met. For example, one life coach stated: "My coaching will produce exceptional results for you in your life and work. Together, we will fashion a life for you of total joy and comfort. And we will do this quickly. You can have the life of your dreams, with loving relationships, a perfect career, and financial independence—all just waiting for you if you sign up now for life coaching." If a client believes these results are a promise of your services, pays you thousands of dollars for months of sessions, and these claims never fully materialize, you are liable for problems.

We suggest: Underpromise, and then overdeliver. Offer only what you are sure you can provide. Coach your clients well, so you can have the pleasure of seeing your clients exceed their expectations, time and time again. Only state the results you feel you can guarantee. What coaching services and results can you deliver without fail? Many clients can move forward and take big steps in life as a result of some very basic coaching services.

Example: A life coach made a list of the basic skills she could guarantee to deliver to all her clients and spent 6 months keeping notes of current client outcomes. She then translated this data into straightforward Web site text. Her Web site read, in part: "I listen carefully and give honest feedback. I have no agenda other than wanting to help you meet your stated goals. I will offer ways to structure your goals into manageable action steps. I will hold you accountable for those goals, by checking with you weekly to see your progress. My clients report that they feel heard as a result of our coaching sessions. They say that they gain clarity by getting a chance to talk openly about important goals, and the process of accountability helped them follow through to see desired goals become reality."

Her Web site stated: "By hiring me as your coach, you can expect to:

- gain clarity about the challenges you face in your life and work
- set goals that reflect the time you have taken to think them through
- have my enthusiastic support to help motivate you
- receive constructive feedback from me to further your agenda
- know that I am checking on your progress weekly, holding you accountable for your progress, and celebrating with you when you reach your goals."

Don't Take on Multiple Roles

To lessen your risk, stay with one role. Be your client's coach. Don't take on conflicting functions, such as being both coach and close friend, or coach and psychotherapist, to the same client. Later in this chapter we will define the way functions conflict as we explore the problems of dual relationships, but a good business practice is to keep your dealings with clients as uncomplicated, aboveboard, and professional as possible.

Maintain professional boundaries. While mixing socially with clients may be essential and part of the culture in which you are coaching, avoid all situations, especially sexual or financial situations, which could lead to a conflict of interest. Don't have a romantic or sexual relationship with a coaching client. Don't invest in a business deal with a coaching client. See the section in this chapter on ethical standards. Define your coaching and business policies, make sure that they mirror the accepted coaching standards defined by the ICF in the next section, and stick to them.

We suggest: Refer out to others at the hint of complications in role. If you are a life coach and your client needs a therapist or a financial adviser, refer to others. If you are an executive coach and your client needs parenting advice, refer. Give at least three referrals each time, not just one. That way you don't have any vested interest in whom your client chooses to hire.

Example: Jill is a business coach and works with the CEO of a small lumber company, to help him increase sales and improve communication among the staff. One afternoon, the CEO came to her and said that he and his wife were very upset about how their financial planner had managed their money. Jill, who had previously worked as an accountant and then as a stockbroker before becoming a business coach, mentioned her prior experience. Her client immediately asked her to take a look at his personal financial statement over the weekend and make some suggestions the next time they met.

Jill looked at his personal taxes and investment statements. She spotted several questionable deductions and also noted some large losses he had with investments. She felt torn about what to do. She had some specific advice to offer, but personal tax and investment advice went far beyond her coaching contract.

Jill called a peer, an executive coach she knew. The peer cautioned Jill against assuming a secondary role of accountant or personal financial adviser, and urged Jill to stay within her established contract. Monday morning, Jill met with her client and handed him back the financial packet. She said that her best advice was that he find and consult with an accountant and financial planner he could trust. She asked if he wanted any referrals and gave him several names. One year later, the client and his wife divorced acrimoniously. The wife subpoenaed the accountant and the financial planner. Jill knew she well might have been on that list, had she tried to step into the additional roles.

Document Your Coaching Sessions

Some coaches feel that their discussions with clients are organic, that in session they simply follow a conversational flow, and as a result they take few notes. But documenting what you do as a coach, especially since coaching is primarily a conversation between two people, protects you if a client distorts reality, makes false claims, or decides to sue. Since coaching is a profession without licensure, you stay safer if you provide some record of what you said and recommended in any particular session.

We suggest: Create a system that allows you to take notes on each session easily. This can be as simple as keeping a handwritten notebook and making notes at the end of a session, or, if you work by phone, having a laptop with you so you can jot down notes as you speak. Date your files, and save copies of your notes on disk and store them safely.

Example: Bob is a wellness coach at an upscale spa and health club. He makes recommendations to his clients regarding nutrition, exercise regime, and lifestyle changes. He keeps scrupulous records about his advice and gives each client a written summary at the end of each session, with weekly goals. "Since I am working with health-related coaching issues, taking careful notes and then making the notes immediately available to my clients insures that we take a partnership approach. There is nothing hidden, and I am not the sole expert. We are both on the same page, literally," he says.

One of Bob's clients sustained an injury at the spa during a workout and sued the spa and named her personal trainer in the suit. She did not name Bob, in part because she had copies of his weekly summaries and felt that after reviewing them carefully, she could find no fault with his suggestions or approach.

Maintain Straightforward Payment Policies

Coaching involves a fiduciary relationship, and it's safer and less risky to keep business finances uncomplicated. Some new coaches, hungry for business, accept bartering as a way to avoid losing a client who can't pay their fee. This is a bad idea. Resist temptation to try to equate your intangible coaching services with other, more tangible services, to avoid feelings of resentment. Keep your dealings with clients legitimate. Don't set yourself up for a conflict of interest by investing with clients. Don't complicate your fee with additional financial transactions outside the realm of coaching.

We suggest: Follow accepted billing and accounting procedures. Don't barter or slide your fee without giving this careful thought and talking to a mentor coach. Set a fee that you feel is fair and competitive within your niche and stick with it. Need some flexibility with clients? Package your services so that you can offer product and a range of fee options, not just one hourly rate. Don't find yourself in a conflict-of-interest situation by having any financial dealings with your client other than selling coaching services and related products.

Example: Robin, a brand-new life coach, meets Sue, who owns a small bookstore, at a local networking event. They like each other immediately, and decide to barter with books for life coaching. Robin normally charges $100 per hour for coaching, but they figure out a deal: Sue will pay Robin $50 an hour for each life coaching session and give her a coupon worth $50 of books.

One day, during a life coaching session, Sue mentions that she has purchased some expensive travel books to sell at her store. Robin comes into the store the next week with two months' worth of coaching-for-books coupons and redeems them on the expensive travel books. Sue gives her the books but seems angry. At the next scheduled coaching session, Sue tells Robin that she can't trust her as her coach because she took advantage of their bartering arrangement by redeeming the coupons on the expensive travel books.

Robin apologizes and says that they had never discussed that the coupon redemption was limited to only specific books. Sue angrily responds that Robin should have figured this out because Sue mentioned how expensive they were in the coaching session, and Robin knows the details of Sue's struggles to keep her bookstore going. Sue calls Robin's purchase a "betrayal of privileged information and lack of support" and says she is quitting coaching and will not recommend her as a coach to others, based on this experience. Robin spends several sleepless nights wondering how she got herself into such a messy situation and decides that bartering is an expense she can no longer afford in her coaching practice.

Ethical Standards

The International Coach Federation (ICF), the major professional association of coaching, maintains a standard of ethical conduct that each coach needs to read and follow. You can read the complete ethical code at www.coachfederation.org. In brief, the code addresses your need, as a coach, to:

- honor coaching agreements and confidentiality
- respect the creative and written work of others in developing your own materials
- not overstate your coaching qualifications, expertise, training, or experience
- not intentionally mislead or make false claims about the coaching process
- not give clients misleading information or advice beyond your level of competence
- encourage clients to seek other resources when they stop benefiting from your services
- avoid conflicts of interest but openly disclose potential or existing conflicts of interest when they occur

- disclose with a client any compensation from third parties that you may receive for referrals

Become familiar with the ICF ethical code of coaching. You may need to follow additional ethical practices, beyond what the ICF proposes, based on other licensure that you currently hold. Follow the ethics of your professional licensure, especially if you use your professional liability insurance to cover any of your work or if you introduce yourself using your other professional credential. For example, if you hold a mental health license, you can be sued under that licensure for unethical behavior with a client, even if you are working as a coach, not a therapist. The fact that you still hold a mental health license will have more sway in court than your explanation that at the time you were engaged in coaching rather than therapy. If you are a therapist and a coach, we suggest that you:

1. Keep the same practices and policies for both your mental health practice and your coaching business.
2. Don't be both coach and therapist for any clients, past or existing. Keep your boundaries distinct and separate between your therapy work and your coaching. Protect your licensure and your liability insurance agreements regarding dual relationships.
3. Develop a specialty as a coach that is different from your therapy practice. Since the scope of mental health practice is defined in statute and regulation, it is best to keep the nature of therapy and coaching services distinct. (Don't be a couples therapist and a couples coach, or an attention deficit disorder (ADD) therapist and an ADD coach, for example.)
4. Don't engage in social contact with your coaching clients. The problems caused by outside social contact for a mental health professional are many, and it's safest to maintain your boundaries and distance with coaching clients in the same way.

Dual Relationships

Dual relationships occur when a relationship with someone has more than one role or interest. Mike Brickey explained that when coaches offer services, they need to be particularly conscientious that dual relationships do not exploit or disadvantage the client (Brickey, 2002). Even though most dual relationships in coaching are mundane, Brickey warned, dual relations in coaching are like office romances—"Sometimes they result in ideal matches, sometimes they have very destructive consequences, and occasionally they ruin careers."

Coaches work within such a wide variety of settings and cultures—corporations, small businesses, private offices, living rooms—and each setting suggests different standards for relating with clients. In corporations, a leadership coach may be expected to attend social functions with clients. A small-business coach may know the business owner from church. A life coach and her client may watch their kids play soccer together at the local high school. Since the majority of coaching clients come through referrals, it's likely that the coach may have some degree of acquaintance, friendship, or prior association with a client, even before the coaching begins.

With multiple relationships so commonplace in our society, how is the coach to make sure that there is no conflict of interest that would exploit or disadvantage the client when a dual relationship exists? Here are some suggestions that we have found work well in helping coaches to minimize risk when multiple roles with clients exist, are potentially complicated, or are simply ambiguous:

- Keep coaching structured and time limited. The easiest way to make a case for coaching within a dual relationship is if the coaching offered is highly technical, specific, niched, and time-limited, with measurable goals and objectives.
- When in doubt, get supervision or mentoring. If the relationship with your client feels complex, it probably is. If you are a new coach and inexperienced in the industry, don't take on a coaching client with whom you may have a conflict of interest, unless you have talked about the case with others who can steer you in the right direction.
- Be open and transparent about potential conflicts with your clients. Once you identify areas of dual relationships or potential conflicts, be open with your clients. Let them know that you are aware of the potential downside, and check in often to make sure that the coaching is on track. When in doubt, refer out.
- Don't let romance enter into the relationship. Never mix romance or sexual relations with your coaching. If you have sexual feelings about clients, don't act on them. Don't date your clients or place yourself in situations that could be sexually charged or misconstrued by others.

Confidentiality Conflicts

Your coaching clients deserve and expect a high degree of confidentiality from their coach, but even something as basic as confidentiality can be complicated. Confidentiality means that you keep private all identifying information about your client, except as otherwise authorized by your client, or as required by law. The ICF ethics code defines confidentiality as:

- Respecting the confidentiality of client information, except as otherwise authorized by the client, or as required by law.
- Obtaining agreement with clients before releasing their names as clients or references or any other client-identifying information.
- Obtaining agreement with the person being coached before releasing information to another person compensating the coach.

However, this code does not specifically address some of the complicated scenarios. For example, as a coach, how do you balance confidential information against your own legal risk? If a client is describing an illegal business or personal situation during a coaching session, what do you do to protect yourself? While you are not required by law to report this kind of information to authorities, you still need to create a policy for your business so that you are not complicit with illegal behavior. At the very least, you must decide when you would stop working with a client based on your level of discomfort with information being revealed. Since a coach is a supportive partner, if your client discloses behaviors and choices that go against your personal or professional ethics or standards, you would be wise to end the coaching relationship sooner rather than later. For this reason, every coaching agreement or contract should have a clause that defines the termination procedure of coaching, with equal ease of ending the contract for both the coach and the client. Read the section in this chapter on coaching agreements to see how to create a sound agreement.

Coaches sometimes inadvertently breach client confidentiality by gossiping. A coaching colleague you see at a local coaching event might ask, "Who are you coaching these days?" Or you might be a corporate coach in the company cafeteria after a session with a client, and meet an interested third party—perhaps a manager who knows about the coaching relationship—who asks, "How's the coaching going?" Any direct answer to these kinds of questions challenges client confidentiality and constitutes a form of "coaching gossip." Gossip, in professional and work circles, is common and contagious. Social scientists believe that we are genetically engineered to gossip for important reasons: in a tribal culture, gossip helped us survive by providing social networking, influence within the tribe, and affiliation with those in power. Coaches may name-drop as a way to boost their influence, or want to talk with other coaches or third parties about their coaching clients because they feel isolated and lonely, wishing for feedback about their work. But confidentiality means not gossiping, even for understandable reasons. Don't do it. This means that an ethical answer to "How's it going" would be: "I can't discuss my coaching relationships because it is a breach of client confidentiality."

Endorsement Concerns

Endorsements can be tricky in regard to confidentiality. Coaches often want endorsements to use in promotional literature or on their Web sites, to help validate their services. Endorsements establish a track record. But because of the personal and confidential nature of coaching, you need to think through all the potential problems of asking for endorsements, in terms of the strain it can place on confidentiality and on the nature of the coach-client relationship. Coachville, a large coach training organization, urges coaches to keep all aspects of the coaching relationship confidential, instructing its members:

- Do not mention, hint at, or allude to who you are working with or have worked with.
- Even if your client tells the world about who you are and your coaching role, just keep mum.

Asking for an endorsement can put a grateful client in a bind, because if you are the client, it can be hard to say no to the coach who has helped you and whom you like. But every client should have the right and comfort of saying no to endorsing a coach, as a way of protecting privacy regarding coaching. Coachville recommends coaches not to ask for endorsements from prior clients, saying that endorsements send a signal to new clients of the expectation that a coach may have to use the new client for future promotion. We think that this recommendation has merit and suggest that coaches limit endorsements to those of a corporate, business, or organizational nature, and maintain anonymity for personal coaching clients, to protect confidentiality.

Confidentiality in Corporate Settings

The Society for Industrial and Organizational Psychology warns coaches about the conflicts of confidentiality that can surface when an external or internal coach is working in an organizational setting. Although trust is a critical component of successful coaching, coaches may not be able to guarantee full confidentiality for an executive client within a corporate setting. Hall, Otazo, and Hollenbeck (1999) explained that the promise of confidentiality is especially jeopardized for internal corporate coaches (those who are corporate employees) and that outsourcing the coaching can offer a higher level of confidentiality because the coaches may not have to report to the corporate management.

Both internal and external executive coaches may be considered agents of their hiring organizations and may be called as witnesses if an employment lawsuit arises regarding an executive who was coached and then fired. This is especially problematic because some corporations bring in a coach to deal with problem executives, as a last-ditch effort to improve a managers' performance.

In general, good business practices for executive coaches involve being very clear about the levels of confidentiality that can and can't be offered to a client. Do this in writing. According to the Executive Coaching Forum, a Web site think-tank for executive coaches, the executive coach may be obligated to provide the sponsoring organization with a summary of conclusions on the executive's current and potential ability to serve in his role. If the corporation seeks such a report, they suggest that the coach can maintain a degree of integrity by first sharing the summary with the client to get the client's input. Before the coaching begins, the coach should obtain a detailed understanding from all parties involved as to what this summary will and will not include, written as part of a coaching agreement. In some business situations, a coaching client may have no expectations of confidentiality, which then changes the nature of the coaching relationship and must be spelled out clearly so that all parties understand the limitations placed on the coach.

Coaching Agreements

Experienced business owners learn, over time, the necessity of having a clear, signed agreement when money is exchanged for services. A coaching contract or agreement is your best chance at protecting yourself, by clarifying what you offer and what clients can expect. The more transparent you make the process of coaching for clients—your services, role, objectives, goals, timetables, policies, and procedures—the less likely you are to encounter client misunderstandings, unhappiness, and lawsuits.

As we surveyed the coaching industry, we noted differences between personal coaching contracts and business coaching contracts. We conducted an informal review of real-life coaching agreements and contracts by asking coaches to share their agreements with us. We also reviewed the ICF Ethics Statement (available at http://www.coachfederation.com) that defines commonly understood coach-client practices. We attended ethics discussions at ICF conferences and reviewed two separate teleclasses on the topic of coaching ethics and agreements. One teleclass was offered through Mentorcoach and featured Eric Harris (consultant to the APA on ethics and coaching); a second featured David Goldsmith (ethics advisor to the International Association of Coaches). Based on all of the above, we suggest that your personal coaching agreement include eight specific sections. Your professional contract (for working within a business or corporate setting) needs those eight plus several added parameters.

1. *Services:* Your services need to include a precise definition of what you do as a coach, your coaching model, and an explanation of what a coach is and is not.

   Sample wording: Coaching is a professional, paid service conducted by weekly phone sessions of 45 minutes that can help you to learn new skills and make significant behavior changes. I, the Coach, will assist you by listening carefully and offering nonjudgmental feedback, thinking through decisions, and asking questions to help you gain clarity, and support you by offering accountability, affirmation, and an action plan through the implementation phase, in order to help you achieve your goals for life and work. As the Client, you will set the agenda for our coaching conversations. I expect you to evaluate your own progress, and to be proactive in the goals you have defined. Coaching does not offer any guarantee of success.

2. *Payment Procedure:* Define your payment and fee schedule clearly and specifically.

   Sample wording: I am paid $380 dollars per month, in advance of our monthly coaching calls, by credit card. This arrangement continues monthly as long as you decide to retain me as your coach. The first coaching session will begin after this agreement is signed and the first payment is received.

3. *Cancellations:* Cancelled or missed sessions are a reality of any ongoing coaching relationship. You must define your policy for cancelled sessions, by you or by your client.

   Sample wording: If you need to cancel or change the time of a coaching session I will need 24 hours' notice in order to not charge you for that session. With advance notice of more than 24 hours, you will not be charged and/or I will make every effort to reschedule with you. If I need to cancel a session for illness, travel, or emergency, I will make every effort to give you adequate advance notice and to reschedule with you.

4. *Termination:* Good endings make complete good coaching and open the door for possible referrals. Think through how you want to help your clients end well.

   Sample wording: Either of us may end the coaching relationship at any time, with 1 week verbal or written notice. I would like to offer support to all the phases of your work with me as a coach, including when you decide to leave coaching. I can best support your decision to leave if you give me several sessions' notice prior to actually leaving. The notice allows you to leave well, having an experience of completion.

5. *Confidentiality:* Define what you provide and guarantee in this regard. Coaches who are licensed in other professions (mental health, medical doctors, lawyers) need to follow the confidentiality requirements of their licensure and should state that in their agreement.

   Sample wording: I protect the confidentiality of all communications with my coaching clients. I will only release information about our work to others with your written permission. I will not release any identifying information about you or our work together without your express permission.

   Addition for mental health professionals: As a licensed therapist, there are some situations in which I am legally obligated to breach your confidentiality in order to protect others from harm, including if I have information that indicates that a child or elderly or disabled person is being abused, I must report that to the appropriate state agency and if a client is an imminent risk to him/herself or makes threats of imminent violence against another person, I am required to take protective actions. If such a situation does occur, I will make every effort to discuss it with you before taking any action.

6. *Definition of Coaching and Psychotherapy:* Clarify the difference between coaching and psychotherapy for clients, to ensure that your services will be understood as coaching, not counseling.

   Sample wording: Although coaching can be confused with other professions, such as counseling, my work with you will be coaching, not psychotherapy. My coaching services are intended for well-functioning individuals who want to take action and make behavior changes in the service of their goals for life and work. Psychotherapy is a health care service that diagnoses and treats the symptoms of mental disorders.

   Addition for mental health professionals: I believe that it is ethically inappropriate for me to be both coach and psychotherapist with a client. If either of us recognizes that you have a problem that would benefit from psychotherapy, I will refer or direct you to appropriate resources.

7. *Nondisclosure and Intellectual Property:* Define mutual protection for yourself and your client, regarding shared information, methods, or materials.

   Sample wording: I will not voluntarily communicate your future plans, business strategy, customer information, or financial information to any other third party. To protect my intellectual property, you agree not to disperse or reuse the coaching materials I may give you, unless you have my written permission.

8. *Hold Harmless Provision:* Include a clause that prevents clients from seeking compensation from coaches if the coaching goes badly, to help inform your client about the shared responsibility of coaching.

   Sample wording: You understand that as your coach, I provide a variety of services as listed above to assist you in achieving your goals. I do not guarantee, and will not be responsible for any damage or loss related to, our coaching sessions. I do not bear responsibility for any consequence and in no event shall be liable for any direct, indirect, incidental, special, or consequential damages relating directly or indirectly to any action or inaction that you take based on the services offered, information provided, or other material obtained through our coaching.

A business or executive coaching contract would address all of the above aspects and might also include parameters regarding areas of potential conflict of interest, including:

- a clear definition of the primary client, the stakeholders, and the coach's role
- objectives, goals, and timetables
- boundaries for coaching multiple levels in the organization, especially when there are direct reporting relationships
- standards for the handling of internal information, both inside and outside the organization
- policies and procedures for selling coaching or products by the coach to other potential coaching candidates or managers inside the organization

Liability Insurance

To practice safely as a coach, you may want to purchase liability insurance. The advantage of liability insurance is that, just as with any other type of liability insurance, you will be better protected in case of a lawsuit. The insurance tends to be expensive, so new coaches may feel it hard to justify the expense when they have just a few clients. Each company offering liability insurance to coaches has differing policies, so query them and find out which policy is best for you. Current options for liability insurance for coaches include:

1. *Hartford Insurance* (through First Niagra Risk Manager, contact phone number: 888-425-2460, Web site: http://www.coachinginsurance.com). Hartford excludes those with special licenses, such as therapists or any other profession. If you are qualified and fit into Hartford's underwriting guidelines, your premiums will be approximately $1,000 a year for $1 million coverage. Less comprehensive coverage is available.
2. *American Professional Association* (through the National Association of Social Workers, contact phone number: 800-421-6694). This insurer of mental health professionals will cover you as a coach if you are a mental health professional and have purchased a mental health liability insurance policy from them and if your coaching falls into the realm of mental health concerns (stress reduction, improved communication). APA will not cover coaching if there is a financial aspect to your coaching, for example, if you offer business coaching that involves reviewing or advising a client about finances.
3. *Lockton* (offered in affiliation with the International Association of Coaches, Web site: http://www.internationalassociationofcoaches.org.)

This liability plan for personal and professional coaches is the most accessible of the three mentioned, and offers full-blown comprehensive coverage for coaches starting at a cost of approximately $200 per year for $1 million per incident and $3 million annual aggregate coverage.

The Practice of Coaching

So far in this book we have examined the business of coaching via a business model that emphasizes positioning, differentiation, and entrepreneurship. Now it's time to see how this model translates into actual coaching practices. In the next section we introduce you to coaches from around the world, so that you can better understand how others have built their coaching businesses. Part 4, Profiles in Coaching, is focused on seven highly profitable coaching areas and profiles coaches who work within these specialty areas:

- executive and leadership coaching
- business coaching
- skills coaching
- career coaching
- life coaching
- wellness coaching
- creativity, relationship, and spiritual coaching

In each chapter we will help you understand the parameters of the coaching specialty and niche, including the services coaches offer and the fees they charge. Then we present a profile based on interviews of one or more coaches who we think represent that type of coaching. You get a behind-the-scenes look into the practice of coaching, through the perspectives of coaches who talk about how they broke into the field, how they work with clients, their marketing approaches, and how they gravitated to their coaching specialty. As you read their stories, it may help crystallize your own decisions and choices about the coaching business you have already created, or the business you will create in the future. The Appendix contains Web sites, books, organizations, and other information for your coaching success.

PART IV

PROFILES IN COACHING

CHAPTER 11

Executive and Leadership Coaching

Executive and leadership coaching are the two coaching specialties that are the best established within the corporate world, and, as a result, tend to be the most lucrative areas of coaching. The two specialties have substantial overlap in that many executive coaches offer leadership coaching programs (and vice versa), but they also have some aspects of separateness in terms of approach, delivery systems, clientele, and focus.

Executive coaching is a bit of a catch-all term, broadly used to mean coaching that targets CEOs, directors, senior or not-so-senior managers, or small-business owners. The executive coach helps clients with a wide range of organizational and management concerns as well as some purely personal issues, and often wears both coach and consultant hats. Executive coaches need a strong résumé of prior executive or business experience of their own, including a good understanding of the politics of the workplace, since they regularly offer managerial know-how and help executives set and achieve organizational goals. They are called on to help executives in trouble save their job or become more effective within current positions. Executive coaches can help a boss effect a culture change, or a stressed-out CEO cope with the stressors of a busy work and home life.

The coach needs to be savvy about the corporate environment and complex organizational dynamics. Executive coaches are hired in one of two ways: as external contractors or as internal staff, depending on an organization's need and budget. The coaching services may be delivered on-site or off-site. Ideally, the executive coach should have actual career experience at or above the level of the executive being coached.

Leadership coaching differs from executive coaching in that the topics of leadership coaching veer away from "functional" coaching topics (management, profitability, team building, or performance-related issues) to focus on an executive's career path, often aligning that path with corporate sustainability. Leadership coaching helps an executive define corporate legacy and implement succession planning. As one leadership coach explains, "We don't help executives learn to manage; we show those executives who already excel as managers and have been identified as the leadership team how to move to the next level." Leadership coaching can be delivered in one-on-one sessions, but most corporations purchase leadership coaching services in the form of seminars or workshops that are delivered to a group of chosen executives.

The actual coaching services of executive and leadership coaching often overlap and can include:

- Conducting a needs analysis of an executive, a team of executives, or a division of a company
- Strategic planning and goal setting
- Measuring and reporting via assessments
- One-on-one coaching sessions
- Facilitating meetings with staff or leading seminars
- Transitioning a client into a longer-term development program
- Identifying strengths and leadership needs
- Imparting skills that define corporate direction
- Encouraging outstanding interpersonal practices
- Increasing ability to delegate tasks and manage organizational conflicts

The executive-leadership coach needs to speak the language of business and understand how to value and at times administer traditional assessments and measures, such as DiSC (dominance, influence, steadiness, conscientiousness) profile, a personality behavioral profile widely used in business settings, or 360-degree feedback assessments (an interview, assessment, and feedback process provided to an executive client that queries those above, below, and lateral to the client to rate the client's effectiveness, strengths, and need for improvement). The coach may or may not be a graduate of coach training program, but will likely be well educated in business, with a business-related or industrial psychology degree, having a range of knowledge about management, team building, conflict resolution, and process reengineering.

Executive-leadership coaching should provide measurable results for the client. The highest paid coaches often distance themselves from the "softer" or intangible benefits of coaching. One high-profile executive and leadership coaching company states: "We are not lifestyle coaches. We do not provide counseling on stress, balance, or personal relationships. We do not provide advice on life planning. We are neither sounding boards nor 'scratching posts' for organizational complaints. We do not coddle our clients. We expect them to actively seek out new executive and leadership practices, experiment with new behaviors, and put in place new standards of personal performance. We see our role as guides, facilitators, and educators."

Global leadership coaching, a subset of leadership coaching, helps the top executives of global companies operate with more confidence within politically complex and culturally diverse contexts. Global leadership coaches show executives how to integrate disparate cultures during mergers, acquisitions, and alliances. They address the threats and the opportunities of global operations and offer programs to attract, develop and retain the human talent necessary to achieve long-term corporate success.

Most executive-leadership coaches are either self-employed or associates within a small coaching firm, although one emerging trend is for large, human-resources consultancies to get into the executive coaching market. For example, a firm such as Hewitt Associates boasts a network of about 200 executive coaches and charges upward of $15,000–$20,000 for up to a year of a senior coach's time. Typical fees for a self-employed executive-leadership coach range from $150 to $450 per hour, and up to 5% of an executive's salary for a specific coaching project. Leadership training programs range in price from $2,000 to $100,000 per employee, per year, offering a combination of off-site workshops, one-on-one coaching, and on-site facilitation.

Coaching in Action

Now meet three coaches who represent the dynamic range of executive and leadership coaching. Eva Parsons successfully relied on her prior experience in human relations to co-develop a classic coaching firm that looks at the needs of executives and then delivers coaching programs that specifically address those needs. Gary Russell went from being a youth social worker to the head of a global leadership coaching company in Australia and built his coaching platform, in part, by teaching coaching for CoachU Australia, a branch of the large coach training organization. At the same time he was teaching, he built a coaching company that incorporated his social awareness, bringing leadership programs to large organizations that serve the neediest global populations. Tanja Parsley, a coach from Ontario, is one of those rare coaches who loves sales and marketing. She parlayed prior sales experience into a training and consulting role, and now offers team building and sales coaching for executives and leaders. All three of these coaches display mental toughness and sharp acuity that help them coach within a corporate culture.

Eva Parsons, Executive Coach
Executive Coaching Network, Inc.
www.excn.com
phone: (858) 551-3950
La Jolla, California

Eva Parsons is that atypical executive coach who made the shift from couch to boardroom. She started her career as a psychotherapist, practicing therapy for 15 years, before she moved into the field of corporate human relations. During Eva's career in human relations, executive coaching emerged as the one skill she enjoyed the most. Coaching was the culmination of everything she had learned to do in psychotherapy and HR. She got her coach training from the Goldsmith Coaching Process, which trains HR professionals who seek to become internal and external coaches.

When Eva and her husband moved to San Diego in 1996, she joined the Executive Coaching Network (EXCN), a coaching firm founded by Alyssa Freas. Eva loves the fact that she gets to work with the best and the brightest, the highly successful and motivated executives who are often at the peak of their careers. "The executives I coach are usually highly successful. They are often thrilled with their jobs and just want to learn to be more effective," she says. "They welcome the opportunity to use executive coaching as a form of career enhancement."

EXCN lists 50 affiliate coaches within their organization coaches in Europe, Asia, South America, and South Africa; their client list includes Fortune 100 companies in various industries, including software, airlines, banks, telecommunications, both in the United States and abroad. Most of the coaches at EXCN have been former executives and have backgrounds in organizational development or psychology, and coaching.

In addition to coaching executives, Eva also facilitates executive, management, and board retreats as well as team-building sessions. Typical executive coaching contracts are long-term and center on a 360-degree feedback process. Eva conducts the 360 interviews both in person and by phone, and then meets with clients for a "feedback findings" session (a debrief of the process) at the executive's office.

"With the 360s, we are providing subjective perceptions from those individuals who interact with our clients," Eva explains. With subsequent coaching, there will often be definite changes in an individual's first 360-degree measurement and the terminal measurements. "The executives are already functional experts," she says. "They often need to learn how to be more effective managers or leaders."

The findings session forms the basis for the coaching process. Together with the coach, the executive determines what the action plan will be, based on the feedback received, and this establishes the basis for a 6–9-month coaching engagement. At the end of the contract period, Eva conducts a mini-assessment to see how well the executive has implemented the action plan.

As a psychotherapist in her earlier career, Eva is very attuned to the distinctions between executive coaching and therapy and says she benefits from having one foot in personal dynamics and the other in organizational dynamics, seeing that there is "a constant interplay between interpersonal and intrapersonal dynamics." But she holds her boundaries between the two professions. "I never let myself veer off into therapy," she says. "Executive coaching differs from therapy because coaching is very results-oriented, with all eyes on focused action-plans, observable changes, and business results."

Eva thinks fast on her feet. She is a good listener, asks probing questions, and loves a challenge. She's not intimidated by arrogant individuals and enjoys working with those who have strong personalities, which is true for most of her executive clients who have come far in their careers. She counters their strength with her own coaching stance. "I don't let a client off the hook," she says.

In one case study highlighted on her coaching company's Web site, the shifting demands of the executive coach—moving between organizational development, coaching, and team building—is detailed. In this case study, the client was the CEO of an organization that had recently spun off from its parent organization. EXCN was hired to conduct a strategic analysis. In order to understand the scope of the assignment, EXCN coaches interviewed a large cross-section of employees from the CEO to frontline supervisors to individual contributors worldwide. During the interviews they asked questions to determine the image the new organization wanted to project. They discovered that the company vision was not clearly defined. Employees understood the organizational strategy, but they did not understand how some business decisions fit into the strategy. Employees needed to put more emphasis on innovation, sense of urgency, diversity, and financial risk management.

With facilitation by EXCN, the vision and mission of the organization to achieve results were made clear to all employees. The CEO also targeted certain top managers as executive coaching candidates. The quantitative follow-up research related to the coaching process indicated extremely positive outcomes, which contributed to the financial well-being of the organization as well as the overall moral of the stakeholders during a critical start-up period.

Gary Russell, Global Leadership Coach
The Human Dimension, Pty LTD
www.humandimension.com.au
phone: (61-2) 6296 4133
Canberra, Australia

Gary Russell provides leadership development programs to organizations across Australia, in the Pacific, and in Africa. He has contracts for government and nonprofit programs as well as those for private sector corporations. Some of his company's clients include World Vision, the World Food Program, and the government of Uganda (the Ugandan prison system and the Ugandan Army), as well as major Australian public sector organizations and private companies such as American Express. Over the past 2½ years, he has been working within Uganda and Rwanda in the areas of effective team relations in highly demanding environments, focusing on ethical leadership, conflict resolution in postconflict and reconciliation processes, and women and leadership. His coaching company, which he cofounded with his wife, Lyn, has five or six coaching and training contracts going at any one time.

Gary started as a youth worker (a social work position that assists young people to identify and meet their needs and make a satisfactory transition to adult life). He continued in social work, then became focused on organizational change, and in the 1990s made a jump into business to develop a training, facilitation, and consulting business for organizations. He added coach training to his management and consultancy experience and became a teacher-trainer for CoachU Australia for several years, as well as helping establish the ICF in Australia.

Gary designed two leadership programs that he sells to organizations: One increases productivity between leaders and teams, effects culture change within an organization, and offers a personal change within the participants. The second program, based on advanced leadership, is offered after productivity goals have been met, targeting key players for increasing personal leadership capacity. Gary's vision for his coaching reflects his own leadership values: he believes in individual responsibility, combined with the need for continual contribution to create a more harmonious world. "I follow Ghandi's advice," he says. "Be the change you wish to see in the world. I coach others to use their 'soul force,' which is essentially a plan of action that develops inner lives while working to transform society. This requires us to learn the skills, strategies and insights that will give us access to our unique twenty-first-century toolbox, leaving us better equipped to handle what happens in our busy and often chaotic lives."

Gary distinguishes coaching from organizational development (OD), explaining that "coaching grows leaders, shapes cultures, transforms people, and improves the productivity of teams, all within the context of developing more resources and knowledge," as opposed to OD, which "focuses on the analysis of an organization or advising structural and systemic changes.

"Leadership coaching is an opportunity for my clients to develop new insights, choices, and learning. Through the uncovering of their courage, confidence, and empowerment they can move forward in ways they didn't think possible," he says.

Gary says he doesn't sell his coaching; instead, he builds a relationship. He feels an informal couple of hours at a coffee shop talking to a lead member in an organization will often help him better understand what the organization needs and what contribution he can make than spending time pitching a coaching package in the boardroom. His company has six associates, all of whom have degrees in psychology, social work, or behavioral work as well as certification from a coach training organization. Associates must demonstrate their ability to work well within complex dynamics, and new associates are mentored for 12 to 18 months before they are allowed to manage their own contract.

Tanja Parsley, Executive and Leadership Coach
Partners in Performance
partnersinperformance.ca
phone: (905) 877-5808
Toronto, Ontario

Tanja Parsley works with senior executives in companies who want to create what she calls "results-focused cultures." She herself came from a sales background, and as one who says she loves marketing, she has some advice for executive and leadership coaches about networking.

"Start networking at the top, with other leaders," she says. "Want to target a particular organization? Where do the senior executives hang out? What associations are they a part of? Go directly to the source. Ask everyone you know for help and referrals." Tanja learned early on the value of networking as a career builder. With a degree in physical and health education, she started working as a fitness counselor in a medically based, high-end fitness club that catered to corporate executives. She became the vice president and manager, and counted all the club's members as friends by the time she left.

She moved on to work with Outcomes, Inc., an organizational development company that worked with executives and leaders using a systems-based approach. Tanja attended an advanced coaching program with B/Coach Systems and completed a certification program in strategic change management at the University of Toronto. With her partner, Peggy Cleary, she developed Partners in Performance, a coaching firm with a focus on peak executive performance and increased corporate revenue. Their firm offers several programs, such as one geared to emotionally intelligent leadership (similar to Goleman, Richard, & McKee [2002], which shows that leaders with well-developed emotional competencies use the power of emotion as a source of information, energy, motivation, creativity, and trust; this translates into effective performance at work and better bottom-line results). Tanja says that they have a variety of programs to deliver, and the first objective is to "get in the door" of a corporation. Then they follow up with additional executive and team coaching services that focus more on the development of business needs.

"I have leveraged my years in sales and consulting to understand how organizations work. I am always very curious about organizational dynamics," she says. Tanja takes a bottom-line approach to coaching executives and talks with them about increasing sales and creating a strong customer base. "If a corporation hasn't hit their numbers, my models and processes can absolutely help them get there. I always ask myself, 'How can we leverage our success for even greater impact?' The corporations are so large that the positive changes they achieve will have ripple effects to many, many people," she says.

Tanja's personality and coaching style mirror the toughness she finds within many CEOs. "I have strong personality traits and when I need to be, I am very assertive. That makes me well suited to work with leaders. I am direct and have the courage to say what needs to be said. I won't pussy-foot around. I listen for both context and content. I use my NLP [neurolinguistic programming] skills to do this. The power of language transcends any differences and helps me connect with senior executives quickly."

During the initial meeting with a company, she uses a strategic questioning framework to uncover the corporate needs and clarify outcomes. Then she presents the highlights of her signature package, the organization alignment road map (OAR). Her coaching package results in improved team building and goal setting, and clarifies managerial focus. She helps executives build commitment or a "hard intent" regarding their behavior change and company goals. "Research shows conclusively that outstanding performance requires three essentials: strong leadership, innovative strategies, and confident, self-motivated performance from every employee. Leadership is the linchpin."

Too often, she says, teams just go through the motions without having strong leadership to get a total buy-in. "My coaching focuses on helping leaders communicate their message. We help them learn how to engage their people and align them to the concrete business results that are most important. That includes having 'fierce conversations,' stepping up to the edge that needs to be addressed, and modeling leadership for all. Executives quickly learn that the more confident they are about the company goals and vision, the better they can lead their teams."

Exercise: Is Executive or Leadership Coaching for Me?

Use the following checklist and written questions to see if executive or leadership coaching is the right fit for you. Note the areas of prior experience, and favorite clients, topics, and coaching strengths and skills. Check the statements that are true. Then answer the questions to determine your projected impact and current readiness to pursue this specialty. Scoring: Checking off 16 or more total answers out of a possible 20, plus positive answers to the additional questions, all indicate that this can be a very satisfactory choice.

My Prior Experience:
❑ I have solid past experience in the for-profit or nonprofit business world, as an executive.
❑ I have been well trained in methods of leadership, coaching, organizational development, systems thinking, management, human relations, or psychology.
❑ I am an executive or leader myself today in my professional life as well as in my community or within volunteer organizations. I rise to the top levels of management of whatever work I do.
❑ I am familiar with business concepts, philosophy, assessments, and measures, and understand how to use data to help senior executives, managers, and CEOs increase their effectiveness and enlarge their role.
❑ I am very comfortable within a corporate culture and can talk in a way that senior executives can hear and understand.

Type of Client: My favorite clients to coach include
❑ Intelligent, strong-willed executives and entrepreneurs
❑ Visionaries who are hiring me for tangible results
❑ Executives who enjoy the status they get via work-related stature
❑ Workaholics who often need to develop a stronger personal life
❑ Adrenaline-fueled cognitive thinkers on a fast track

Coaching Topics: I understand and enjoy coaching about
❑ Work and leadership that are based on value, vision, and purpose
❑ Boosting teamwork, cutting overhead, delegating effectively, and improving morale
❑ Productivity, profitability, and innovation

(continued)

Exercise: Is Executive or Leadership Coaching for Me? (continued)

❏ The benefits and costs of being a top executive
❏ Aligning individual goals with the bottom line of a corporation or organization

My Coaching Strengths and Skills:
❏ I am an analytical thinker and a clear communicator. I can and do deliver a straight, bottom-line message, but one that inspires.
❏ I see the big picture and don't get sidetracked by crises.
❏ I have strong boundaries and can maintain strict confidentiality.
❏ I keep my clients on track with their coaching goals and plans.
❏ I am highly constructive and principled and don't take criticism or negative responses personally.

Answer the following questions:
How will my work as an executive or leadership coach uphold the vision, mission, and purpose statement of my coaching business?

_____

_____

What additional skills and strengths can I, or do I already, provide for clients as an executive or leadership coach? (Refer to Chapter 4).

_____

_____

What tangible benefits and results do I offer clients in this niche market? (Refer to Chapter 5.)

_____

_____

What one word or short phrase describes my particular coaching specialty in a client's mind? (Refer to Chapter 6.)

_____

_____

(continued)

Exercise: Is Executive or Leadership Coaching for Me? (continued)

Do I have the right credentials, coaching materials, pricing, programs, and package of services to move into this market now? If not, what are my next steps in this regard? (Refer to Chapter 9.)

_____

_____

After answering the checklist and above questions, my passion about this specialty of coaching and willingness to take steps to pursue this specialty further are: (high, medium, low) _____

Additional notes:

CHAPTER 12

Business Coaching

Business coaching is a highly strategic specialty. Whereas executive coaches work with those who have chosen to be in the world of business, business coaches work with reluctant entrepreneurs—small business owners such as lawyers, real estate agents, therapists, technological consultants, and inventors, who need help in learning how to successfully own and operate a business. The people who hire a business coach are often highly professional and talented in all aspects of their work except for the way they run their business. The business coach helps these clients develop business acumen, so that they can work more smartly and build a business that showcases their craft. For small business owners in crisis, a business coach can be a lifesaver.

Business coaches are almost always savvy entrepreneurs themselves. Although most offer individual coaching sessions for the business owner, they also provide additional coaching services, including products such as customized computer software, self-authored books or manuals, classes, workshops, or seminars. The business coach offers the client a variety of coaching services and products known as a turn-key system—a full-service package designed to get the client up and running in business so that all that is necessary for the client to do is to "turn the key."

Since the goal of business coaching is specific and strategic, the method is often a combination of consulting (advice based on the coach's prior experience) and coaching (listening skills, questioning, goal setting, client accountability, and motivation). Business coaches are often marketing to a targeted niche, a particular industry that is relevant to their prior experience in business, but they should also have general business experience to talk to a client about aspects of strategic and financial planning, business expansion, and management practices, to address the full range of possible challenges. Business coaches we interviewed for this book focused their coaching agenda on the areas of:

- Time management
- Marketing
- Best business practices
- Finances and cash flow
- Staffing and employee issues
- Personal organization
- Balance between work and family life
- Personal and professional goals and future plans
- Negative or fearful thinking that sabotages constructive action

Their clients included new entrepreneurs, professionals employed by an organization (such as lawyers in a law firm) who want to advance their customer base or their revenue, stake-holders in a family business, and even those seasoned small business owners who want to prepare themselves and their business for sale. Business coaches regularly help their clients to increase their income, decrease their workload, and market effectively.

Business coaches charge hourly, monthly, or by the program. Hourly fees for these coaches range from $100 to $300 an hour, plus product or program sales.

Coaching in Action

Now meet two business coaches who both target small business owners, but have very different coaching styles. Robert Gerrish went from the glamorous world of London public relations to a simpler lifestyle as a coach for solo entrepreneurs in Australia; C. J. Hayden parlayed her extensive and eclectic business experience into a coaching and writing career. Both Robert and C. J. are comfortable "partnering with" the business owners they coach, to help alleviate the isolation and lack of business acumen that a small business owner often faces.

Robert Gerrish, Solopreneur Coach
Flying Solo
www.flyingsolo.org
phone: (61-2) 9337 2600
Watsons Bay, Sydney, Australia

"After a couple of years of coaching anyone with a heartbeat and a credit card," Robert says, "it became apparent to me that specializing my coaching would be a smart move." Robert remembers coaching the owner of a large public relations company. She was having a terrible time managing her staff and all Robert could think of was how nice it was to work in a smaller way in business, to fly solo.

Learning to fly solo was descriptive of his own career. Robert worked with a boutique marketing and promotions agency in London, whose work involved branding, new product launches, and general marketing activities for multinational corporations. The company merged with communications giant Saatchi & Saatchi in the late 1980s.

After working as managing director of the merged business, Robert left to become a solopreneur. His area of expertise is marketing and promotion—and his first solo business was an independent marketing and management consultant for small businesses. He transitioned into a full-time coaching role in 1998. He coaches his clients to create a business that gives them the manageable, yet profitable lifestyle they want. He trained with CoachU and is a certified through the ICF as a Professional Certified Coach (PCC.)

Robert is a passionate person and considers passion an important element in choosing a line of work. "Ventures high on passion and learning; low on income!" is how he described his own early solopreneurial experiences, which matches what many of his clients experience. He built his visibility as a coach by writing monthly columns for *The Telegraph* and *My Business* in Australia, speaking on radio, and contributing to a number of international Web sites dedicated to the solo small-business community.

Robert says that while many coaches target small businesses, *small* can mean anything from 1 to 100 personnel. With his *soloist* tag, he looks for clients who are working alone and have a sense that they're "doing it for themselves, by themselves." By developing the brand for his coaching, *Flying Solo*, he expresses his own high energy that appeals to a creative and upbeat ideal client. As a coach, Robert works by phone, although if the need arises he is happy to meet face-to-face and occasionally surprises his clients by suggesting they meet so he can take a peek at their office and see firsthand how they work.

A typical coaching scenario for Robert is the soloist who's been in business for a couple of years. She probably knows how to run a business but simply isn't having enough fun, is probably not making enough money, and is unsure of where her efforts are headed. "The starting place is often a discussion about her business vision, followed by a clarification of my coaching services: I tell her that I can help with her ability in marketing and promotion, getting and keeping customers, organizing her business systems and business information. By doing this, I can show her how to take her small business to the next developmental level. If she agrees to hire me, from there it's usually right into the exciting world of personal marketing," Robert says without irony. (Robert loves marketing.)

Robert coaches his clients to improve their business practices by giving them examples of when business practice signals an amateur, versus a professional, approach. "Picture this," he explains. "You're driving through the country when you see a scruffy plank of wood loosely nailed to a tree. On this makeshift sign you see the words 'Parachute Lessons, next left' scrawled in paint.

"Would you feel safe in the hands of these instructors based on what you've seen? Chances are, you wouldn't. Now look around your own business. Where are you hanging out signs that say 'I'm small, I'm a bit of a risk,' and so on?"

He starts with the obvious: He asks his clients to note how they answer the phone; the contact details they give out and the professionalism of the information; their letterhead and business card (buy cheap, look cheap); and how they speak and listen to customers (learn when to stop talking and when to start listening). Robert asks his solopreneur clients to take a hard look at their businesses and consider what they have stopped doing that used to work well, what random actions need to become business habits for their businesses to be fit and healthy. The most common client challenges he finds are clients who feel isolated and lack clarity about what they have to offer. A typical time period for coaching is 4–12 months, and a few clients have been with him for 3-plus years. Robert finds that he does best when he draws in high-energy clients with "lots of goals and achievement desires," who move through the coaching process willingly and quickly. Robert offers a few dos and don'ts for those coaches who want to pursue business coaching:

- Do help the clients you work with see their business as a business, not a hobby.
- Do help your clients feel supported; most professionals struggle with business isolation.
- Don't get offtrack. Keep your eye on their profitability.
- Do make sure that you have clear goals in place and that the goals are ones that your client really wants. Make the goals fun, part of a bigger win-win game.

C. J. Hayden, Business Coach
Wings Business Coaching
www.getclientsnow.com
phone: (415) 981-8845
San Francisco, California

"My business background is very eclectic," says C. J. Hayden, business coach. "I had over fifty jobs before I turned thirty and changed careers six times. I find that having experience in many different industries and environments has contributed greatly to my value as a business coach."

Just prior to becoming a coach in 1992, C. J. was working as a productivity consultant for midsize companies, helping redesign workflow, computer systems, forms, and procedures. One aspect that fascinated her was that people constantly sabotaged the systems put in place to make their jobs easier. They persisted in repeating dysfunctional patterns and other unproductive behavior. She became interested in what motivated people to change and decided to start working with people instead of systems.

She was drawn to coach entrepreneurs, because she noticed their high level of motivation compared to others she worked with. "I felt as if this was a population for whom I could really make a difference," C. J. explained. Because most of her clients work alone, they are hungry for partnership. There's no one in the next cubicle to give the business owner a quick piece of feedback on an issue, or listen to complaints for a few minutes to help vent some tension.

C. J. helps fill that gap for her clients. She also helps them to toughen up and not to take rejection personally. "When my clients are essentially selling themselves, it can be hard to hear a lot of no's before something clicks," she says. She helps them see that each no gets them closer to a yes, and reminds them about the bigger picture.

The majority of her clients are sole proprietors, without a board or boss to be accountable to or a staff to manage. "We don't spend much time working on issues like team building, company politics, internal communications, or job performance," she says. A more typical set of issues for a business coach is marketing strategy, profitability, product development, communication with clients, and strategic planning for the business.

Her coaching reaches into the heart of her client's business. C. J. frequently reviews financial statements, sales projections, project plans, marketing materials, book proposals, and more to give her clients guidance in areas where she has expertise. Her business coaching is not life coaching, but at times there can be considerable overlap. She helps her clients with time management, goal setting, and quieting their "inner critic" to stay motivated. She coaches clients to do their own self-inquiry, to seek out their inner wisdom and unique answers.

A typical case is a consultant who contacted her because he was working too hard and not earning enough money. In the prework she assigned him before the first coaching session, he determined that the areas where he most wanted to make a change were increasing his gross income, getting some help with administrative details, packaging his services in such a way that his clients could buy them more readily, generating some passive income, and becoming more widely known as an expert in the field.

Together, they set some specific goals for him in each of these areas and determined what should be his first step in accomplishing each one. In their coaching sessions, they discussed the how-to's of revising his service package, promoting his new package to prospective clients, charging higher fees, choosing and managing support staff, developing products from his intellectual property, and sharing more of his expertise through publishing articles and finding opportunities for public speaking. Over several sessions they also worked through obstacles that hindered his progress: his concerns about charging more, his reluctance to delegate, his difficulty finding the time to work on his new products, and his confusion about which of his talents he most wanted to showcase in his writing and speaking.

After 3 months of working together, he had increased his fees, hired an assistant, completed a prototype of his first product, redesigned his service package, and written the marketing copy to describe it. He had also landed a column in a local newspaper, begun to promote himself as a speaker, and obtained several new clients that increased his income substantially.

C. J. tends to work with a client for a longer term than many coaches; some clients stay with her for up to several years. A familiar pattern is working with a client for 6 months to a year until a period of significant change is set into place—say, redesigning a business model or writing a book. Then clients will take a break and return the next time they have a big project to work through, which may last another year or two.

C. J. is an author and speaker, and has written two books, *Get Clients NOW!* and *Get Hired NOW!* She is a Master Certified Coach (MCC) and was a founding director of the Professional & Personal Coaches Association (which merged with the International Coach Federation). She has taught coaching skills for the Coaches Training Institute (CTI), Marriott International, Wells Fargo Bank, and BP Amoco. She offers a variety of coaching services and products, including classes, books, tapes, and programs on multiple Web sites. To market her business coaching, she located every resource center and professional association in her local area that served small businesses. She attended their public meetings, asked to post her newsletter on their bulletin boards, and tried to meet all the people in charge. She became a volunteer for some organizations and taught work-shops for many others. All of her first clients were either students from her workshops or referrals from those organizations. Currently, clients find her through her speaking engagements at corporations, professional associations, and small businesses, from reading her books and articles, visiting her Web sites, or as a result of hearing her on TV or radio.

C. J. thinks of herself as a gate-crasher. "I never believe anyone who tells me she can't do something because she doesn't have the right credentials, connections, or background," she says. "Owning a business truly gives you the ability to design your own universe. You get to decide how you want to work, who you want to work with, how much you want to earn, and how you want to structure your days." Here are C. J.'s dos and don'ts for coaches who want to pursue business coaching:

- Do hold the concept of possibility for clients, by helping them expand their vision of what they can do, be, and have.
- Do show clients how to create a business model to fulfill their desires.
- Do stay realistic with clients. Help them understand the necessity of planning and follow-through.
- Do be prepared to offer whatever coaching the client needs to stay on track and keep moving forward.

- Don't expect to earn a big income from coaching sessions alone. Most successful coaches teach, consult, train, write, speak, conduct group programs, develop products, or license intellectual property in addition to coaching. They use coaching as a springboard to running a business.

Exercise: Is Business Coaching for Me?

Use the following checklist and written questions to see if business coaching is the right fit for you. Note the areas of prior experience, and favorite clients, topics, and coaching strengths and skills. Check the statements that are true. Then answer the questions to determine your projected impact and current readiness to pursue this specialty. Scoring: Checking off 16 or more total answers out of a possible 20, plus positive answers to the additional questions, indicate that this can be a very satisfactory choice.

My Prior Experience:
❑ I am a professional myself and have owned a business or two, so I know what it takes to succeed.
❑ I have a package of resources, skills, and tools to offer my coaching clients.
❑ I am organized and professional in my own business endeavors (including my coaching business) and can model best business practices and high standards for my clients.
❑ I have a good grasp of money and can help a small business owner become financially solvent and profitable.
❑ I can related to a variety of professions and feel at ease within both the professional and the business culture.

Type of Client: My favorite clients to coach include
❑ Independent thinkers who value their autonomy
❑ People who are highly skilled in their chosen field
❑ Smart, highly creative people
❑ Overly stressed, unbalanced, hard workers who need to set limits
❑ Those who tend to be overly optimistic or pessimistic and live on the edge of business crisis

(continued)

Exercise: Is Business Coaching for Me? (continued)

Coaching Topics: I understand and enjoy coaching about
❑ Money, profit, and budgets
❑ Marketing and attracting clients
❑ Setting up and operating a successful business
❑ Balance between overwork and having a good personal life
❑ Time management and efficiency

My Coaching Strengths and Skills:
❑ I am passionate about business and love to help other people make money.
❑ I can partner with a professional in an easy, respectful way.
❑ I can hold a client accountable to agreed-upon goals.
❑ I have a strong professional background that I integrate into my coaching.
❑ I am equally happy being a coach or a consultant with my clients.

Answer the following questions:
How will my work as a business coach uphold the vision, purpose, and mission statement of my coaching business?

_____

_____

What additional skills and strengths can I, or do I already, provide for clients as a business coach? (Refer to Chapter 4.)

_____

_____

What tangible benefits and results do I offer clients in this niche market? (Refer to Chapter 5.)

_____

_____

(continued)

Exercise: Is Business Coaching for Me? (continued)

What one word or short phrase describes my particular coaching specialty in a client's mind? (Refer to Chapter 6.)

_____

_____

Do I have the right credentials, coaching materials, pricing, programs, and package of services to move into this market now? If not, what are my next steps in this regard? (Refer to Chapter 9.)

_____

_____

After answering the checklist and above questions, my passion about this specialty of coaching and willingness to take steps to pursue this specialty further are: (high, medium, low) _____

Additional notes:

CHAPTER 13

Skills Coaching

Some coaches niche based on the types of clients they work with: executives, leaders, non-business-oriented professionals. But skills coaches work with a broad population and specialize based on the specific skill set they impart. Skills coaches are experts in some specific skill, such as public speaking, sales, writing, peak performance, networking, computer use, image improvement, financial planning, fund-raising, interview techniques, organizing, study, socializing, dating, or networking. They highlight their expertise in this skill to attract clients. As coaches, they offer clients a "twofer": skill-based knowledge plus their overall coaching ability.

The skills coach may offer a skill that is needed and used by a wide population—say, public speaking—or one that is more arcane and targeted to a narrower client population—say, study and organizational skills for teenagers in high school who are diagnosed with attention deficit disorder ADD. Unlike an executive coach or a business coach who may impart a range of tips, suggestions, and skills to a client, the hallmark of a skills coach is the ability to promote measurable results for a client within a specific area of behavior. In this regard, skills coaching probably resembles traditional sports coaching more closely than the other specialties we explore in this book because the results of the coaching are often so clearly focused.

Skills coaches are part teacher, part coach. To bring in new clients, past reputation and résumé counts. But the real measure of their coaching is not only how good the coach is at a particular skill, say, public speaking, but whether or not the coach can help the client improve and become a great speaker. Skills coaches are not just teachers; they are also coaches, and they can't be the stars of the relationship. Their job is to be in the background and help their clients shine and develop as individuals. Successful skills

229

coaches listen well, communicate clearly, and are proficient motivators. They give accurate feedback during the implementation process, inspire their clients to do more than they might ever undertake alone, and in the process may coach clients on additional areas of personal life. Clients that hire a skills coach expect to increase their skills significantly, quickly, and with lasting results, but they also want a coaching relationship with support and connection.

Some examples of how skills coaches converted their past experience into a current coaching specialty are:

- A book marketing coach who helps novice authors get published. This coach was a 30-year veteran of a large publishing house and knows the ins and outs of the publishing world.
- A vocal performance coach who was a well-regarded opera singer and teacher, and now coaches singers to approach a singing career holistically, in a way that encompasses not only vocal excellence, but incorporates mind, body, and spirit.
- A sales coach who earned millions during his 25-year real estate career, overcame a difficult illness, then refashioned his business model to allow him time to make money but work a much shorter week, with extended family time. He now coaches others in the real estate industry how to make million-dollar incomes for themselves, while preserving family time for a balanced life.

At its best, skills coaching is developmental as well as strategic for a client, as the client comes to "own" the skills and, in the process, uses the relationship with the coach to develop and grow as a full person. The coach creates an environment for the client to learn in an accelerated manner, often by having objective tools and a clearly structured coaching model, but attends to other aspects of a client's life and work.

Skills coaches charge fees in the range of executive or business coaches, from $100 an hour up to $250 an hour. Skills coaches can be in demand as keynote speakers or workshop presenters. On-site consulting or presenting fees for a skills coach can be as low as $500 or as high as $8,000 a day.

Coaching in Action

Here are brief profiles of two skills coaches who each tackle a skill that causes fear and loathing in many people. Sandra Schrift went from owning a successful speaking bureau to coaching a variety of performance-shy clients to go beyond their fears and become great public speakers. Sales coach Richard Levinson excelled in his own sales career and coaches his clients to overcome their distaste of self-promotion and marketing, to learn to be successful in selling. Both of these coaches understand learning theory and offer a flexible approach of skill-sets to fit each adult client.

Sandra Schrift, Public Speaking Coach
www.schrift.com
phone: (619) 688-9467
San Diego, California

Sandra Schrift has been part of the speaking industry for over two decades. An agent for speakers, she represented 1,500 local and national speakers within her own speaking bureau and was the founder of the first National Speakers Association (NSA) in San Diego. In 1996, she sold her speaking bureau and turned to coaching emerging and experienced speakers. "I saw that running a speaker's bureau was a silver mine, but coaching speakers could be a gold mine!" Sandra explains. She trained with CoachU and her mentor coach was Robert Alderman, known for his high-powered marketing advice. "I've always been a good coach. I have a lot of credibility with new speakers or those who want to go to another level. I coach them from the presentation development, to promotion, to marketing. Everything I learned to do the hard way, I can now coach people to do the easier way."

Sandra coaches by phone and most of her clients find her through her Web site, by searching the Internet for help with public speaking. She works with a broad professional population such as attorneys, executives, or others who want to become masterful presenters. When Sandra started coaching in 1996, her first clients included seven ministers and two rabbis. "Apparently," Sandra says, "people of the cloth search the Web for help with speaking."

Her Web site is her biggest marketing tool, and she keeps it content-rich, with an extensive list of free information, including hundreds of resources for the would-be speaker: associations, conferences, networking groups, and short articles. Sandra finds that her Web site and full menu of services break the ice with clients.

"I really don't know why there is such a fear of public speaking," she says. "Something triggers the autonomic nervous system and even seasoned professionals get butterflies. The trick is to get the butterflies to fly in *formation!*" She wants to bring her clients into a different perspective of themselves, one that will make their work as speakers more enjoyable and more powerful. She focuses on teaching methods of peak performance, so that clients learn how to overcome what scares them and become effective speakers. When new clients hire her, she asks them to send in a completed "prep form" in advance of each phone session. This gives the clients a sense of accountability and helps to set the calls' agenda. She likes to move fast as a coach. "Next!" is her motto. She also acknowledges that she is constantly optimistic and "a good cheerleader" for her clients.

Sandra offers several coaching packages, including an annual retainer fee (the coaching time is open-ended and these clients can use her as much or as little as they want); a monthly retainer (three 45-minute sessions a month and unlimited e-mail support with a 6-month minimum); and a discount program for prepaying (paying in full for 6 months and then getting the 7th month of coaching free). Sandra's coaching platform includes her Web site, her products of tapes and CDs she has developed to augment her coaching sessions, an e-book (*Speak Like a Pro for Profit*), and classes she regularly offers for those who prefer to learn in a group.

As a model for her clients, Sandra also gives many talks herself, including occasional free classes, so that she is out in front of the public often. Clients stay with her anywhere from 6 months to several years. Sandra sees herself as a constant student of her niche. She considers that part of her coaching job is research and develops substantial additional resources for her clients. She consistently attends to marketing her own practice so that her coaching is not a secret. Not one to rest on her laurels, she says that as a coach in business, networking will always need to be a part of her lifestyle.

Richard Levinson, Sales Coach
RHL Associates
www.salesgohigher.com
phone: (248) 353-1505
Southfield, Michigan

Richard Levinson coaches individuals who want to develop a stronger ability to sell. He coaches salespeople to set and reach high personal and professional goals, and helps non-sales-oriented professionals develop and execute strategies that fit their own innate strengths. He shows executives how to be better salespeople inside their own organizations, and he assists companies to upgrade their sales force.

What began as skills-based, tactical teaching (showing clients how to get the best results from a specific sales call) expanded into a coaching approach (helping clients get unstuck in their sales performance by having them look within themselves). Richard believes that one of his primary strengths is in seeing his clients as whole and fully functional, although they need his help for difficulties in one area. He has a strong faith in the "omnipotent core" of his clients. He doesn't provide advice but instead leads clients through a process of personal inventory in order to identify the internal resources that they already have available, and then transfer those resources to their goals about selling.

Richard coaches clients to enhance and apply their strong suits. For example, a client may be shy about initiating a marketing conversation during a networking event. But this same client is a naturally curious person and able to carry on an active dialogue when her curiosity gets aroused. In a case like this, Richard would find ways to help her stay curious about each new person she met, long enough to keep a dialogue going, and then learn to weave in her marketing pitch.

Richard has been a coach for 12 years. After leaving the Navy, he sold insurance and then became director of financial planning at an accounting firm. He developed his own selling process and wanted to teach it, but found that his system didn't transfer well to others because they didn't get the same results. In 1992, he got trained in the Sandler System (a sales training method), which he determined to be a better sales system, and now, armed with the right tools, felt ready to be in business for himself. He decided to practice what he preached and began to sell his coaching services and brand his system of sales coaching.

Some of his clients use him on an as-need basis. These are salespeople usually requesting coaching to develop or improve a sales strategy for an upcoming specific sales call. Others (usually non-sales people) arrange a longer coaching relationship as they work on generating referrals. He always gives his clients homework and enlists accountability for actions steps.

He distinguishes his coaching niche from sales consulting or sales training because he works with his clients in a discovery relationship in which a process of inquiry is part of the model. He coaches professional clients to get to know themselves in a new way, within the context of their strengths and their blocks regarding sales.

A typical case: A certified public accountant hires him because she's told that in order to make partner, she has to bring in new accounts. She has a problem closing sales. In her first coaching session, she admits that she hates to sell. She has no idea how to make it easier for herself—how to set up functioning networks for referrals, or create achievable and clear sales goals. Richard coaches her to understand that the selling is a process of steps: he breaks down the sales path into small goals, with each client contact carefully scripted and every follow-up action specified. This skill-based approach grounds her so that she no longer feels confused about what to do or say next. He helps her look at her objections to any steps and emphasizes her inner strengths (such as her ability to be a warm listener of others) so that she builds on her strengths, one step at a time. There are homework assignments, practice times, and checking in on her progress. As she becomes more skillful at sales and develops increased confidence, the goals they set together get more substantial.

They agree to work together for 8 weeks and then reevaluate. At the end of 8 weeks, Richard helps her articulate the gains she has made, looks with her at the sales she has closed, and then coaches her to approach her boss to get a clear picture of what more she has to achieve, and in what period of time, in order to be considered a partner. She comes back to him with her boss's response, and he asks her to decide if she really has the commitment to accomplish this partnership goal. Once she agrees, the next level of the coaching process can begin.

As she proceeds in coaching, she recognizes an important reality about her profession and can correct a misperception she held about her job. "I became a CPA so I could avoid all that prospecting and selling stuff," she complained. With understanding about the actual nature of her job and the path to partnership in the firm, she tells Richard that she must accept that her job has to embrace this "selling stuff," too.

Although Richard has a sales system that he is passionate about using, he says he doesn't assume that all of his clients will benefit from one particular method or teaching style. He tailors his sales model to the person, asking clients how they'd liked to be coached and how much accountability they want in their coaching.

Exercise: Is Skills Coaching for Me?

Use the following checklist and written questions to see if skills coaching appeals to you. Note the areas of prior experience, and favorite clients, topics, and coaching strengths and skills. Check the statements that are true. Then answer the questions to determine your projected impact and current readiness to pursue this specialty. Scoring: Checking off 16 or more total answers out of a possible 20, plus positive answers to the additional questions, all indicate that this can be a very satisfactory choice.

My Prior Experience:
❑ I have substantial real-world experience in the skill that I coach others to do.
❑ I am not just a teacher of this skill; I am also trained or certified as a coach.
❑ I have a structured skill-based program that I offer with measurable, tangible results.
❑ I have a track record and a reputation in my skill, including references and endorsements.
❑ I am connected to a larger community of professionals within my skill set, so that when you hire me, you access my network as well.

Type of Client: My favorite clients to coach include
❑ Motivated individuals who have targeted a very real need for my services
❑ Those who want to work on specific, defined goals
❑ People who may want to work short term and will expect results
❑ People who are grateful for tangible, concrete coaching
❑ Challenging clients who appreciate value and don't tolerate incompetence

Coaching Topics: I understand and enjoy coaching about:
❑ My area of skill and expertise
❑ Motivation, purpose, goals, deadlines, and action steps
❑ Measurable evidence as well as subjective experience
❑ Success and achievement for the whole person
❑ Money, financial independence, and excellence

(continued)

Exercise: Is Skills Coaching for Me? (continued)

My Coaching Strengths and Skills:
- ❑ I am a model of my skill for others.
- ❑ I love to teach.
- ❑ I have confidence in my clients' ability to succeed.
- ❑ I am a good listener and give accurate feedback that can be heard and immediately implemented.
- ❑ I am an extrovert, have fun with my clients, and keep the coaching upbeat and optimistic.

Answer the following questions:
How will my work as a skills coach uphold the vision, purpose, and mission statement of my coaching business?

_____

_____

What additional skills and strengths can I, or do I already, provide for clients as a skills coach? (Refer to Chapter 4.)

_____

_____

What tangible benefits and results do I offer clients in this niche market? (Refer to Chapter 5.)

_____

_____

What one word or short phrase describes my particular coaching specialty in a client's mind? (Refer to Chapter 6.)

_____

_____

(continued)

Exercise: Is Skills Coaching for Me? (continued)

Do I have the right credentials, coaching materials, pricing, programs, and package of services to move into this market now? If not, what are my next steps in this regard? (Refer to Chapter 9.)

_____

_____

After answering the checklist and above questions, my passion about this specialty of coaching and willingness to take steps to pursue this specialty further are: (high, medium, low) _____

Additional notes:

CHAPTER 14

Career Coaching

With the global economy in flux and a broad labor pool that is in transition, it's not surprising that career coaching is a specialty both in demand and growing. Career coaching is considered an essential resource for those in and out of the labor market. Career coaches most often work either independently out of their own businesses or as subcontractors to corporations or public organizations.

This specialty is often confused with career counseling. Here is the difference: Career counselors offer aptitude testing, job search services, résumé writing, and some career management advice. Career coaches offer career management advice and coaching specific to career issues. They do not find people jobs. One career coach explains, "We are not an employment agency. We don't match job openings with job seekers. We don't offer career assessments, furnish answers, or find people jobs. We coach. We ask perceptive questions, challenge limiting belief systems or fantasies that stop people from pursuing a happier career path, and work with a client to help improve the client's life and work situation. We help clients adapt their vision to reality and what is available now. If we do any testing, we use assessments selectively. We don't write résumés or cover letters or look through want ads with clients. We see the big picture of a career path and help clients set some goals, take actions, and be accountable to us for those actions."

Career coaches help clients gain clarity about what they want in their next career. They have coaching conversations that help people evaluate and analyze their next steps and career choices. They may help clients design job-search strategies and learn interviewing, networking, and negotiating skills, and how to craft a strong verbal pitch. They help clients manage the change and stress of work, ready themselves for promotion, and map out career strategies. Most coaches in this specialty narrow their niche to targeted populations, coaching one of the three following categories: those who are between jobs; those still employed who want to advance within their existing company; or those who want to leave one job and find a better one.

Career coaching services help clients to:

- Become "career self-reliant" by taking control and ownership of their own career development
- Speed up a job search by setting priorities and getting highly strategic with their actions
- Translate experience into job opportunities
- Improve interviewing, networking, and negotiating styles
- Use assessment tools to increase understanding and credibility
- Find "right work"—a career path that feels valid and best
- Remove blocks to career progress
- Learn communication styles
- Promote a win-win balance of work-life priorities

Career coaches charge by the session (typical fees range from $75 to $150 per hour), by the package (monthly sessions, on-site training, and résumé help from $250 a month and up), or, for corporate accounts, by the project.

Coaching in Action

Deborah Brown Volkman is a career coach from New York who converted her own checkered career path into a coaching specialty, one that recognized the value of helping each person she coached to find a dream career.

Deborah Brown-Volkman, Career Coach
Surpass Your Dreams, Inc
www.surpassyourdreams.com
phone: (631) 874-2877
East Moriches, New York

Deborah Brown-Volkman came to career coaching after a long career in the corporate arena. She learned about "the good, the bad, and the ugly" of career advancement through firsthand experience, but found ways to change jobs and improve her career, sometimes against all odds. For a while, Deborah was switching corporate jobs almost every 2 years. People teased her that she was too picky, but she kept looking for a job that was truly fulfilling. She learned exactly what to say in job interviews and how to negotiate a good salary. She broke established job-seeking rules (stay at a career for several years to establish your loyalty, accept less money at first to get your foot in the door), but kept getting new and better jobs. She had faith in herself and her career path. She brings this sense of optimism to her work as a career coach.

Deborah says she has always loved to motivate people, and she wanted to figure out how to make a living helping others find good ways to make a living. Coaching seemed to be the right fit. She trained with CoachU and was a founding member of Coachville, the online coaching community and training center. At first she gravitated toward a specialty of life coaching, but she didn't want to just help people feel better; she wanted to help them get better jobs. She went from telling clients "You can have a life that you love" to "You can have a career that you love."

Deborah believes that who she coaches and what she coaches about are directly related to her own experience and background. "You can't coach everyone, so you have to ask yourself, 'What have I gone through and what can I give back?'" Her career coaching targets those clients who are out of work and in crisis, helping them find a better career and get back into the workforce. She also coaches those who are employed and overworked how to prioritize, manage their time, and be more effective. Deborah offers her own experience as a model for time management: for 3½ years she worked a full-time day job in corporate sales and marketing, went to school at night, and built her coaching business on the side. "I had to learn how to be really efficient," she says, "and I can show others how to do that."

She offers several in-person coaching, telephone coaching, and e-mail coaching programs. Her Web site also offers a free "personal transformation" worksheet to pique a potential client's interest. Deborah found that writing books opened the most doors for her coaching practice. She also teaches teleclasses at teleclass.com (a Web site that sponsors and broadcasts teleclasses by coaches), has published three books, appears on TV, writes a monthly newsletter, and writes articles for career-oriented Web sites.

Because of her prior marketing background, she believes in continual networking to build her coaching business. She stays active in the chamber of commerce, the Rotary Club, networking groups, and women's groups to build visibility. She regularly seeks out existing career groups to see how she might link her coaching to their resource lists.

Many clients are at a low point when they hire her and don't believe finding a new job is possible. She has a strong faith in her coaching process, and this gives her clients courage to go through the steps, even though they must traverse a while in the unknown. "Clients ask me, 'How did I lose this job?' and want to look for a new career that has more meaning. It takes courage to stick with it. That's where the collaboration of coaching comes in," she says. Deborah designed a structured, five-step coaching program. Her clients respond well to the structure, which makes them feel more secure. Usually clients hire her for 1–6 months. The longer they work with her, the lower her price becomes. One month's coaching costs $550 per month; 6 months' coaching costs $450 per month. Her fees are clearly listed on her Web page, so her clients know exactly what they are getting into, and this transparency serves as a self-screening device.

Her coaching is "as virtual as possible." She coaches by phone and uses an e-mail coaching contract, credit card authorization for payment of fees, and an e-mail intake form. The first 90 days of coaching comprise "personal foundation work"—clearing out fears and negative mind sets and designing specific life goals. The career-focused coaching really starts in the second 90-day period. After 6 months, her clients have met most of their goals. If they are really stuck, she may suggest that they consider some psychotherapy at this point to help them move forward.

Deborah makes a distinction between career coaching and counseling. "Career counseling is more of a consulting process. People take assessments and then are told what they should do. In career coaching, the answer comes from the client. It is a harder process but ultimately more rewarding. You come to an answer that truly reflects who you are. Sometimes people just need to know an answer in a very short period of time and just want career counseling. But if in your gut you really feel something is missing, then coaching is the way to go."

A trial lawyer wanted to go in a new direction. He had his own practice, but didn't like it and didn't know what else he wanted to do. During coaching, Deborah observed that he expressed great enjoyment whenever he needed to interact with the media. He loved working with the press and TV, and also enjoyed the few marketing duties he had in regard to advertising, occasional speaking, and sending out direct-mail promotions.

Deborah helped him name his new direction as marketing. "Every career has an association that is a gold mine for the client. He did research and found out what a career in marketing would be like." She also coached him to gather information through interviews by calling people who were already successful in this arena. She directed him to go to trade shows, read books, and find an occupational handbook published by the Department of Labor. Once he decided that this was his area, she coached him to rework his résumé by emphasizing his experience and strengths that fit this type of career, advising him how to fill in certain gaps and what to emphasize. The career transition process took him 1 year. "Most people wait until the breaking point, until they are really fed up with a career," Deborah says. "They need to start earlier. The answer is always out there."

Deborah offers some advice for new coaches who might want to pursue a specialty as a career coach:

- Don't select a niche because it is lucrative. Don't be a career coach unless you love talking about careers. Get into a niche you enjoy. Having some career training is good, but prior experience relating to career change is better.
- Do learn about your niche in the field. Go to career-oriented workshops, talk to people, and keep taking your personal career to a different level. Do build your coaching business based upon yourself and your strengths. Have courage and you will find that someone will pay you for your skills, your strengths, and your courageous approach.
- Have a comprehensive menu of coaching services that take into account that not everyone can or will hire you right away, but still might want to know your underlying message.

Exercise: Is Career Coaching for Me?

Use the following checklist and written questions to see if career coaching is the right fit for you. Note the areas of prior experience, and favorite clients, topics, and coaching strengths and skills. Check the statements that are true. Then answer the questions to determine your projected impact and current readiness to pursue this specialty. Scoring: Checking off 16 or more total answers out of a possible 20, plus positive answers to the additional questions, all indicate that this can be a very satisfactory choice.

My Prior Experience:

❑ I have training or certification in the field of coaching, career development, or career planning or a related field, and am knowledgeable about the dynamics of human behavior.

❑ I have had personal experience in the job market over time and have been through at least one successful career transition myself.

❑ I can interpret and understand career assessments, their scoring, and performance evaluations to help clients further their goals.

❑ I have knowledge of career resources, occupations, and workplace trends.

❑ I am familiar with methods of negotiation and strategies for career planning, and am comfortable analyzing salary and benefit packages.

Type of Client: My favorite clients to coach include

❑ Frustrated out-of work individuals who want a better job or a different career direction

❑ Those who desire to find a calling, not just a job

❑ People in crisis who need to move forward

❑ Employees, managers, and others still employed who want to advance in their careers

❑ People who can appreciate a good dose of clarity, hope, and possibility

Coaching Topics: I understand and enjoy coaching about

❑ Aligning individual strengths and skills with career

❑ Finding the best balance between work and personal life

❑ Crafting a winning résumé, self-marketing, personal promotion

(continued)

Exercise: Is Career Coaching for Me? (continued)

❑ Personal and professional vision, purpose, and mission
❑ Career choices, self-esteem, overcoming roadblocks to change

My Coaching Strengths and Skills:
❑ I am fascinated the process of vocation and the world of work.
❑ I am optimistic, yet pragmatic, a very good listener and clear communicator.
❑ I am resourceful and calm in the midst of crisis.
❑ I have a huge reserve of career-related information, tips, resources, ideas, and strategies at my fingertips.
❑ I apply structure and accountability to my coaching sessions.

Answer the following questions:
How will my work as a career coach uphold the vision, purpose, and mission statement of my coaching business?

_____

_____

What additional skills and strengths can I, or do I already, provide for clients as a career coach? (Refer to Chapter 4.)

_____

_____

What tangible benefits and results do I offer clients in this niche market? (Refer to Chapter 5.)

_____

_____

What one word or short phrase describes my particular coaching specialty in a client's mind? (Refer to Chapter 6.)

_____

_____

(continued)

Exercise: Is Career Coaching for Me? (continued)

Do I have the right credentials, coaching materials, pricing, programs, and package of services to move into this market now? If not, what are my next steps in this regard? (Refer to Chapter 9.)

_____

_____

After answering the checklist and above questions, my passion about this specialty of coaching and willingness to take steps to pursue this specialty further are: (high, medium, low) _____

Additional notes:

CHAPTER 15

Life Coaching

Life coaching is a general term that designates coaching whose focus is on a client's personal lifestyle, as opposed to a focus on business challenges, professional skills, or career concerns. Life coaching appeals to clients who consider themselves lifelong learners and are interested in self-actualization. Clients often seek out a life coach when in transition between one developmental stage of life and another, such as leaving college, becoming a parent, approaching midlife, or negotiating retirement. The life coach is a partner in planning—listening carefully and giving pragmatic yet constructive feedback to help a client clarify values, desires, goals, and plan of action. Throughout this process, the coach is a collaborator who is involved and interested in the client, the coaching process, and the coaching results.

Life coaching can be the most challenging coaching specialty for the coach. Because the topic of discussion is the client's personal life, not business, life coaching comes close to mirroring therapy. The coach must be cognizant of the distinctions between therapy and coaching (see Chapter 2) and know how to keep the conversation on a coaching, not a therapy, track. Although the topics of life coaching may touch on some of those that arise in psychotherapy, life coaches stay focused on present-day, here-and-now behavioral goals and actions. They work with "coachable" clients who use the coaching process to create tangible results. They don't delve into historic complex issues or process difficult feelings.

The life coach is friendly, but not a friend, a professional for hire who needs to set boundaries to not incur dual relationships or create conflicts of interest (see Chapter 10). Although life coaching is considered by some executive, leadership, and business coaches to be the less demanding or "softer" side of coaching, life coaches must be rigorous and adept at helping clients look at and change important core aspects of themselves. Life coaches help clients define a life vision and set goals, prompt their clients to action, hold clients responsible for weekly progress with accountability, challenge their setbacks, and cheer on their successes. Life coaching is not therapy, but when it is working well, clients do change internally and externally as they take steps to improve their lives and achieve desired goals.

The best life coaches are models of their services. They present an example of a well-lived life. This pushes life coaches to look at all areas of their own lives and make sure they set an example of integrity, happiness, and responsibility. Life coaching conversations need structure, and coaches must be discriminating about their coaching process, by using a method of coaching based on accepted coaching standards and having some form of ongoing coaching supervision in place (that is, they are continually getting coached themselves or are part of a peer coaching mentoring group). The most successful life coaches we interviewed for this book have been coached themselves and completed a program of coach training in order to develop an effective coaching style and demonstrate a "moral compass"— an awareness and use of coaching ethics that establish the coach as a solid, resourceful professional.

Life coaches may niche their coaching in terms of population, age, gender, or focal point, but most life coaches examine similar topics of lifestyle and quality of life, vision, values, goals, habits, attitudes, barriers to success, perceptions and beliefs, balance, fulfillment, passion, and happiness. Questions that a life coach may ask a potential client to consider include:

- What matters most to you in life?
- If you knew you were going to die in a year, would you stop what you're doing now? And do what?
- What is the one goal you wish you could accomplish that would make your life terrific?

According to the recent coaching surveys, life coaches charge less than executive or business coaches. The average fee is $70–$125 per hour, although some senior life coaches charge $175 per hour. Most life coaches work with clients in individual sessions, in person, or by phone, on a weekly or biweekly basis. A few also offer coaching classes for small groups; some give workshops.

Coaching in Action

Here are profiles of two life coaches who use developmental, structured coaching models in their work with clients. Karen Andrews, a former therapist and now a coach, niches her practice for women in their 40s and 50s who are going through midlife transitions. She uses a life coaching model based on adult developmental stages and the client-centered coach training she received at Coaches Training Institute. Kathy Gates came from a human relations business background and has a broader client base but narrows her life coaching by theme: the importance of making good choices in life. She takes her clients through a stage-related process of life planning that she has written in manual form, to help them establish priorities.

Karen Andrews, Women's Life Coach
Heart Source Coaching
www.blazinghormones.com
phone: (970) 922-0399
Snowmass Village, Colorado

Karen's coaching niche is women who find themselves in midlife transition. She offers individual coaching, information, and insight to assist those challenged by change of life—common physical health, emotional, and situational transitions. "It is so sad to see women basically crumble in many areas of their lives during middle age," she says. Karen sees that the overall themes in coaching women at midlife involve concerns about aging, fertility, body image, self-worth, health, illness, living life to the fullest, productivity, and balance. "And yet," Karen points out, "those are the very challenges that can also motivate women to move ahead in their lives."

Karen's own personal experiences influenced her coaching specialty. She has been married 31 years and has gone through conflict, separation, and renewal in her marriage. She has two grown daughters and has traveled widely, living in two different foreign countries. She tells her clients that nothing they tell her can alarm her. "Wherever they are, I can go there with them. I am a soul friend who will walk their life's journey with them."

Karen has a master's in psychology and worked as a group and marriage counselor. She is a Certified Spiritual Director (a 2-year theology program) and completed professional coaching training with the Coaches Training Institute (CTI), a multiyear coach training program. She began to write a quarterly e-mail newsletter called *Blazing Hormones*, to research and write about the various changes experienced by women at midlife.

"My clients are beautiful mirrors because often what I need to look at in my own life seems to appear with each new client. My goal as a coach is always one that is 'win-win' with each client. It always encompasses seeing their uniqueness, beauty, and potential," she says. Karen sends out a welcome packet to new clients and sets a contract for 3 months minimum for the individual coaching. By phone or in person, she meets with clients either two or three times a month.

Karen stays open to topics ranging from the personal to the professional during sessions and lets her clients define what they want to focus on, no matter how big or small the issue. Two case examples describe her coaching style:

A woman executive was unhappy and needed coaching about the possible end of her career within an organization in financial trouble. Whereas an executive coach might have focused on just the business concerns, Karen took a life-coaching approach and allowed the coaching to move back and forth between the topics of personal and professional life. They started with a goal to separate and set boundaries between the woman's business and personal life, so that as her career came to an end, her personal life could become more compelling. The coaching lasted for 6 months with very satisfactory results. A year later, the client returned after a diagnosis of breast cancer. The coaching then focused on a supportive stance, with Karen listening and providing careful, reflective feedback so that her client could eventually make difficult decisions about her health care and future lifestyle.

The second case was a female professional athlete, at the top of her high-risk sport for almost 20 years. Now in her 40s, she found that the professional competition was getting younger and began to face the reality of aging and the inevitable transition of stepping away from her competitive sport. Not wanting to fully disengage from her professional world, Karen's client transformed her athletic skills into other areas of her life, both personally and professionally. Karen coached her to look at her life in a new way and make appropriate but desirable choices, based on her current stage in life.

Karen trusts herself to use her instinct and intuition with her clients. She goes beyond her coaching training asks not superficial questions, but rather questions that change a person's life and outlook. She talks to her clients as if she were a trusted friend, but still allows herself to be tough and respectful of boundaries. She sees herself as a catalyst for change, and is not afraid to disclose who she is as a person to a client—including voicing her beliefs and opinions: it makes her more credible and real.

Kathy Gates, Life Coach
Real Life Coach
www.reallifecoach.com
phone: (480) 998-5843
Scottsdale, Arizona

"Living well is a daily habit," says Kathy Gates, who comes to life coaching from a background worked in human relations. Her coaching clients are people who are working very hard, but don't necessarily have happy lives. She introduces them to the concept of abundance. "I believe that good habits, extra money, and supportive relationships are essential to a happy life, and they are things that I've learned and practiced myself."

Early in her coaching career, Kathy got some advice from her coach: Think about the statement she wanted to make via her coaching. If she had 1 minute to speak to others on CNN, what would she really want the world to know? Her answer: You always have a choice. Make good choices. Good choices will help you build the life you want.

Kathy describes herself as a linear, logical thinker who can take complicated concepts and translate them into very simple terms. She is a strategic life coach who helps clients cut through the strings attached to their challenges. She offers a bit of sympathy and some cheerleading, but warns clients that she is not there to commiserate with them. "I have high standards and give my best as a coach. I hope that with this modeling, my clients will do the same."

In her prior human resources career, Kathy learned how to relate to a wide variety of professional people during the course of a day (lawyers one minute, laborers the next), and the value of staying highly organized, skills that she now uses as a life coach. She trained with CoachU.

Kathy works with clients by phone and e-mail. She offers the e-book she wrote, *7 Secrets to a Great Life*, as a manual for clients, to help them plan their lives, establish priorities, and create a reserve of resources. She doesn't think a client can create a vision or determine a life purpose when surrounded by clutter, disorganization, or the clatter of daily life. She shows clients how to tackle the basic steps of getting rid of mess, clearing out both physical and mental space, and bringing in some quiet time to think and plan, the sometimes "less glamorous" tasks of getting a life back on track, the prep work. "I coach clients to simplify, clarify, hone, polish, and work, work, and work to achieve goals in important areas of one's life—more time, better career, nicer physical space, better relationships, improved finances, better health, and improved self-confidence," she says. "We find those goals that are honest and practical to accomplish."

Kathy asks potential clients who want to work with her to also interview at least two other coaches in order to make an informed decision. As a result of this interview process, when a client decides to hire her, Kathy finds that it is a good working relationship. A typical client was a single mother of a young child who had a high-stress professional job with long hours. Kathy asked the client to determine one "big goal." In this case, the client decided to create a home-based business. Then she helped the client define the intentions and benefits of that goal: more control over time, more time with the child, having a business that reflects a particular work ethic. She asked her client to set up a series of "reserves"—a financial savings of 6 months' salary to live on while building the new business, a housekeeper who would assist with errands and babysitting to free up her time. She asked her client to pay down her credit card balance and cut her expenses for the next year. She suggested a plan for daily exercise, more sleep, and good nutrition. Each week they discussed specific actions to further each goal. The weekly coaching calls help to keep the client focused and moving forward one step at a time, prioritizing and making the goal manageable, instead of being overwhelmed by the big picture.

Kathy has advice for those who are thinking about becoming life coaches. She suggests that new coaches recognize that it is very difficult to coach a person to take steps to change the "familiar unhappiness" that we all can live in. Life coaches need to be patient. A typical coaching client may need 4–6 months to see deep, lasting lifestyle changes. Positive results come from clients taking action, so that they move away from a lifestyle that isn't working. New coaches should not let clients get discouraged about the process of change. Sometimes the way to a more aligned personal and professional life seems like a defeat at first. It can be difficult to give up on something even if it's dragging you further and further away from your goals.

When you instill commitment into the process of coaching and a commitment to change, then half the work of coaching will be done. Make sure every goal is unified with a client's head *and* heart.

Exercise: Is Life Coaching for Me?

Use the following checklist and written questions to see if life coaching is the right fit for you. Note the areas of prior experience, and favorite clients, topics, and coaching strengths and skills. Check the statements that are true. Then answer the questions to determine your projected impact and current readiness to pursue this specialty. Scoring: Checking off 16 or more total answers out of a possible 20, plus positive answers to the additional questions, all indicate that this can be a very satisfactory choice.

My Prior Experience:
❏ I have prior training, degree, or certification in the field of human behavior and coaching.
❏ I have been through significant transition myself in my personal life and understand what a process of life change requires.
❏ My passions and interests coincide with my area of coaching.
❏ I rely on a developmental model to help clients reach their goals. My life coaching process with clients is not random or unstructured.
❏ I have built extensive resources including reading material, community links to associations, and networks to offer to my clients.

Type of Client: My favorite clients to coach include
❏ Individuals who want to make a change in their personal lives
❏ Functional people who are stuck and may be frustrated, but are not without resources
❏ Women and men who are ready to take action, not just talk about action
❏ Verbal, savvy, goal-oriented individuals
❏ People who want a collaborative partner, not an expert to help them figure out life choices

Coaching Topics: I understand and enjoy coaching about
❏ Facing down normal fears and overcoming obstacles or challenges
❏ Setting and achieving specific goals and defining weekly action steps
❏ Happiness, balance, vision, passion, legacy
❏ Wanting more faster, with more success
❏ Possibility, abundance, and choice

(continued)

Exercise: Is Life Coaching for Me? (continued)

My Coaching Strengths and Skills:

❏ I have the ability to listen carefully, ask probing questions, and work with a person on multiple levels in order to facilitate change.

❏ I think clearly and offer constructive, laserlike communication.

❏ I am optimistic and pragmatic; I have a big vision for my clients, but want to see results.

❏ I base my coaching methods on a coaching model, my experience of being coached myself, my coach training, and professional supervision, not guesswork.

❏ I am fascinated with people and human behavior and find I can talk to anybody about anything.

Answer the following questions:

How will my work as a life coach uphold the vision, purpose, and mission statement of my coaching business?

_____

_____

What additional skills and strengths can I, or do I already, provide for clients as a life coach? (Refer to Chapter 4.)

_____

_____

What tangible benefits and results do I offer clients in this niche market? (Refer to Chapter 5.)

_____

_____

What one word or short phrase describes my particular coaching specialty in a client's mind? (Refer to Chapter 6.)

_____

_____

(continued)

Exercise: Is Life Coaching for Me? (continued)

Do I have the right credentials, coaching materials, pricing, programs, and package of services to move into this market now? If not, what are my next steps in this regard? (Refer to Chapter 9.)

_____

_____

After answering the checklist and above questions, my passion about this specialty of coaching and willingness to take steps to pursue this specialty further are: (high, medium, low) _____

Additional notes:

CHAPTER 16

Wellness Coaching

Wellness coaching is similar in some ways to life coaching, but it provides a singular focus on the physical well-being and overall health of a client. Wellness coaching programs are becoming an established element of holistic health care because they help individuals take greater responsibility for their own health and modifying their behavior in beneficial ways.

Wellness coaching has strategies aimed at three distinct populations:

- Coordinated interventions and communications for people with chronic conditions
- Support and motivation those who are moderately well and have specific health-related goals
- Increasing self-care efforts for those who are fully healthy, yet want to enhance their quality of life.

Given this broad scope of coaching, wellness coaches often narrow their work to distinct areas such as illness prevention or managing existing health concerns. Some coaches focus on helping healthy clients sustain healthful behaviors. Others implement programs for weight loss or other step-by-step lifestyle changes. As a result of this focus on health maintenance and illness prevention, wellness coaches need to be educated about health, safety, behavioral consistency, and the special needs of each client.

Wellness coaching does not use a medical model or mirror a hierarchical doctor-patient relationship. Instead, as with all coaching, it relies on a partnership model: a client who is ready and able to make behavioral changes, and a coach who can suggest and guide a client to set goals and adopt a healthier lifestyle. Coaches may define a plan of action, but wellness coaching can only succeed when the client is ready to take action. Wellness coaches help clients:

- assess health concerns and set wellness goals
- reduce stress
- prepare for surgery or recover from surgery or medical procedures
- incorporate new understandings about health into daily practices
- manage pain and discomfort
- stay motivated over the long term in order to sustain weight loss, exercise routines, meditation practices, or other healthy behaviors

Wellness coaches often work in combination with other health care providers. Because of the complimentary nature of wellness coaching, many coaches have a "day job" as a traditional health care provider and offer wellness coaching part-time. We see examples of personal trainers, massage therapists, chiropractors, nurses, mental health practitioners, and nutritionists adding wellness coaching to their list of services.

Many wellness coaches are licensed to sell products, such as vitamins, exercise equipment, or motivational and relaxation tapes, along with their coaching sessions. These coaches offer a variety of services, including online, telephone, or face-to-face coaching, health assessments, facilitated support groups, and informational resources. They often coordinate their coaching with other health care providers, and at times generate activity or outcome reports for both the client and the client's team of health professionals.

Coaches interested in this specialty can obtain coach training specific to health and wellness. For example, the International Life Coach Training (ILCT), an accredited coaching program, offers a certificate program in wellness as part of its life coach training. The popular Dr. Phil of TV fame has a coach training program to certify coaches in his "Ultimate Weight Loss Solution." Corporate Coach U, an accredited coach training program, offers executive coaches a course in executive and employee wellness coaching, to address employee wellness as a fundamental component of overall productivity, innovation, and retention.

Wellness coaches charge by the hour or by the program and hourly fees range from $55 to $125. Wellness programs, which may include facilitated support groups, coaching in the field (akin to personal training sessions), assessments, and other coaching services, are priced on a monthly or complete-program basis.

Coaching in Action

Tom Robinson is a wellness coach who learned how to coach those with chronic illness based on his own, firsthand experience with chronic disease. He combines a diverse professional background with his knowledge of healing to develop a coaching specialty for infirmed clients.

Tom Robinson, Chronic Illness Coach
Chronic Illness Coach
www.chronicillnesscoach.com
phone: (805) 965-8412
Santa Barbara, California

For several years, Tom Robinson, a 25-year veteran of the software engineering industry, wanted to make a career change. Part of his desire to change careers was based on a life-changing spiritual experience; as that experience began to take root, he began to be less satisfied with the technical work he did every day and wanted more contact with people. In 1995, he went back to school and obtained a graduate degree in management, in a program that emphasized the human side of managing organizations. He had a career path in organization and team building mapped out, but then the California economy collapsed and some previously open doors slammed shut. He hired a coach to help him sort everything out and also joined the online training organization Coachville.

A few years later, Tom started his own coaching business. First, he took time to define his specialty and niche. With the help of a close friend, he decided to combine his innate and learned coaching skills with his personal experience in overcoming chronic illness. Diagnosed with Crohn's disease (a debilitating and potentially life-threatening illness) in 1996, Tom had been very proactive in investigating and designing his own treatment. He tried out many different remedies and, through trial and error, became proficient as his own case manager, in collaboration with his doctors and other medical practitioners. "In a way I became my own doctor. Not only did I learn a valuable set of skills, but along the way I developed a special and helpful type of empathy for others with chronic illnesses," Tom explained.

Through market research he learned that there was barely a handful of coaches working with the chronically ill. "I naively thought that people would flock to me once I got my Web site up. It didn't take long to discover the fallacy of that assumption," he said. "However, as I started coaching people with chronic illnesses I found that I was very good at it and really enjoyed it; my enjoyment and satisfaction have continued to grow ever since." Tom knew he could coach in other areas, such as management or career transition, but chronic illness was so core to him, he felt that this is where he could distinguish himself.

Tom only offers individual coaching via short maintenance weekly sessions of 30 minutes or regular sessions of 1 hour in length. He plans to offer group coaching by teleclass in the future. To market his coaching, he gives free talks to chronic illness support groups. After each talk, he offers a free short coaching session to interested audience members. He also passes around a sign-up sheet where people can check off if they would like a complimentary coaching session, receive his newsletter, or join a coaching group.

Tom says that his major coaching skill is the way he listens. "I have a gift for listening to others in a nonjudgmental way that makes them feel understood and supported. It creates a safe place that enables my clients to look within and share what they find. I also have a gift for getting to the heart of a problem, then engaging in and supporting others in creatively brainstorming to solve it. From my profound spiritual experiences I've come to know that we are more than our personalities. Knowing that helps me, in a subtle way, get beyond my own and my clients' personas. This is very effective in helping my clients find out what they really want, and then helping them achieve it. Getting out of pain is only one goal of many that emerge in that process."

When he first started to build his coaching business, Tom would jump into working with a client as soon as they verbally agreed to start. He's since learned that a written coaching agreement is needed to make coaching successful. Now he verbally prepares his clients for what the coaching process will entail. He follows that by e-mailing them an agreement form that tells them about the work they need to do in the coaching process and asks them to agree, in writing, to signify their commitment to do the work.

Tom is clear that wellness coaching is not social work. "Social workers provide a needed service for the chronically ill. They teach them how to adapt to the limitations brought on by their illnesses. They teach them specific coping skills. They teach them how to get their social and support needs met. But that's about as far as hospital social workers go. As a coach for people with chronic illnesses, I support them in adapting to their limitations, but my main job is to empower them to live satisfying lives, lives that even healthy people would envy."

A woman with chronic pain syndrome who feels her disease is starting to run her life calls Tom, and he offers her a complimentary coaching session. He sends her a five-page questionnaire to be filled out and returned before the first coaching session. In addition to the questions that coaches typically ask their clients, he asks:

- how the illness has impacted her life
- what medical options and treatments she has explored and tried
- to list the ways she feels supported or unsupported in her illness by friends and family
- what she has learned due to her illness
- to name someone the client admires who has the same illness, and why
- to describe any dreams she had in the past for her future that have been forgotten or abandoned because of her illness

Tom also sends her a coaching agreement and reviews his policies about payment, cancellations, and termination. The first paid coaching session takes about 2 hours. Tom goes over the answers to her questionnaire. His goal is to learn as much relevant information as he can about her, and he pays special attention to the topics that elicit enthusiasm and passion. These are times when her aliveness is so strong and intense that he literally feels something resonating inside himself. He has learned that these will be very fruitful areas for their coaching.

At the end of the initial session Tom and his client decide on the coaching schedule. Tom recommends that they start with one 1-hour session per week. As long as the coaching is providing her value and she is moving forward in her life, he will stay flexible with the schedule she prefers.

Over the first month of sessions, Tom and his client talk about her satisfaction or dissatisfaction with her current medical care and treatment, and Tom encourages her to take responsibility for getting excellent care. He supports her in doing anything she has to in order to make this true. She reports that this is the most valuable aspect of the coaching so far. She uses resources that Tom provides and networking research to find answers for herself.

In subsequent sessions, he broaches other aspects of life coaching, such as how she can cope effectively with her limitations, getting in touch with and finding outlets for passions she has put in limbo since her illness, and dealing with her self-image and self-esteem issues. "The latter is a common theme for clients with chronic illness and I often act as a very positive and true mirror for them," Tom says.

Tom's clients stay with him from a few months up to 1 year. He tries to stay flexible with his policies because his clients are often in crisis due to the ramifications of their illness. Sometimes their money runs out, or clients are not used to paying out of pocket for health-related services. He keeps his schedule flexible because his ill clients may have bad days or "brain fog" that result in missed sessions. He also stays flexible in his willingness to slow down the pace of the coaching. Many chronically ill clients have spent years feeling disappointed due to significant needs not getting met. Tom says that his clients need validation and help in getting basic needs met, even though some of these needs are hard for them to speak about or even identify. The coaching process teaches Tom about patience, and teaches his clients about the value of open and clear verbal communication, improved self-awareness, and increased self-actualization. Tom advises those coaches who want to work in the wellness arena to consider the following:

- Do become informed about physical and psychological complications that can affect clients within your area of coaching.
- Don't think you have to be an expert about all of the health problems your clients may have. Your clients are and will be well versed in their condition and treatments. Be their coach, not their physician.
- Don't have compassion be your only strong coaching skill. You need to help your clients get results, not just feel cared for. (For example, results that Tom sees with his clients include: clients creating and sticking with a daily schedule to accomplish small goals of getting tasks done around the house, getting to work regularly, and making follow-up calls with health professionals. He uses accountability to help clients take action steps, even when they want to just stay in bed, based on illness. He also helps them determine when it is wise to delay a task and stay in bed to recover.)
- Don't project your experience onto clients. Everyone is different in regard to illness and health.

Exercise: Is Wellness Coaching for Me?

Use the following checklist and written questions to see if wellness coaching is the right fit for you. Note the areas of prior experience, and favorite clients, topics, and coaching strengths and skills. Check the statements that are true. Then answer the questions to determine your projected impact and current readiness to pursue this specialty. Scoring: Checking off 16 or more total answers out of a possible 20, plus positive answers to the additional questions, all indicate that this can be a very satisfactory choice.

My Prior Experience:

❑ I have a professional background, certification, license, or degree in health or human behavior.

❑ I am trained in motivational and behavioral strategies required to create and sustain healthy behaviors.

❑ I have a passion and desire to help people achieve their health and wellness goals.

❑ I have faced health issues firsthand and know what it takes to maintain an extremely healthy lifestyle.

❑ I have a referral network of medical experts so that I can refer clients out for additional advice or get consulting for my coaching regarding health and wellness questions.

Type of Client: My favorite clients to coach include

❑ People who are focused on health and wellness

❑ Those engaged in a process of recovery and healing from illness, addiction, or injury

❑ Otherwise healthy individuals who are determined to enhance their physical and mental well-being

❑ Courageous, unsung heroes who are living with chronic physical conditions

❑ Clients with a single-minded focus about coaching

Coaching Topics: I understand and enjoy coaching about

❑ Action plans for optimum health and wellness

❑ Behavioral modification strategies that get results

❑ Peak performance, motivation, and "personal best"

❑ Setting boundaries, raising standards, and self-accountability

❑ Stress, energy, and patience

(continued)

My Coaching Strengths and Skills:
❑ I love research and naturally collect and distribute resource materials.
❑ I am a cheerleader at heart.
❑ I understand inherent motivational strategies.
❑ I listen carefully and take my client's concerns seriously.
❑ I can be tough and encourage a "just do it" approach for clients when necessary.

Answer the following questions:
How will my work as a wellness coach uphold the vision, purpose, and mission statement of my coaching business?

_____

_____

What additional skills and strengths can I, or do I already, provide for clients as a wellness coach? (Refer to Chapter 4.)

_____

_____

What tangible benefits and results do I offer clients in this niche market? (Refer to Chapter 5.)

_____

_____

What one word or short phrase describes my particular coaching specialty in a client's mind? (Refer to Chapter 6.)

_____

_____

(continued)

Do I have the right credentials, coaching materials, pricing, programs, and package of services to move into this market now? If not, what are my next steps in this regard? (Refer to Chapter 9.)

_____

_____

After answering the checklist and above questions, my passion about this specialty of coaching and willingness to take steps to pursue this specialty further are: (high, medium, low) _____

Additional notes:

CHAPTER 17

Creativity, Relationship, and Spiritual Coaching

In this final chapter, we explore three coaching specialties that all concentrate on interior, as opposed to exterior, aspects of human development. We present these three categories as considerations of a trend in coaching: an integration of coaching with the personal growth movement.

Creativity, relationship, and spiritual coaching might be considered subsets of life coaching, except that coaches who identify themselves with one of these three categories consider the focus of their coaching as distinct from any other specialty. They study coursework within their chosen specialty (for example, relationship coaches often attend one of the half-dozen relationship coaching trainings offered nationally by a variety of organizations), use coaching methods that are developed for their particular specialty—rather than more general life coaching methods—and position their coaching businesses for clients who want coaching within their specialty area.

A creativity coach does not call her specialty life coaching, because she is focused primarily on improving her client's creative ventures, whereas a life coach may or may not attend to creative matters. A relationship coach sees her work with clients first and foremost through the lens of improving clients' relationships. A spiritual coach relies extensively on intuitive, religious, or other spiritual, innate beliefs to define her particular coaching services.

Coaches we interviewed who identified with one of these three disciplines had all trained specifically as creativity, relationship, or spiritual coaches, and they promote themselves as such. They generally combine their coach training with additional personal growth or former professional training. For example, one spiritual coach got her coach training from an organization that offered courses into finding one's spiritual path and analyzing dreams; she completed a 3-year course as an interfaith minister, which she added to her previous degree as a pastoral counselor. As a coach, she combined all of these disciplines to offer spiritual coaching that focuses on helping clients live a peaceful, meditative life.

Creativity coaching focuses on encouraging a person's need and desire to create or engage in artistic endeavors. Creativity coaching addresses the balance between the demands of daily life and finding the time and capacity to pursue original, imaginative interests and passions. Coaches support clients with identifying, planning, and implementing goals that directly point to artistic and authentic self-expression. This can include any of the arts—writing, painting, singing, inventing—and may involve performance skills, starting or developing a pastime, or turning a beloved hobby into a profession. Coaches offer clarification, encouragement, feedback, suggestions, information, and accountability to help clients overcome blocks to creative pursuit, plan projects, and take projects from planning stages to fruition.

Relationship coaching helps people find and create loving, fulfilling relationships. Coaches offer skills, ideas, support, and strategies to show clients how to improve existing relationships, open up to new potential interactions, and have healthy, joyful, rewarding contact with others. Relationship coaching comes close to overlapping with psychotherapy, since both focus on interpersonal concerns and tap into topics of communication, conflict resolution, and improved interaction. But relationship coaches are skill-based and focus on present-day, here-and-now goals, without attempting to resolve issues from past relationships or family-of-origin material. Relationship coaching focuses on strategies and tools that enhance communication and strengthen self-confidence. Coaches encourage people to adopt new behaviors to improve ongoing or new relationships. The relationship topics include parenting, couples, singles, dating, and families.

Spiritual coaching incorporates spirituality and theology, as well as religious, intuitive, and spiritual methods into coaching. The coaching may subscribe to a specific theory or religion or combine and incorporate aspects of many spiritual practices to create a holistic approach. Spiritual coaching encourages clients to be guided by spiritual concepts, to discover the deeply held values and principles that have meaning for them, and then orient their life and work around those principles. While other coaches, especially life and wellness coaches, discuss topics of mind, body, and spirit as part of the natural course of a coaching conversation, spiritual coaches orient each coaching session around a framework of spiritual path. Spiritual coaching covers topics such as cause and effect, life purpose, collective wisdom, dreamwork, higher self, finding a calling versus a career, and how religious or "higher power" tenets integrate into coaching goals.

All three varieties of inner-self coaching charge similarly to other life coaches, with fees between $55 and $150 per hour. Many offer low-cost classes and groups, and some have a pro bono or scholarship component to their coaching.

Coaching in Action

Harriett Simon Salinger is a veteran coach who has worked as a coach in many traditional settings and describes her work as "coaching the essence." Her coaching represents an intuitive, spiritual approach to coaching. Coach Toni Coleman incorporates her interest in human nature and former background as a psychotherapist, as she helps her single clients find and develop loving relationships.

Harriett Simon Salinger, Heart-to-Heart Coach
Wise Woman Coaching
www.hssalinger.com
phone: (800) 487-4599 or (323) 931-0594
Los Angeles, California

Harriett Simon Salinger describes her style as "coaching the essence." She believes that coaching unlocks a client's ability to gain clarity, remove self-imposed limitations, access inner wisdom, and find a sense of purpose. She sees her role as a coach as one of sparking and sustaining positive change. Her 10-year coaching business has gone through many iterations, twists, and turns, which she feels is normal and necessary to finding one's coaching home.

Harriett was a psychotherapist for over 30 years in clinical practice with a master's in social work from Columbia University. She credits her experience as a therapist with teaching her how to feel very comfortable talking with all types of people. In 1994, Harriett was looking for new expression in her work and found it in the profession of coaching. She became a teacher-trainer with CoachU and was one of the first tier of coaches to achieve the Master Coach Certification (MCC). In the early years of her coaching, with the coaching business still in its infancy, she didn't even know what to call her style of spiritual, heart-felt relating, but stuck with her methods and found a way to coach others that reflected her values and greater purpose. Harriett also adapted a classic social-work maxim, "Start where the client is," and applied it to her coaching. In coaching sessions, Harriett helps clients to:

- Discover what they want, both personally and professionally
- Develop a strategy to get from their wishes to actualized goals
- Remove obstacles and self-imposed limitations that hinder their dreams
- Discover their deepest passions and the things that bring them true joy
- Find choices where none seem to exist
- Come home to their true self

"Most of my clients come to me at a time when they know that they need to somehow change their story, reweave or find their own voice, or change in some way the patterns of their life," she says. "Perhaps they're not as successful as they'd like to be. Perhaps they're curious about what is hidden from them, what they cannot yet see in their lives. Whatever the issue, it is my privilege to coach clients to reexamine their lives, to unlock new perspectives and see new realities that have been previously hidden from them."

She says it initially took her about 6 months as a coach to get away from her therapy mind-set. For Harriett, coaching is less about empathetic listening, a skill she relied heavily on as a therapist, and more about intuition and truth-telling. She will listen to a client talk during a coaching session, but then may interrupt the client to silently "check inside" with herself, to tap into her intuitive, innate wisdom and sensing. In this way she tries to get a deeper, more discerning awareness about the person she is coaching, not just talk about the content being discussed. Then, unlike a therapist who might also use intuition or awareness, but withhold directive comment, she speaks out, in a blunt manner, to truthfully and unreservedly communicate what she intuitively notes. Because so much of her work is by phone, Harriett relies on these intuitive inklings and direct communications to get to the heart of the coaching matter quickly. Harriett took her style of coaching into different settings, including doing some corporate training for several years, but now prefers to coach individual clients. She is a mentor coach for many new coaches who need to experience coaching firsthand to help build their coaching practices. Regardless of the topics she addresses in coaching, she considers her work of helping others part of a spiritual path. Although phone coaching is verbal and cognitive, she tries to "see" her clients beyond just their words and helps them articulate their human needs through a partnership she builds with them, that goes "right to their hearts." Harriett explains, "My coaching style includes deliberate straight talk, laughter, and committed purposeful action. I am challenging and compassionate, empathic and direct. I will always start where you are, have you embrace that place and move to where you want to be. I am trustworthy and trusting."

One client was a new coach and a former psychotherapist who hired Harriett to help her start up her coaching business. The client had completed a course of coach training, but needed to hire a mentor coach to help her experience coaching while she built a coaching business, and wanted one who could help her understand the differences between therapy and coaching. Harriett asked the new coach to write a broad vision statement, including a description of the kinds of clients she hoped to attract as a coach. Harriett then questioned the coach specifically about how coaching would help these clients, and how the coach would work with each type of client as a coach, not a therapist. This back-and-forth process of dialogue, along with the experience of being coached herself by Harriett, helped the new coach formulate distinctions about therapy and coaching.

As the new coach began to talk about her marketing ideas, Harriett would often stop and say, "That's interesting, but let me check inside" and then quietly and silently check in with her own intuitive sense. Once, when the new coach wanted to understand why so few of her referrals were becoming paying clients, Harriett "checked inside" and then said, "I think you know the answer yourself, but I will tell you what I get from my intuition. I believe you need to strengthen your personal and unique identity as a coach before you will be able to attract and retain clients consistently. If you want to work with me toward making this shift, I am game."

The new coach thought this was a good assessment of her problem. She could see how her lack of confidence and insecurity were sabotaging her efforts at retaining new coaching clients. The new coach used the next several months of coaching to identify specific steps and actions that would help her strengthen her confidence as a coach. As a result she was able to retain more potential coaching clients.

Another client, a corporate trainer, says that Harriett is as much an alchemist as she is a coach, and has the capacity to see and sense those gold nuggets within her clients. According to this client, "She doesn't just listen to me. She possesses an agility that allows her to climb behind my words and sense what is really going on."

Harriett says she works well with clients who are willing to look at their limiting beliefs and self-created limitations, in order permit change to happen. "Your life is a testament to who you are and how you live. I invite clients to ask, 'Am I ready to live more fully than ever before?'"

Antoinette Coleman, Singles Coach
Consum-mate
www.consum-mate.com
phone: (703) 847-1768
McLean Virginia

During Toni Coleman's long career as a psychotherapist, she counseled single men and women and saw reoccurring patterns of loneliness, isolation, and frustration due to difficulties in meeting compatible singles and forming healthy relationships. As a psychotherapist she worked with the depression that these problems exacerbated in her clinical clients. Over time, she began to think that she could help singles more as a coach, to show the skills and resources necessary for successful relating. As she began to shift the nature of her work from symptomology to skills, from therapy to coaching, she decided to target those singles seeking healthy, lasting relationships.

Within this niche, she offers a full range of services. Toni assists singles to becoming relationship-ready by integrating the skills of mind-set and expert communication. She works with those actively involved in dating, to teach them the skills of making good choices and relationship problem-solving. Her goal is to help her clients find and sustain lasting love.

Toni's past professional experience included being a social worker, both in public agencies and in her own private practice. Her personal and professional interest in understanding the rhyme and reason of dating and relationships developed over a long period of time. "I was a single woman who married for the first and only time at age thirty-five," she says. "I dated actively in my local area of Washington, D.C., and had many good and bad experiences." She used herself as a test case to study her dating process and learn more about who she was attracted to, and why. The careful analysis paid off. "All of this led me to meet the right man, get married, have four kids, and have a stable marriage for over sixteen years (and counting)."

Toni knew that she had found the right coaching specialty because her interest in the coaching possibilities of working with singles excited her. She accumulated resources that could be put to good coaching use for singles. Although she trained as a life coach and attended workshops that addressed other niches, she kept coming back to her passion: singles.

Toni, who lives adjacent to Washington, D.C., is an expert in the ever-transient singles market. "Singles in metropolitan areas often report that their social support systems are lacking. Many singles who live in DC move from someplace else and find it hard to connect in a town that values workaholism. They often feel isolated and fill up their time by getting very busy with activities that don't lead them to much fulfillment.

"As a coach, I am a constant partner. I use e-mail a lot to touch base and remind my clients that I am there. My work with them helps them stay patient and focus on developing a good personal foundation first," she says. Because there is often a sense of urgency among singles to find any partner in order to fight loneliness, her coaching relationship helps her clients stem the pattern of rushing into short-term, dysfunctional encounters that just end up reinforcing feelings of failure and desperation.

A typical coaching client is a man, a bachelor in his 30s, who wants to be married. Toni begins with an assessment she calls the "Pillars of Life." Her client rates his level of satisfaction in 10 different areas of his life. In the coaching session, as they go over this assessment together, he has the opportunity to decide which areas of his life are fine just as they are and which areas need work. Toni sees this initial process as the personal growth that will lead this client to his relationship goal.

The client has decided to curtail dating until the coaching progresses further. Toni hears two reoccurring themes from him in his discussions about dating: he always chooses a certain type of woman who is unavailable in some way, and he chooses women to date who make him feel complete or better about himself. Through the coaching sessions, he discusses how and why he chooses women, and then, with Toni's help, begins to set goals to shift these problem areas. Toni and her client periodically assess whether he is "relationship ready," and soon he begins to date again.

New goals and behaviors always emerge as the coaching (and the dating) advance. He learns how to flirt effectively and appropriately; how to approach a woman he is interested in; and first-date tips to effect straight, friendly, uncomplicated communication. When a first date turns into a second and beyond, Toni helps him understand the stages of a relationship, so he can anticipate and normalize each stage. She recommends specific behavioral strategies he can use to help him through inevitable relationship challenges, such as conflict resolution skills. They work together for 6 months, and he feels pleased with his new sense of self-confidence and a new, promising relationship.

Exercise: Is Creativity, Relationship, or Spiritual Coaching for Me?

Use the following checklist and written questions to see if creativity, relationship, or spiritual coaching appeals to you. Note the areas of prior experience, and favorite clients, topics, and coaching strengths and skills. Check the statements that are true. Then answer the questions to determine your projected impact and current readiness to pursue this specialty. Scoring: Checking off 16 or more total answers out of a possible 20, plus positive answers to the additional questions, all indicate that this can be a very satisfactory choice.

My Prior Experience:
❑ I have a background and understanding of human development, creative arts, or spirituality.
❑ I am dedicated to my own personal growth and continually engage in my education through trainings, workshops, courses, reading, and other enlightening resources.
❑ I have completed a coach training programs or certification so that my coaching is based on solid coaching skills and methods.
❑ I have a strong sense of integrity and ethical behavior that supports the discipline needed to be effective in this area of coaching.
❑ I have a wealth of information, tools, techniques, and ideas for those who want to enhance their inner self-development.

Type of Client: My favorite clients to coach include
❑ True believers in the importance of inner work
❑ Artists, designers, craftspersons, performers, or others on their creative journey
❑ Insight-oriented professionals who live according to values and vision

(continued)

Exercise: Is Creativity, Relationship, or Spiritual Coaching for Me?
(continued)

❑ Free spirits, new-agers, spiritual seekers
❑ People who are successful in their careers but not fulfilled in their personal lives

Coaching Topics: I understand and enjoy coaching about
❑ Vision, values, passion, joy, and peace of mind
❑ Loving relationships with self and others
❑ Achieving creative and artistic goals
❑ Enlightenment, attraction, inspiration, resourcefulness
❑ Making a living, getting grounded in reality, financial independence

My Coaching Strengths and Skills:
❑ I can maintain clarity despite a number of conflicting statements and options.
❑ I am an optimistic and pragmatic.
❑ I can strategize a workable plan for achieving a bold vision.
❑ I come from the best in me, to connect with the best in my client.
❑ I am a careful, nonjudgmental listener who asks challenging questions and offers insightful feedback.

Answer the following questions:
How will my work as a creativity, relationship, or spiritual coach uphold the vision, purpose, and mission statement of my coaching business?

_____

_____

What additional skills and strengths can I, or do I already, provide for clients as a creativity, relationship, or spiritual coach? (Refer to Chapter 4.)

_____

_____

(continued)

Exercise: Is Creativity, Relationship, or Spiritual Coaching for Me?

(continued)

What tangible benefits and results do I offer clients in this niche market? (Refer to Chapter 5.)

_____

_____

What one word or short phrase describes my particular coaching specialty in a client's mind? (Refer to Chapter 6.)

_____

_____

Do I have the right credentials, coaching materials, pricing, programs, and package of services to move into this market now? If not, what are my next steps in this regard? (Refer to Chapter 9.)

_____

_____

After answering the checklist and above questions, my passion about this specialty of coaching and willingness to take steps to pursue this specialty further are: (high, medium, low) _____

Additional notes:

APPENDIX OF HELPFUL INFORMATION

A. AUTHOR CONTACT INFORMATION

Lynn Grodzki, LCSW, PCC
910 La Grande Road
Silver Spring, MD 20903
Phone: (301) 434-0766
E-mail: lynn@privatepracticesuccess.com
Web sites: www.privatepracticesuccess.com;
        www.businessandpracticeofcoaching.com

Wendy Allen, Ph.D., MFT
1207 De La Vina
Santa Barbara, CA 93101
Phone: (805) 962-2212
E-mail: weallen@earthlink.net
Web sites: www.wendyphd.com; www.privatepracticesuccess.com

B. LEVELS OF COACH CERTIFICATION

The following three levels of certification are offered by the International Coach Federation (ICF) (www.coachfederation.org) to strengthen the coaching profession and establish industry regulations. See the ICF Web site for a full explanation of each level and information about the application process.

MCC: Master Certified Coach. The highest level of certification for graduates of a certified coach and mentor training; requires 2,500 hours of documented coaching.

PCC: Professional Certified Coach. The midlevel certification for graduates of a certified coaching–mentoring training program; requires 750 hours of documented coaching.

ACC: Associate Certified Coach. A temporary certification good for up to 3 years, after which time the ACC must proceed to PCC or ACC certification.

C. COACH TRAINING ORGANIZATIONS

The current list of accredited coach training organizations numbers about 24 schools and training organizations. It can be found under the auspices of the ICF: www.coachfederation.org. The ICF maintains the official list of accredited organizations, which changes as more schools complete the process.

D. COACHING ASSOCIATIONS

The following are a few of the recognized professional coaching associations.

Association for Coaching (UK): The largest British association for coaches, offering a list of coaches and conferences in the UK. associationfor-coaching.com

International Association of Coaches (IAC): Professional association for coaches, sponsored by the Coachville.com training organization (www.cvcommunity.com) and the late Thomas Leonard, offering information, community news, certification process, and membership liability insurance. internationalassociationofcoaches.org

International Coach Federation (ICF): Professional organization of personal and business coaches that exists to build, support, and preserve the integrity of the coaching profession. The ICF offers an accreditation for coaches and training schools and provides its members with research, information, and the chance to attend their well-regarded and usually packed conferences. coachfederation.com

Worldwide Association of Business Coaches: An international association dedicated to represent all internal and external coaches working at business organizations and the government. wabcoaches.com

E. HELPFUL JOURNALS AND PERIODICALS

American Psychologist: The periodical for the American Psychological Association (APA), one of the few psychological associations to address coaching. The APA list of journals at their site (apa.org) includes *Consulting Psychology Journal*, published by Division 13 of the APA, with articles on coaching. apa.org/journals

Entrepreneur Magazine: One of the best periodicals, for any kind of entrepreneur, that covers a wide spectrum of issues from mind-set to franchises. Edited by Rieva Lesonsky. http://www.entrepreneur.com

Fast Company: An informative and entertaining magazine that helps businesspeople think "out of the box," featuring columnists such as Seth Godin and Richard Leider. http://www.fastcompany.com

Inc Magazine: Another good business magazine that sees itself as a broad resource for small businesses and entrepreneurs. Published by Gruner and Jahr USA. http://www.inc.com

The Independent Practitioner: Publication from the APA, reviews coaching studies and published coaching articles for psychologists. http://www.division42.org/MembersArea/IPfiles/Pubhome.html

The International Journal of Coaching in Organizations (IJCO): A professional coaching journal published for the purpose of presenting reflection on and critical analysis of coaching in organizations, sponsored by the World Association of Business Coaches (WABC). http://www.wabc-coaches.com/advantage/internationaljournal.htm

The International Journal of Mentoring and Coaching: A range of international papers representing a cross section of sectors from consultants working in businesses, practicing managers, academics to promote good practice and the expectation of good practice in mentoring and coaching across Europe. http://www.emccouncil.org/frames/journalframe.htm

The Journal of Applied Behavioral Science: Affiliated with NTL (National Training Labs) and published by Sage Publications. http://www.sagepub.com

The Journal of Leadership Education: An international, refereed journal that serves scholars and professional practitioners engaged in leadership education. http://www.fhsu.edu/jole

The New Economy Magazine: An online e-zine that helps readers think "out of the box" by developing organizational readiness in turbulent times. Edited by Marcia L. Conner. http://www.linezine.com

Organizational Dynamics: A quarterly review of organizational behavior for professional managers. Published by Elsevier Press, University of Helsinki. http://www.ingenta.com/journals/browse/mcb/502, http://www.elesevier.com

Personnel Psychology: Loosely affiliated with the Society for Industrial and Organizational Psychology. Occasional articles on executive coaching. http://www.personnelpsychology.com

Psychotherapy Finances: Addresses insightful ways for therapists to make more money. Features up-to-date status on financial information for those in private practice. Edited by John Klein. http://www.psychotherapyfinances.com

Psychotherapy Networker: One of the most popular psychotherapy journals in the United States. Has embraced coaching and often runs articles by coaches. http://www.psychotherapynetworker.org

F. COACHING BOOKS

General Coaching Information

Auerbach, J. (2001). *Personal and executive coaching: The complete guide for mental health professionals.* Ventura, CA: Executive College Press.
A comprehensive, hands-on guide to what it takes to be a personal or business coach, written for mental health therapists. Includes helpful information about how to coach clients with learning disorders such as ADD.

CoachU, Inc. (2005) *The CoachU personal and corporate coach training handbook.* Hoboken, NJ: Wiley.
A complete and elegant coaching curriculum for the new or experienced coach to consider and utilize.

Flaherty, J. (1999). *Coaching: Evoking excellence in others.* Burlington, MA: Elsevier.
A guide for the coach to develop new protocols and language to form a strong, reciprocal relationship with the client through mutual influence and growth. Also, useful and practical coaching skill-sets are detailed.

Fortgang, L. B. (1998). *Take yourself to the top: The secrets of America's #1 career coach.* New York: TimeWarner.
Career coaching action-oriented plans to help readers take big steps, make changes, and become responsible for the choices they make.

Goleman, D., Boyatzis, R., & McKee, A.(2002). *Primal leadership: Realizing the power of emotional intelligence.* Cambridge, MA: Harvard University Business School.

Applying Goleman's important concepts and skill sets to coaching leaders in today's marketplace.

Goldsmith, M. (Ed.) (2000). *Coaching for leadership: How the world's greatest coaches help leaders learn.* San Francisco: Jossey-Boss.
Essays from top executive coaches and case studies give the reader an understanding of the how to help leaders make the best use of the coaching process.

Grodzki, L. (Ed.) (2003). *The new private practice: Therapist-coaches share stories, strategies, and advice.* New York: Norton.
Sixteen behind-the-scenes essays from therapists-turned-coaches who share how they successfully broke into the coaching field, what they do, and how they charge.

Hargrove, R. (2003). *Masterful coaching.* New York: Wiley.
Sees the coach as a critical agent in transforming organizational cultures and defines the coaching competencies and skills necessary for excellence in coaching.

Hudson, F. (1999). *The handbook of coaching: A comprehensive resource guide for managers, executives, consultants and human resource professionals.* New York: Jossey-Bass.
A compendium of basic information about the burgeoning field of adult coaching from one of the leading authorities on coaching.

Leonard, T. J., & Byron, L. (1998). *The portable coach: 28 sure-fire strategies for business and personal success.* New York: Scribner.
The founder of the new coaching profession gives his explanation of coaching principles to help readers improve life, career, and relationships.

O'Neill, M. B. (2000). *Executive coaching with backbone and heart: A systems approach to engaging leaders with their challenges.* San Francisco: Jossey-Bass.
A systems approach to engaging leaders with their challenges that asks the coach to use both an engaged relationship and a "tough love" mind-set.

Pilzer, P. Z. (2002). *The wellness revolution: How to make a fortune in the next trillion-dollar industry.* New York: Wiley.
Insights into the health care industry and how entrepreneurs fit into the wellness industry of the future.

Prochaska, J., Norcross, J., & DiClemente, C. (1995). *Changing for good.* New York: Perennial Currents.
Resource for professionals interested in research about stages of behaviorial change.

Reardon, K. K. (2000). *The secret handshake: Mastering the politics of the business inner circle.* New York: Currency.
Understanding the politics of the corporate world.

Seligman, M. (2002). *Authentic happiness: Using the new positive psychology to realize your potential for lastig fulfillment.* New York: Free Press.
Psychological research regarding happiness and suggestions for implementation.

Vaillant, G. (2002). *Aging well: Surprising guideposts to a happier life from the landmark Harvard study of adult development.* Boston: Little, Brown.
How to increase the likelihood of living a happy, healthy, and fulfilling life into old age.

Whitworth, L., Kimsey-House, H., & Sandahl, P. (2004). *Co-active coaching: New skills for coaching people toward success in work and life.* Palo Alto, CA: Davies-Black.
The importance of the relationship between the coach and the client and how to use this coaching model to frame an effective and powerful coaching collaboration.

Williams, P., & Davis, D. C. (2002). *Therapist as life coach: Transforming you practice.* New York: Norton.
How to transform a psychotherapy practice into a coaching practice from the founder of Institute of Life Coach Training.

Zeus, P., & Skiffington, S. (2001). *The Complete guide to coaching at work.* Sydney: McGraw-Hill.
Straightforward explanation of how to bring coaching skills into the workplace, to coach teams, to further strategic planning, and for leadership.

Business Aspects

CoachVille.com. (2003). *The coaching starter kit: Everything you need to launch and expand your coaching practice.* New York: Norton.
A resource of forms, advice, and start-up information for new coaches in practice.

Csikszentimihalyi, M. (2003). *Good business: Leadership, flow, and the making of meaning.* New York: Penguin.
Business advice on leadership, flow, and meaning.

Edwards, P., Edwards, S., & Douglas, L. (1998). *Getting business to come to you*. New York: Penguin.
A thorough how-to guide for finding clients and referrals through methods of attraction.

Fairley, S. G., & Stout, C. E. (2004). *Getting started in personal and executive coaching*. New York: Wiley.
A clear business plan and many practical how-to's of building a coaching practice.

Fisher, D., & Vilas, S. (2000). *Power networking: 59 secrets for personal and professional success*. Austin, Texas: Bard Press.
Tips and ideas for achieving personal and professional networking goals, with a self-assessment quiz to get started.

Gerber, M. (1995). *The E-myth revisited: Why most small businesses don't work and what to do about it*. New York: HarperBusiness.
Required reading for anyone thinking about starting a business or for those who have already taken that fateful step. Outlines an accessible and organized plan, so that daily details are scripted, freeing the entrepreneur's mind to build long-term success.

Godin, S. (1999). *Permission marketing: Turning strangers into friends and friends into customers*. New York: Simon & Schuster.
Opt-in marketing strategies, essential for e-mail and direct-mail campaigns.

Godin, S.(2002). *Survival is not enough: Zooming, evolution, and the future of your company*. New York: Free Press.
Understanding the evolutionary process behind business and how to take advantage of the nature of change, without fear.

Grodzki, L. (2000). *Building your ideal private practice: A guide for therapists and other healing professionals*. New York: Norton.
A best-selling guide to practice-building for therapists and other healing professionals. Offers strategies and addresses how small business owners develop an entrepreneurial mind-set and learn to succeed in business ownership.

Grodzki, L. (2003). *Twelve months to your ideal private practice: A workbook*. New York: Norton.
A yearlong workbook that implements the concepts in Grodzki's previous book plus new material to help those in private practice develop a successful small business.

Harlow, S. (2002). *Selling yourself without selling your soul.* New York: HarperResource.
A woman's guide to marketing with integrity.

Jones, L. B. (1998). *The path: Creating your mission statement for work and life.* New York: Hyperion.
Inspiring and practical advice that leads listeners through every step of defining and fulfilling a mission.

Leonard, T. (1978). *Working wisdom: The top ten lists for improving your business!* Austin, TX: Bard Press.
A fun and accessible book full of business ideas for the coach.

Richmond, L.(1999). *Work as a spiritual practice.* New York: Broadway Books.
Offers a practical Buddhist approach to inner growth and job satisfaction that has some significant things to say about how to achieve your heart's desire and be successful.

Ries, A., & Ries, L. (2002). *The 22 immutable laws of marketing.* New York: HarperBusiness.
A clear explanation of business branding and how it can help you achieve a broad base of recognition with an aligned marketing approach.

Money Matters
Barnhart, T. (1995). *Five rituals of wealth: Proven strategies for turning the little you have into more than enough.* New York: HarperBusiness.
How people of all incomes can increase their financial status.

Carlson, R. (1997). *Don't worry, make money: Spiritual and practical ways to create abundance and more fun on your life.* New York: Hyperion.
A quick read offering commonsense practical steps anyone can take to increase their income.

Cole, H. P., & Reese, D. (2004). *Mastering the financial dimension of your practice.* New York: Brunner-Rutledge.
A unique perspective for service-oriented practitioners. Focuses on financial concerns such as the best investments for a solopreneurs.

Kinder, G. (1999). *The seven stages of money maturity: Understanding the spirit and value of money in your life.* New York: Delacorte Press.
The stages of development regarding money, values, and spirit.

Kioyaski, R. T, & Lechter, S. L. (2000). *Rich dad, poor dad*. New York: Warner.
How to make money that works for you instead of you working for it.

Mellan, O. (1994). *Money harmony: Resolving money conflicts in your life and relationships*. New York: Walker.
Resolving money conflicts in life and relationships.

Stern, L. (1997). *Money-smart secrets for the self-employed*. New York: Random House.
Helpful resource that outlines a series of logical, easy-to-apply techniques addressing all of the major economic issues faced by a solo enterprise today— including taxes, expenses, and record keeping.

Personal Growth

Adrienne, Carol. (1998). *The purpose of your life: Finding your place in the world using synchronisity, intuition, and uncommon sense*. New York: Eagle Press.
For coaches or clients working with their vision, mission, and purpose statement.

Grabhorn, L. (1999). *Excuse me, your life is waiting*. Olympia, WA: Hara.
Help with the concept of abundance and attraction, and how to use energy and thinking to come into better alignment with one's world.

Katie, B. (2003). *Loving what is: Four questions than can change your life*. New York: Harmony House.
How to develop a true paradigm shift by using a deceptively simple cognitive process of questioning.

Leider, R. (1997). *The power of purpose: Creating meaning in your life*. San Francisco: Berrett-Koehler.
A down-to-earth guide for people who are struggling to find their professional calling, from a well-known executive coach and trainer.

Lewis, T., Amini, F., & Lannon, R. (2000). *A General theory of love*. New York: Vintage.
Accessible explanation about the importance of attachment in relationships. Helpful for coaches who want to understand developmental stages of relating.

Maslow, A. H., & Lowry, R. (Eds.). (1998). *Toward a psychology of being.* 3rd ed. New York: Wiley.
Maslow's theory of self-actualization, hierarchy of human needs, and ideas of agency (motivation).

Peterson, C., & Seligman, M. (2004). *Character strengths and virtues: A handbook and classification.* Oxford, UK: Oxford University Press.
Source material that classifies categories of human strengths and makes a solid contribution to the new positive psychology field.

Richardson, C. (1998). *Take time for your life: A personal coach's seven-step program for creating the life you want.* New York: Broadway.
How to transform one's life and become a model of the services you offer.

Rock, D. (2003). *Personal best: Step by step coaching for creating the life you want.* Sydney: Simon & Schuster Australia.

Tolle, E. (1999). *The power of now: A guide to spiritual enlightenment.* Novato, CA: New World Library.
Part philosophy, part spiritual awareness, this book can help the coach understand how "the present is perfect" and live by intentions.

Wilber, K. (2000). *A theory of everything: An integral vision for business, politics, science and spirituality.* New York: Random House.
A unified theory of science, religion, and psychology that can be very helpful in constructing a fundamental belief system for coaches. Read with a dictionary handy.

Zander, R., & Zander, B. (2000). *The art of possibility: Transforming professional and personal life.* Boston: Harvard Business School Press.
A set of breakthrough practices for creativity in all human endeavors.

G. WEB SITES FOR COACHES

authentichappiness.com—Martin Seligman's Authentic Happiness Web site offers more than 20 assessments based on positive psychology research that can be scored instantly and assessed for free, just by registering. Includes assessments for signature strengths, happiness scales to use as pre- and post tests for coaching, and measures of capacity for relational attachment.

executivecoachingforum.com—The Executive Coaching Forum, a Web site filled with articles and suggestions for advancing the highest standards and best practices of executive coaching, including a free handbook that can be downloaded.

ezineville.com—E-goodies served daily, many available for reprint.

mind-map.com—The basic elements of mind-mapping; a creative and visual way for designing marketing plans.

motivation123.com—A useful newsletter that offers useful tips and steps for getting and keeping motivated, sponsored by Jason Michael Gracia, author of *The Motivated Mind*.

nsaspaker.org—The National Speakers Association is an international, professional organization of experts who speak for a living. They have state and regional chapters nationwide and can be a great resource for coaches who want to develop more expertise and be savvy as public speakers.

practicepaysolutions.com—Practice Pay Solutions is a merchant account company that provides services to help coaches accept credit cards and process billing information. It is sensitive to the needs of coaches in business and offers competitive rates.

privatepracticesuccess.com—Lynn Grodzki's Web site, full of practice-building advice, e-mail newsletter, resources, and links.

schrift.com—Coach Sandra Schrift's personal Web site, with the an excellent compilation of resources and links for those who want to become professional speakers.

speakers.com/web site/speakersonline.asp—Listing of professional speakers and their fees.

teleclass4u.com—Find or advertise a teleclass.

teleclassinternational.com—Listings of teleclasses worldwide.

thinksmart.com—Encourages and teachers members to take the initiative in innovation.

vistaprint.com—Easily accessible and affordable graphics–paper materials for the coach, including business cards, and stationary.

writers-publish.com—Self-publishing how-to's for publishing books and e-books.

writersservices.com—Get published, find an agent in the United States or UK, write the perfect proposal that sells, and other valuable resources online for the coach-author.

H. COACHING ASSESSMENTS

authentichappiness.org—Dozens of free tests and immediate scoring, to use as pre- and postmeasures for life coaching clients, referenced in Seligman (2002) and coaching program. All the assessments are copyrighted and may not be distributed in print version without express permission of the owners of the tests, but they can be fully accessed for online use by coaches and clients by registering at the Web site.

Coachingdynamics.com—Good selection of coaching assessments and training seminars for using the assessments, including: TTI, HBDI, TriMetrix system, and T.E.A.M.S. from coaches Winston and Barb Connor. The Connors are well-regarded trainers within the coaching industry and certifying agents for several of the assessments they offer.

coachingwell.com—Find access to common assessments including: 360 Degree Performance Feedback, DiSC, and Highlands.

enneagramcentral.com—Clearinghouse for information on the Enneagram, including how to coach using this method of personality assessment.

knowyourtype.com/mbti.html—MBTI (Myers Briggs Types Index) is a personality test used by individuals and businesses to help employees work better in teams.

References

Anonymous (2003, November 13). Corporate therapy. *The Economist.* Retrieved March 11, 2005, from www.economist.com/business/displayStory.cfm?story_id=2212916

Brickey, M. (2002). Dual relations: Can coaches be pragmatic? *The Independent Practioner, 22,* 2. Retrieved March 11, 2005, from http://www.division42.org/MemberArea/oIPfiles/IPSpring_2002/articles/prof.practice/dual_relations.html.

Carter, A. (2001). *Executive Coaching: Inspiring performance at work.* Report 379, Brighton, UK: Institute for Employment Studies.

CoachU, Inc. (2005). *The CoachU personal and corporate coach training handbook.* Hoboken, NJ: Wiley.

Coachville.com. (2001). *Full practice 100 program, lesson #89: Multiple revenu streams.* Retrieved March 9, 2005, from http://www.coachville.com/fullpractice/x89pdf.pdf

Cole, D. (2002, October 29). Even executives can use help from the sidelines. *The New York Times,* section G, p. 5.

Crawford, F. (2002, November). The psychology of coaching. *Macquarie University News.* Retrieved March 11, 2005, from http://www.po.mg.edu.au/macnews/ShawItem.asp?ItemID=146

Dean, B. (2000, Spring). *Niche criteria for a successful coaching practice.* American Psychological Association: Division 42 Online. Retrieved March 9, 2005, from http://www.division42.org/MembersArea/IPfiles/IPSpsoo/Marketing/Dean.html

Domino, M. (2000, November). *The economics of mental health. For Richer or Poorer.* Opening presentation of panel discussion conducted at the American Associate of Family and Marriage Therapy National Conference, Denver. CO.

Easterbrook, G. (2004). *The progress paradox: How life gets better while people feel worse.* New York: Random House.

Fairley, S. G., & Stout, C. E. (2004). *Getting started in personal and executive coaching: How to create a thriving coaching practice.* New York: Wiley.

Fleischman, G, & Bryant, J. (2000, Spring). C corporation, LLC, or sole proprietorship: What form is best for your business. *Management Accounting Quarterly, 1*(3), 14–21.

Forster, S. (2002). *Seven coaches share their success stories.* Retrieved November 1, 2004, from www.Coachville.com/fullpractice/x99pdf.pdf

Gerber, M. (1995). *The E-myth revisited: Why most small businesses don't work and what to do about it.* New York: HarperBusiness.

Gladwell, M. (2002). *The tipping point: How little things can make a big difference.* Boston: Back Bay Books.

Godin, S. (2002). *The big red fez: How to make any website better.* New York: Free Press.

Goleman, D. (1997). *Emotional intelligence: Whay it can matter more than IQ.* New York: Bantom Books.

Goleman, D., Boyatzis, R., & McKee, A. (2002). *Primal leadership: Realizing the power of emotional intelligence.* Cambridge, MA: Harvard Business School Press.

Hall, D. T., Otazo, K. L., & Hollenbeck (1999, Winter). Behind closed doors: What really happens in executive coaching. *Journal of Organizational Dynamics, 29,* 39–53.

Hargrove, R. (2003). *Masterful coaching.* New York: Wiley.

Hart, V., Blattner, J., & Leipsic, S. (2001). Coaching vs. therapy: A perspective. *Consulting Psychology Journal, 53,* 229–237.

Hyatt, J. (2003). The inner game of business. *Fortune Small Business Magazine, 13*(4). Retrieved March 9, 2005, from http://www.fortune.com/smallbusiness/articles/0,15114,449263,00.html

Kremer, C., Rizzuto, R., & Case, J. (2000). *Managing by the numbers: A commonsense guide to understanding and using your company's financials.* New York: Basic Books.

Leider, R. (1997). *The power of purpose: Creating meaning in your life and work.* San Francisco: Berrett-Koehler.

Leonard, T. J., & Byron, L. (1998). *The portable coach: 28 sure-fire strategies for business and personal success.* New York: Scribner.

Levine, T. (2003). Was coaching just a fad? PR Web. Retrieved August 1, 2004, from http://wwwprweb.com/releases/2003/g/prweb79235.htm

Lewis, T., Amini, F., & Lannon, R.(2000). *A general theory of love.* New York: Vintage.

Mellan, O. (1994). *Money harmony: Resolving money conflicts in your life and your relationships.* New York: Walker.

Naughton, J. (2002, July). The coaching boom. *Psychotherapy Networker Magazine, 26.* Retrieved March 11, 2005 from http://wwwpsychotherapynetworker.org/coaching_boom.html

Peters, T. (1997, August). The brand called you. *Fast Company Magazine, 10,* 83. Retrieved August 10, 1997, from www.fastcompany.com/online/10/brandyou.html

Petersen, K. (2002, August 6). Life coaches all the rage. *USA Today.* Retrieved March 11, 2005, from http://www.usatoday.com/news/health/2002-08-04-lifecoach_x.htm

Peterson, C., & Seligman, M. (2004). *Character strengths and virtues: A handbook and classification.* Oxford, UK: Oxford University Press.

Prochaska, J. O., Norcross, J. C., & DiClemente, C. C. (1995). *Changing for good.* New York: Perrenial Currents.

Ray, S. *Loving relationships.* Berkeley, CA: Celestial Arts.

Ries, A., & Ries, L. (2002). *The 22 immutable laws of marketing.* New York: HarperBusiness.

Schein, E. H. (2000). Coaching and consultation: Are they the same? In M. Goldsmith, L. Lyons, & A. Freas (Eds.), *Coaching for leadership: How the world's greatest coaches help leaders learn* (pp. 65–73). San Francisco: Jossey-Bass.

Schulte, B. (2002, August 17). No fat cats allowed. *The Washington Post,* p. c.01.

Schwartz, B. (2004). *The paradox of choice: Why more is less.* New York: Ecco Press.

Seligman, M. (1995). The effectiveness of psychotherapy: The consumer reports study. *American Psychologist 50*(12), 965–974.

———. (2002). *Authentic happiness: Using the new positive psychology to realize your potential for lasting fulfillment.* New York: Free Press.

Shevlin, S. (2002). Beyond insight to vision. In L. Grodzki (Ed.), *The new private proactice: Therapist-coaches share stories, strategies, and advice* (pp. 115–127). New York: Norton.

Simon C. C. (2003, June 10). A coach for team you. *The Washington Post, HE* 01.

Sommer, C. (2002). Uncommon-sense coaching. In L. Grodzki (Ed.), *The new private proactice: Therapist-coaches share stories, strategies, and advice* (pp. 161–177). New York: Norton.

Trout, J. (2001). *Differentiate or die: Survival in our era of competition.* New York: Wiley.

Vaillant, G. (2002). *Aging well: Surprising guideposts to a happier life from the landmark Harvard study of adult development.* Boston: Little, Brown.

Walker, R. (2004, December 5). The hidden (in plain sight) persuaders. *The New York Times Magazine,* 68–75.

Wheatley, M. J., & Kellner-Rogers, M. (1996). *A simpler way.* San Francisco: Berrett-Koehler.

Whitworth, L., Kimsey-House, H., & Sandahl, P. (1998). *Co-active coaching: New skills for coaching people toward success in work and life.* Palo Alto, CA: Davies-Black.

Wilder, H. S. (2002). The leadership edge. In L. Grodzki (Ed.), *The new private practice: Therapist-coaches share stories, strategies, and advice* (pp. 37–50). New York: Norton.

Williams, P. (2002). Life coaching in addiction counseling: How to get the most from the 12 steps. *Counselor Magazine.* Retrieved March 9, 2005, from http://www.counselormagazine.com/display_article.asp?a:d=Opinion %20%20DECEMBER.htm

Index